Geospatial Development By Example with Python

Build your first interactive map and build location-aware applications using cutting-edge examples in Python

Pablo Carreira

BIRMINGHAM - MUMBAI

Geospatial Development By Example with Python

Copyright © 2016 Packt Publishing

All rights reserved. No part of this book may be reproduced, stored in a retrieval system, or transmitted in any form or by any means, without the prior written permission of the publisher, except in the case of brief quotations embedded in critical articles or reviews.

Every effort has been made in the preparation of this book to ensure the accuracy of the information presented. However, the information contained in this book is sold without warranty, either express or implied. Neither the author, nor Packt Publishing, and its dealers and distributors will be held liable for any damages caused or alleged to be caused directly or indirectly by this book.

Packt Publishing has endeavored to provide trademark information about all of the companies and products mentioned in this book by the appropriate use of capitals. However, Packt Publishing cannot guarantee the accuracy of this information.

First published: January 2016

Production reference: 1250116

Published by Packt Publishing Ltd.
Livery Place
35 Livery Street
Birmingham B3 2PB, UK.

ISBN 978-1-78528-235-5

www.packtpub.com

Credits

Author
Pablo Carreira

Reviewers
Brylie Christopher Oxley
Vivek Kumar Singh
Claudio Sparpaglione

Commissioning Editor
Sarah Crofton

Acquisition Editor
Meeta Rajani

Content Development Editor
Rashmi Suvarna

Technical Editor
Shivani Kiran Mistry

Copy Editor
Akshata Lobo

Project Coordinator
Judie Jose

Proofreader
Safis Editing

Indexer
Hemangini Bari

Graphics
Disha Haria

Production Coordinator
Nilesh Mohite

Cover Work
Nilesh Mohite

About the Author

Pablo Carreira is a Python programmer and a full stack developer living in São Paulo state, Brazil. He is now the lead developer of an advanced web platform for precision agriculture and actively uses Python as a backend solution for efficient geoprocessing.

Born in 1980, Brazil, Pablo graduated as an agronomical engineer. Being a programming enthusiast and self-taught since childhood, he learned programming as a hobby and later honored his techniques in order to solve work tasks.

Having 8 years of professional experience in geoprocessing, he uses Python along with geographic information systems in order to automate processes and solve problems related to precision agriculture, environmental analysis, and land division.

> I would like to thank my mother and father for the support given through all my life. I also would like to thank my wife for her help and patience in face of my absence during all the writing sessions.
>
> I thank my university teacher José Paulo Molin, who first introduced me to geoprocessing and precision agriculture and created in me a deep interest in the area and gave the means for my development. Finally, I thank my good friend Gerardo F. E. Perez for all the opportunities that he presented me with and for the uncountable hours of good technical discussions.

About the Reviewers

Brylie Christopher Oxley enjoys working on technology projects that improve the human and environmental commons. He is dedicated to working for open source, open web, and open knowledge movements.

He regularly contributes to open source projects primarily built with web platform technologies, including a wellbeing visualization application for aging populations and a community portal for refugee support.

> Thank you Elvin, Lauri, Antti, Marjo, and Lynne for being the shining stars of my life.

Vivek Kumar Singh is a research scholar at the center of atmospheric science, Indian Institute of Technology, Delhi (IIT Delhi). He has completed his master's in technology in Remote Sensing and GIS from the Indian Institute of Remote Sensing, ISRO, in Dehradun, Uttarakhand, India. He focused on the different applications of Remote Sensing and GIS using geocomputational modeling with satellite observations during his time in graduate school. His main research expertise is in the application of satellite remote sensing for air quality monitoring and assessment, urban heat island and remote sensing, and geographical systems around the world. He is also interested in researching the air quality in growing megacities, spatial and temporal trends in aerosols over urban regions, the radiative effects of aerosols, the development of statistical models to estimate surface level particulate matter air quality, aerosols and clouds data validation, and the retrieval of cloud products from UV satellite measurements. He is also an associate with the BhuNak science team on the development and validation of new GIS products for climate studies. He also currently participated in developing and conducting remote sensing technical workshops and capacity building activities for the BhuNak Program, where he teaches the application of satellite imagery to environmental decision-making activities with a focus on urban living quality.

> I would like to thank Vaibhav Kumar, PhD Scholar at the Center of Urban Science and Engineering, Indian Institute of Technology, Bombay (IIT-Bombay), for his contribution (cofounder of BhuNak Research Group). A special thank you to ML Singh (father), Prashant Kumar Singh (brother), and Kimeera Tummala (friend) for their contribution in my life.

Claudio Sparpaglione is a CTO at WalletSaver, an Italian startup rocking in the mobile phone tariff comparison landscape. His work experience includes the design and building of geospatial applications and web-oriented systems in the online advertisement industry. A passionate Pythonista and open-source advocate, he's a maintainer of the PyOWM project and actively involved in the community with contributions to projects such as Python-Requests and Reactive Manifesto. His main interests include high-scalable web architectures, APIs design, and cloud computing.

www.PacktPub.com

Support files, eBooks, discount offers, and more

For support files and downloads related to your book, please visit www.PacktPub.com.

Did you know that Packt offers eBook versions of every book published, with PDF and ePub files available? You can upgrade to the eBook version at www.PacktPub.com and as a print book customer, you are entitled to a discount on the eBook copy. Get in touch with us at service@packtpub.com for more details.

At www.PacktPub.com, you can also read a collection of free technical articles, sign up for a range of free newsletters and receive exclusive discounts and offers on Packt books and eBooks.

https://www2.packtpub.com/books/subscription/packtlib

Do you need instant solutions to your IT questions? PacktLib is Packt's online digital book library. Here, you can search, access, and read Packt's entire library of books.

Why subscribe?

- Fully searchable across every book published by Packt
- Copy and paste, print, and bookmark content
- On demand and accessible via a web browser

Free access for Packt account holders

If you have an account with Packt at www.PacktPub.com, you can use this to access PacktLib today and view 9 entirely free books. Simply use your login credentials for immediate access.

Table of Contents

Preface	**vii**
Chapter 1: Preparing the Work Environment	**1**
Installing Python	**2**
Windows	2
Ubuntu Linux	2
Python packages and package manager	**3**
The repository of Python packages for Windows	3
Installing packages and required software	**4**
OpenCV	4
Windows	4
Ubuntu Linux	5
Installing NumPy	**5**
Windows	5
Ubuntu Linux	5
Installing GDAL and OGR	**5**
Windows	8
Ubuntu Linux	8
Installing Mapnik	**8**
Windows	8
Ubuntu Linux	9
Installing Shapely	**9**
Windows	9
Ubuntu Linux	10
Installing other packages directly from pip	**10**
Windows	10
Ubuntu Linux	10

Table of Contents

Installing an IDE — 11
  Windows — 11
  Linux — 11
Creating the book project — 12
Programming and running your first example — 15
Transforming the coordinate system and calculating the area of all countries — 18
Sort the countries by area size — 24
Summary — 25

Chapter 2: The Geocaching App — 27
Building the basic application structure — 28
  Creating the application tree structure — 28
  Functions and methods — 29
  Documenting your code — 30
  Creating the application entry point — 31
Downloading geocaching data — 34
  Geocaching data sources — 35
  Fetching information from a REST API — 36
  Downloading data from a URL — 37
  Downloading data manually — 39
Opening the file and getting its contents — 41
  Preparing the content for analysis — 43
Combining functions into an application — 43
Setting your current location — 46
Finding the closest point — 49
Summary — 54

Chapter 3: Combining Multiple Data Sources — 55
Representing geographic data — 56
  Representing geometries — 57
Making data homogeneous — 60
  The concept of abstraction — 61
  Abstracting the geocache point — 61
  Abstracting geocaching data — 63
Importing geocaching data — 64
  Reading GPX attributes — 67
  Returning the homogeneous data — 72
  Converting the data into Geocache objects — 75
  Merging multiple sources of data — 77
Integrating new functionality into the application — 79
Summary — 81

Chapter 4: Improving the App Search Capabilities — 83
- Working with polygons — 84
  - Knowing well-known text — 85
- Using Shapely to handle geometries — 87
- Importing polygons — 89
- Getting the attributes' values — 97
- Importing lines — 99
- Converting the spatial reference system and units — 101
- Geometry relationships — 106
  - Touches — 107
  - Crosses — 107
  - Contains — 108
  - Within — 108
  - Equals or almost equals — 108
  - Intersects — 109
  - Disjoint — 109
- Filtering by attributes and relations — 109
- Filtering by multiple attributes — 113
  - Chaining filters — 115
- Integrating with the app — 117
- Summary — 120

Chapter 5: Making Maps — 121
- Knowing Mapnik — 122
  - Making a map with pure Python — 122
  - Making a map with a style sheet — 124
- Creating utility functions to generate maps — 126
  - Changing the data source at runtime — 127
  - Automatically previewing the map — 130
- Styling maps — 131
  - Map style — 131
  - Polygon style — 132
  - Line styles — 134
  - Text styles — 135
  - Adding layers to the map — 136
  - Point styles — 139
- Using Python objects as a source of data — 141
- Exporting geo objects — 145
- Creating the Map Maker app — 149
  - Using PythonDatasource — 151
  - Using the app with filtering — 158
- Summary — 160

Table of Contents

Chapter 6: Working with Remote Sensing Images	**161**
Understanding how images are represented	**162**
Opening images with OpenCV	164
Knowing numerical types	166
Processing remote sensing images and data	**168**
Mosaicking images	169
Adjusting the values of the images	174
Cropping an image	176
Creating a shaded relief image	179
Building an image processing pipeline	**181**
Creating a RasterData class	182
Summary	**190**
Chapter 7: Extract Information from Raster Data	**191**
Getting the basic statistics	**191**
Preparing the data	193
Printing simple information	194
Formatting the output information	196
Calculating quartiles, histograms, and other statistics	198
Making statistics a lazy property	199
Creating color classified images	**201**
Choosing the right colors for a map	203
Blending images	**210**
Showing statistics with colors	**212**
Using the histogram to colorize the image	213
Summary	**215**
Chapter 8: Data Miner App	**217**
Measuring execution time	**218**
Code profiling	**222**
Storing information on a database	**223**
Creating an Object Relational Mapping	225
Preparing the environment	226
Changing our models	227
Customizing a manager	228
Generating the tables and importing data	232
Filtering the data	235
Importing massive amount of data	**236**
Optimizing database inserts	237
Optimizing data parsing	239
Importing OpenStreetMap points of interest	242
Removing the test data	246
Populating the database with real data	247

Searching for data and crossing information	251
Filtering using boundaries	253
Summary	**255**
Chapter 9: Processing Big Images	**257**
Working with satellite images	**257**
Getting Landsat 8 images	259
Memory and images	**263**
Processing images in chunks	**266**
Using GDAL to open images	266
Iterating through the whole image	270
Creating image compositions	**273**
True color compositions	274
Processing specific regions	278
False color compositions	280
Summary	**283**
Chapter 10: Parallel Processing	**285**
Multiprocessing basics	**285**
Block iteration	**289**
Improving the image resolution	**295**
Image resampling	295
Pan sharpening	305
Summary	**309**
Index	**311**

Preface

From Python programming good practices to the advanced use of analysis packages, this book teaches how to write applications that will perform complex geoprocessing tasks that can be replicated and reused. The book contains three sample applications. *Chapter 1* shows how to prepare a development environment. From *Chapter 2* to *Chapter 4*, the reader goes deep into Python functionality using classes, inheritance, and other resources in order to read, manipulate, combine, and search information in vector data. *Chapter 5* to *Chapter 7* presents techniques to render beautiful maps, and handle and analyze raster data. In the final three chapters, the book approaches code optimization and presents solutions to handle large datasets common in geoprocessing tasks. All the examples are modular and can be rearranged to achieve countless different results. During the book, the code is deduced step by step until it reaches the final form. The reader is led to edit, change, and improve the code, experimenting with different solutions and organizations, subtly learning the mental process of the development of a geoprocessing application.

What this book covers

Chapter 1, *Preparing the Work Environment*, shows the processes of installing all the libraries that you will need to go through the examples in the book, as well how to set up an integrated development environment (IDE) that will help organize the code and avoid mistakes. Finally, it will present the first contact with one of the geospatial libraries.

Chapter 2, *The Geocaching App*, will go through the important steps in geoprocessing applications, such as opening files, reading data, and preparing it for analysis with the tools at hand. Going through these steps, the user will learn how to organize and use the resources provided by the language to write consistent applications.

Chapter 3, *Combining Multiple Data Sources*, will cover the process of combining sources, and how to use Python classes to create your own representation of geospatial data. Geographic data tends to be heterogeneous, so writing programs that are able to combine multiple sources of data is a fundamental topic in geoprocessing.

Chapter 4, *Improving the App Search Capabilities*, will add new functionalities to the application. Users will write a code capable of filtering features by geographic boundaries and by any field in the data. In the process, they will see how to work with polygons and how the relations between geometries can be analyzed in a geoprocessing application.

Chapter 5, *Making Maps*, starts a new application that will be able to produce nice maps from the vectors of the data. Mapnik, one of the most used mapping packages, will be used. The user will understand how it works and how to adapt it to consume the data presented in the previous chapters.

Chapter 6, *Working with Remote Sensing Images*, will present a process of deduction that will result in a versatile and powerful software structure able to combine, crop, and adjust the values of images to prepare them for presentation.

Chapter 7, *Extract Information from Raster Data*, will approach the process of extracting information from raster data, which can be analyzed in order to produce valuable information. Going beyond simple numerical values, it will show how to display this information on beautiful color maps.

Chapter 8, *Data Miner App*, will show how to use databases and how to import data into it in order to minimize processing time and allow huge datasets to be processed. Geospatial data tends to be extensive and its processing demands a lot of computer power. To make the code more efficient, the reader will learn techniques of code profiling and optimization.

Chapter 9, *Processing Big Images*, will show how to process big satellite images. It will focus on how to perform sustainable image processing and how to open and make calculations with many big images while keeping the memory consumption low with efficient code.

Chapter 10, *Parallel Processing*, will teach the reader how to use the full available computer power. In order to speed up tasks, it will show how to distribute them among processor cores for parallel processing.

What you need for this book

To run the examples of this book, you will only need a computer with at least 4 GB of RAM with the Ubuntu Linux or Microsoft Windows operating system. All the programs and libraries that we will use are either free of charge or open source.

Who this book is for

This book is intended for beginners or advanced developers in Python, who want to work with geographic data. The book is suitable for professional developers who are new to geospatial development, for hobbyists, or for data scientists who want to move into simple development.

Conventions

In this book, you will find a number of text styles that distinguish between different kinds of information. Here are some examples of these styles and an explanation of their meaning.

Code words in text, database table names, folder names, filenames, file extensions, pathnames, dummy URLs, user input, and Twitter handles are shown as follows: "A Python package is a directory containing one or more Python files (that is, modules) plus one __init__.py file."

A block of code is set as follows:

```
import ogr
# Open the shapefile and get the first layer.
datasource = ogr.Open("../data/world_borders_simple.shp")
layer = datasource.GetLayerByIndex(0)
print("Number of features: {}".format(layer.GetFeatureCount()))
```

When we wish to draw your attention to a particular part of a code block, the relevant lines or items are set in bold:

```
if __name__ == '__main__':
    gdal.PushErrorHandler('CPLQuietErrorHandler')
    vector_data = PointCollection("../data/geocaching.gpx")
    vector_data.print_information()
```

Preface

Any command-line input or output is written as follows:

```
Collecting django
  Downloading Django-1.9-py2.py3-none-any.whl (6.6MB)
    100% |################################| 6.6MB 43kB/s
Installing collected packages: django
Successfully installed django-1.9
```

New terms and **important words** are shown in bold. Words that you see on the screen, for example, in menus or dialog boxes, appear in the text like this: "Proceed with the default options by clicking on the **Next** button."

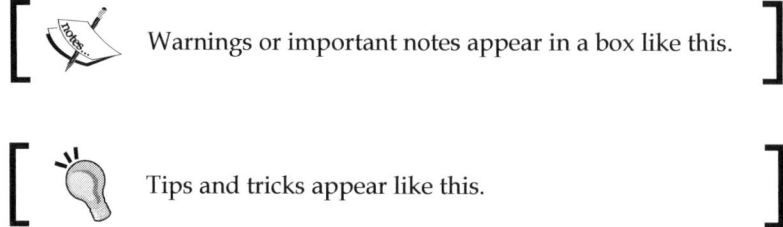

> Warnings or important notes appear in a box like this.

> Tips and tricks appear like this.

Reader feedback

Feedback from our readers is always welcome. Let us know what you think about this book—what you liked or disliked. Reader feedback is important for us as it helps us develop titles that you will really get the most out of.

To send us general feedback, simply e-mail feedback@packtpub.com, and mention the book's title in the subject of your message.

If there is a topic that you have expertise in and you are interested in either writing or contributing to a book, see our author guide at www.packtpub.com/authors.

Customer support

Now that you are the proud owner of a Packt book, we have a number of things to help you to get the most from your purchase.

Downloading the example code

You can download the example code files from your account at http://www.packtpub.com for all the Packt Publishing books you have purchased. If you purchased this book elsewhere, you can visit http://www.packtpub.com/support and register to have the files e-mailed directly to you.

Downloading the color images of this book

We also provide you with a PDF file that has color images of the screenshots/diagrams used in this book. The color images will help you better understand the changes in the output. You can download this file from `https://www.packtpub.com/sites/default/files/downloads/GeospatialDevelopmentByExampleWithPython_ColorImages.pdf`.

Errata

Although we have taken every care to ensure the accuracy of our content, mistakes do happen. If you find a mistake in one of our books—maybe a mistake in the text or the code—we would be grateful if you could report this to us. By doing so, you can save other readers from frustration and help us improve subsequent versions of this book. If you find any errata, please report them by visiting `http://www.packtpub.com/submit-errata`, selecting your book, clicking on the **Errata Submission Form** link, and entering the details of your errata. Once your errata are verified, your submission will be accepted and the errata will be uploaded to our website or added to any list of existing errata under the Errata section of that title.

To view the previously submitted errata, go to `https://www.packtpub.com/books/content/support` and enter the name of the book in the search field. The required information will appear under the **Errata** section.

Piracy

Piracy of copyrighted material on the Internet is an ongoing problem across all media. At Packt, we take the protection of our copyright and licenses very seriously. If you come across any illegal copies of our works in any form on the Internet, please provide us with the location address or website name immediately so that we can pursue a remedy.

Please contact us at `copyright@packtpub.com` with a link to the suspected pirated material.

We appreciate your help in protecting our authors and our ability to bring you valuable content.

Questions

If you have a problem with any aspect of this book, you can contact us at `questions@packtpub.com`, and we will do our best to address the problem.

1
Preparing the Work Environment

Working with a programming language as a tool for geoprocessing provides the opportunity to construct a personalized application that can more optimally perform the task required by the user. This means that repetitive tasks can be automated, file inputs and outputs can be customized, and processes can be tuned to perform exactly what you want to be done.

Python is a powerful programming language that is gaining special attention as a tool for geoprocessing and scientific analysis. A number of factors may have contributed to its popularization, and three among them are worth mentioning: it's a scripting language, it's flexible and easy to learn, and it has a wide range of libraries available as open source software.

The number of available libraries and packages allow users to spend less time in programming basic functionalities and more in building processes and workflows to reach their goals.

In this first chapter, we will go through the process of installing all the libraries that you will need to go through the examples; it's likely that these same libraries will also satisfy most of your needs in real-world applications. Then, we will set up an **Integrated Development Environment** (**IDE**) that will help organize code and avoid mistakes. Finally, we will write a sample program with one of the libraries. Therefore, here are the topics that will be covered:

- Installing Python and the packages that you need for the examples in this book
- Learning the basics of the packages that you will use

- Installing an IDE to write and organize your code
- Creating a project for this book
- Writing your first code

Installing Python

For this book, we suggest using Python 2.7; this version of Python is fully compatible with the libraries and packages that we will use in the examples and also has precompiled binary files available on the Internet for Windows users. We will keep all the examples as compatible as possible with Python 3.4 so that it would be easy to port future upgrades.

Windows users may find compatibility problems with the 64-bit packages, so we recommend the 32-bit version of Python for them.

For Linux users, we will show the installation procedures for Ubuntu Linux distribution and use package managers, so you don't need to worry about versions and requirements; the package managers will do this for you.

The libraries that you will install are written in Python and other languages, the most common being C and C++. These libraries can abstract classes, methods, and functions to Python objects or have an extra layer that makes the connection; when this happens, we say that the library has *Python bindings*.

Windows

Here are the steps to perform for the installation of Python on Windows:

1. Go to `https://www.python.org/downloads/windows/` and click on Download the latest Python 2.7 release for Windows.
2. On the next page, roll down, and you will find a list of files; make sure that you download **Windows x86 MSI installer**.
3. After the file is downloaded, open the installer by clicking on the file and following the instructions. Proceed with the default options by clicking on the **Next** button.

Ubuntu Linux

Ubuntu already comes with Python installed, so there is no need to install it. If for any reason, it's not available, you can install it with the following command:

```
sudo apt-get install python
```

Python 2.7.9 comes with Pip, but if you use an older version, you need to install Pip with the following command:

```
sudo apt-get install python-pip
```

Python packages and package manager

A Python package is a directory containing one or more Python files (that is, modules) plus one __init__.py file (this can be just an empty file). This file tells Python Interpreter that the directory is a package.

When writing Python code, we can import packages and modules and use them in our code. The Python community does this a lot; many packages use other packages and so on, forming an intricate network of requirements and dependencies.

In order to facilitate the installation of packages and all the requirements for it to run, Python has a package manager called pip.

Pip looks for packages in a central repository (or on a user-defined place), downloads it, then downloads its dependencies, and installs them. Some packages also use libraries in other languages, such as C. In these cases, these libraries need to be compiled during the installation. Ubuntu users don't have problem with this because many compilers are already installed on the system, but this won't work on Windows by default.

The repository of Python packages for Windows

Python makes it easy to install libraries and packages through pip. However, since Windows doesn't include any compiler by default, the installation of packages that needs the compilation of libraries fails. Instead of going through the process of installing a compiler, which is out of this book's scope, we can get the packages ready to use.

These packages come prebuilt for various types of system and don't need a compilation of its libraries. This type of package is called a wheel.

 Christoph Gohlke did a favor to all of us by building these packages and making them available for download at http://www.lfd.uci.edu/~gohlke/pythonlibs/.

[3]

Preparing the Work Environment

Installing packages and required software

In this topic, we will go through the installation process of every package used in the book.

OpenCV

OpenCV is an optimized C/C++ library intended for video and image processing with hundreds of functions ranging from simple image resizing to object recognition, face detection, and so on. OpenCV is a big library, and we will use its capabilities of reading, transforming, and writing images. It's a good choice because its development is active, and it has a large user community and very good documentation.

Windows

Here is the installation procedure for Windows:

1. Go to http://www.lfd.uci.edu/~gohlke/pythonlibs/.
2. Press *Ctrl* + *F* to open the search dialog of your browser and then search for OpenCV.
3. You will find a list of files; choose opencv_python-2.4.11-cp27-none-win32.whl or any OpenCV version that contains cp27 and win32. This means that this is the 32-bit version for Python 2.7.
4. Save the downloaded file to a known location.
5. Open Windows Command Prompt and run the following command:
   `c:\Python27\scripts\pip install path_to_the_file_you_downloaded.whl`
6. You should see an output telling you that the installation was successful, as follows:
   ```
   Processing c:\downloads\opencv_python-2.4.12-cp27-none-win32.whl
   Installing collected packages: opencv-python
   Successfully installed opencv-python-2.4.12
   ```

> You can drag and drop a file into the command prompt to enter its full path.

Ubuntu Linux

Here is the installation process for Ubuntu Linux:

1. Open a new terminal with *Ctrl + T*.
2. Then, enter the following command:
   ```
   sudo apt-get install python-opencv
   ```

Installing NumPy

NumPy is a package for scientific computing with Python. It handles multidimensional arrays of operations in a very efficient way. NumPy is required by OpenCV to run and will be used by many raster operations that we will perform in the examples. NumPy is also an efficient data container and will be our tool to calculate massive image data.

Windows

Repeat the same procedure as you did to install OpenCV; however, this time, search for NumPy and choose a file named `numpy-1.9.2+mkl-cp27-none-win32.whl`.

Ubuntu Linux

NumPy is automatically installed as a dependency of OpenCV on Ubuntu, but if you want to install it without OpenCV, follow these steps:

1. Open a new terminal with *Ctrl + T*.
2. Then, enter the following command:
   ```
   sudo pip install numpy
   ```

Installing GDAL and OGR

GDAL (Geospatial Data Abstraction Library) is composed of two packages that come together: OGR handles geospatial vector file formats, including coordinate system transformations and vector operations. GDAL is the raster part of the library, and in version 1.11, it comes packed with 139 drivers that can read, and some even create rasters. GDAL also comes packed with functions for raster transformations and calculations such as resizing, clipping, reprojecting, and so on.

Preparing the Work Environment

In the following tables, there's an excerpt of the list of GDAL and OGR drivers with the most common formats that you may find:

Long format name	Code	Creation
Arc/Info ASCII Grid	`AAIGrid`	Yes
Arc/Info Export E00 GRID	`E00GRID`	No
ENVI .hdr Labelled Raster	`ENVI`	Yes
Generic Binary (.hdr Labelled)	`GENBIN`	No
Oracle Spatial GeoRaster	`GEORASTER`	Yes
GSat File Format	`GFF`	No
Graphics Interchange Format (.gif)	`GIF`	Yes
GMT Compatible netCDF	`GMT`	Yes
GRASS ASCII Grid	`GRASSASCIIGrid`	No
Golden Software ASCII Grid	`GSAG`	Yes
Golden Software Binary Grid	`GSBG`	Yes
Golden Software Surfer 7 Binary Grid	`GS7BG`	Yes
TIFF / BigTIFF / GeoTIFF (.tif)	`GTiff`	Yes
GXF (Grid eXchange File)	`GXF`	No
Erdas Imagine (.img)	`HFA`	Yes
JPEG JFIF (.jpg)	`JPEG`	Yes
NOAA Polar Orbiter Level 1b Data Set (AVHRR)	`L1B`	No
NOAA NGS Geoid Height Grids	`NGSGEOID`	No
NITF	`NITF`	Yes
NTv2 Datum Grid Shift	`NTv2`	Yes
PCI .aux Labelled	`PAux`	Yes
PCI Geomatics Database File	`PCIDSK`	Yes
PCRaster	`PCRaster`	Yes
Geospatial PDF	`PDF`	Yes
NASA Planetary Data System	`PDS`	No
Portable Network Graphics (`.png`)	`PNG`	Yes
R Object Data Store	`R`	Yes
Raster Matrix Format (`*.rsw`, `.mtw`)	`RMF`	Yes
RadarSat2 XML (`product.xml`)	`RS2`	No
Idrisi Raster	`RST`	Yes
SAGA GIS Binary format	`SAGA`	Yes

Long format name	Code	Creation
USGS SDTS DEM (*CATD.DDF)	SDTS	No
SGI Image Format	SGI	Yes
SRTM HGT Format	SRTMHGT	Yes
Terragen Heightfield (.ter)	TERRAGEN	Yes
USGS ASCII DEM / CDED (.dem)	USGSDEM	Yes
ASCII Gridded XYZ	XYZ	Yes

The following table describes the OGR drivers:

Format name	Code	Creation
Arc/Info Binary Coverage	AVCBin	No
Arc/Info .E00 (ASCII) Coverage	AVCE00	No
AutoCAD DXF	DXF	Yes
Comma Separated Value (.csv)	CSV	Yes
ESRI Shapefile	ESRI Shapefile	Yes
GeoJSON	GeoJSON	Yes
Géoconcept Export	Geoconcept	Yes
GeoRSS	GeoRSS	Yes
GML	GML	Yes
GMT	GMT	Yes
GPSBabel	GPSBabel	Yes
GPX	GPX	Yes
GPSTrackMaker (.gtm, .gtz)	GPSTrackMaker	Yes
Hydrographic Transfer Format	HTF	No
Idrisi Vector (.VCT)	Idrisi	No
KML	KML	Yes
Mapinfo File	MapInfo File	Yes
Microstation DGN	DGN	Yes
OpenAir	OpenAir	No
ESRI FileGDB	OpenFileGDB	No
PCI Geomatics Database File	PCIDSK	Yes
Geospatial PDF	PDF	Yes
PDS	PDS	No
PostgreSQL SQL dump	PGDump	Yes
U.S. Census TIGER/Line	TIGER	No

Preparing the Work Environment

>  You can find the full GDAL and OGR API documentation and the complete list of drivers at `http://gdal.org/python/`.

Windows

Again, we will use a wheel for the installation. Repeat the same procedure as before:

1. Go to `http://www.lfd.uci.edu/~gohlke/pythonlibs/`.
2. Now, search for GDAL and download the file named `GDAL-1.11.3-cp27-none-win32.whl`.
3. Finally, install it with `pip`, as we did before.

Ubuntu Linux

Perform the following steps:

1. Go to the terminal or open a new one.
2. Then, enter the following command:
   ```
   sudo apt-get install python-gdal
   ```

Installing Mapnik

Mapnik is a map rendering package. It is a free toolkit to develop mapping applications. It produces high-quality maps and is used on many applications, including OpenStreetMaps.

Windows

Mapnik isn't available for installation as other libraries are. Instead, you need to go to `http://mapnik.org/` and follow the download link:

1. Download the Windows 32-bit package of Mapnik 2.2.
2. Extract the `mapnik-v2.2.0` to `C:\` folder.
3. Then, rename the extracted folder `c:\mapnik`.
4. Now, add `Mapnik` to your **PATH**.

5. Open **Control Panel** and go to **System**.
6. Click on the **Advanced System Settings** link in the left-hand side column.
7. In the **System Properties** window, click on the **Advanced** tab.
8. Next, click on the **Environment Variables** button.
9. In the **System variables** section, highlight the **PATH** variable and click on **Edit**. Add the following paths to the end of the list, each separated with a semicolon, as follows:

    `c:\mapnik\bin;c:\mapnik\lib`

10. Now, click on the **New** button; then, set the variable name to `PYTHONPATH` and value to `c:\mapnik\python\2.7\site-packages`.

Ubuntu Linux

For this, perform the following:

1. Go to the terminal or open a new one.
2. Then, enter the following command:

    `sudo apt-get install mapnik`

Installing Shapely

Shapely is a package for the manipulation and analysis of two dimensional geometries. It can perform operations such as union and subtraction of geometries. It also can perform tests and comparisons, such as when a geometry intersects other geometries.

Windows

Here's what you need to do:

1. As before, download the prebuilt wheel; this time, look for a file named `Shapely-1.5.13-cp27-none-win32.whl`.
2. Then, install it with `pip`.

Ubuntu Linux

Here are the steps you need to perform:

1. Go to the terminal or open a new one with *Ctrl + T*.
2. Enter the following command:
   ```
   sudo pip install shapely
   ```

Installing other packages directly from pip

Some packages do not require compilation steps. For Windows users, these are easier to install because they can be obtained and installed directly with `pip` with a single command.

Windows

You need to simply type the following command in your Command Prompt:

```
c:\Python27\scripts\pip install django tabulate requests xmltodict psycopg2
```

Ubuntu Linux

In the terminal, type the following command:

```
sudo pip install django tabulate requests xmltodict psycopg2
```

For each package, you should see the progress of the installation, similar to the following:

```
Collecting django
  Downloading Django-1.9-py2.py3-none-any.whl (6.6MB)
    100% |################################| 6.6MB 43kB/s
Installing collected packages: django
Successfully installed django-1.9
```

Installing an IDE

IDEs are fancy text editors with tools and inspections regarding programming languages. You can surely use any text editor or IDE of your preference; none of the tasks in this book depends on the IDE, but an IDE will facilitate our work a lot because the suggested configuration will help you avoid mistakes and save time on typing, running, and debugging your code. The IDE checks the code for you and detects underlying errors; it even guesses what you are typing and completes the statements for you, runs the code with a simple command, and if there are exceptions, it provides links to the place where the exception occurred. For Windows or Linux, go to http://www.jetbrains.com/pycharm/ and click on the big orange button **Get Pycharm Now**. On the next page, select the free community edition.

Windows

Here are the steps you need to perform:

1. After the download finishes, open the downloaded file; the **Setup Wizard** will pop up.
2. Click on **Next**, and in the installation options, check both of the boxes: **Create Desktop shortcut** and **Create associations**.
3. Click on **Next** and continue the installation.

Linux

Perform the following steps:

1. Unpack the downloaded file in a directory.
2. To open PyCharm, run pycharm.sh from the bin subdirectory. You can create a shortcut to it if you wish.

>
> **Downloading the example code**
>
> You can download the example code files for all Packt books you have purchased from your account at http://www.packtpub.com. If you purchased this book elsewhere, you can visit http://www.packtpub.com/support and register to have the files e-mailed directly to you.

Creating the book project

Perform the following steps:

1. After installation, open Pycharm, and you will be prompted to create your first project:

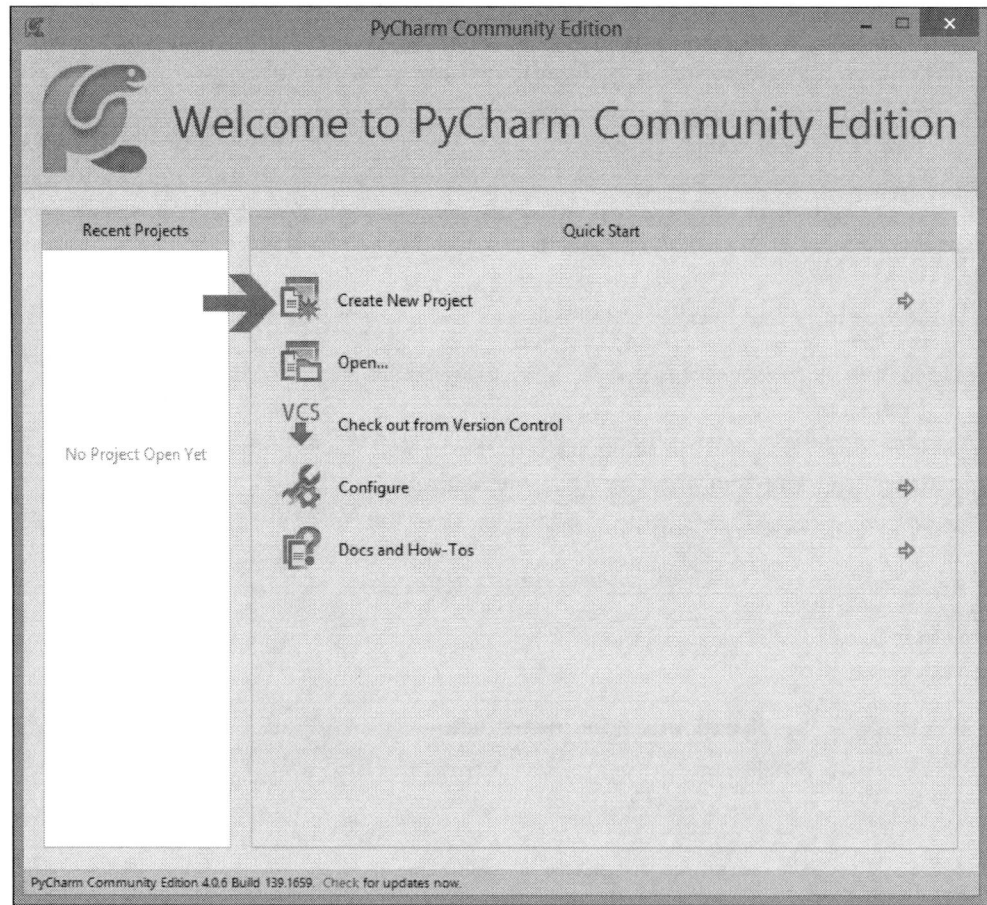

Chapter 1

2. Click on create new project and then choose `c:\geopy` as your project location. In Linux, you can put the project inside your home folder—for example, `/home/myname/geopy`. Click on **Create** to create the project.

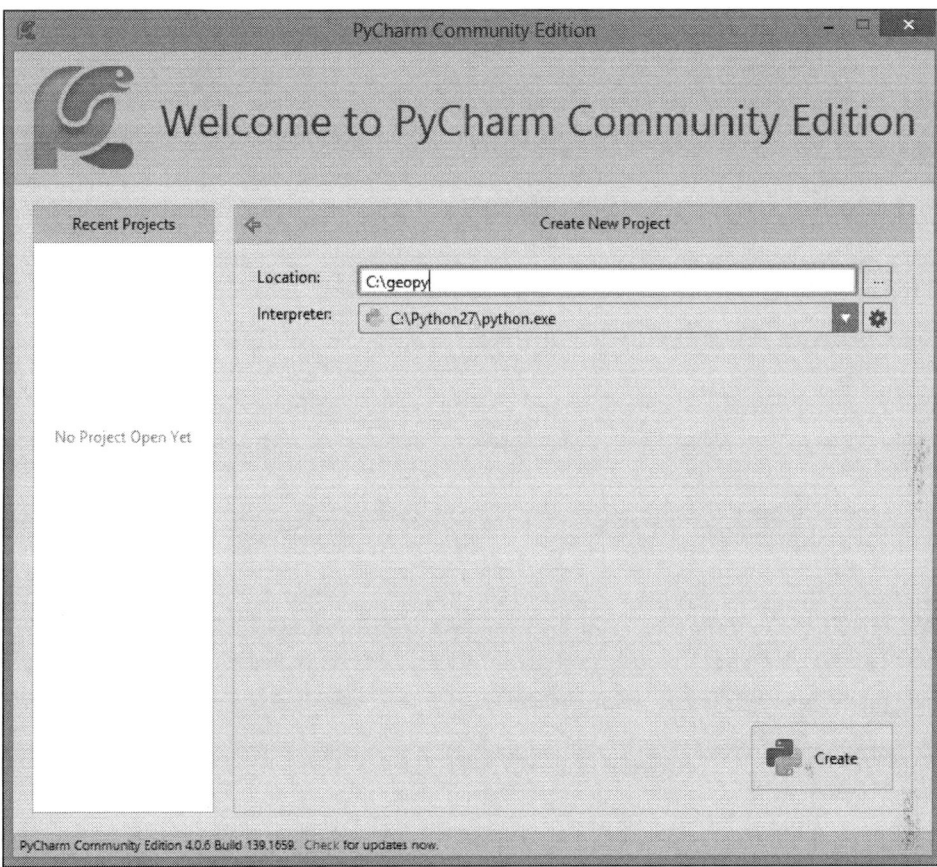

Preparing the Work Environment

3. In Windows, you will receive a security alert; this is Pycharm trying to access the Internet. It's recommended that you allow it so that you can later check for updates or download plugins:

4. Finally, you should see the following window on your project workspace. Take some time to explore the menus and buttons, try right-clicking on your project folder to see the options:

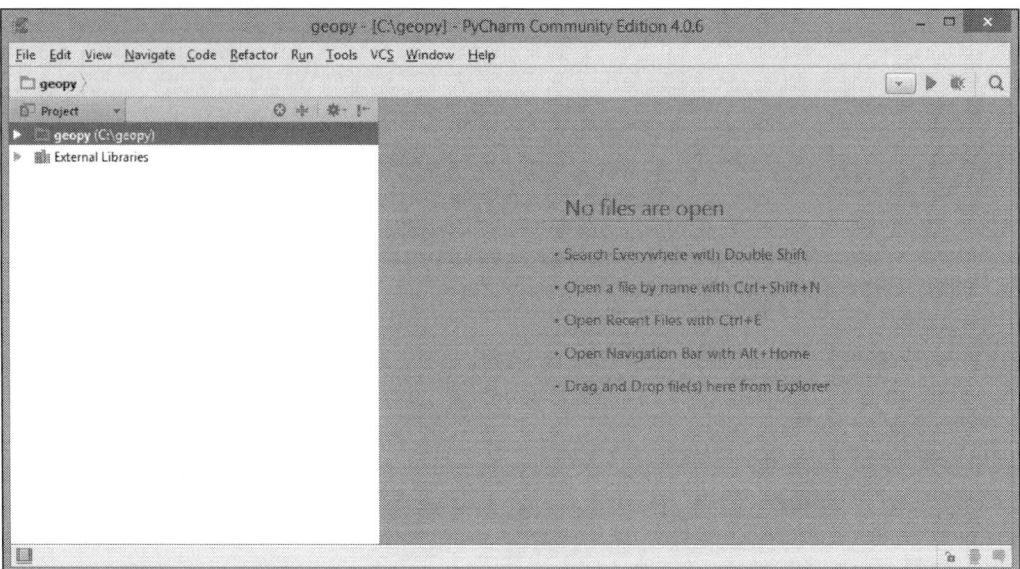

Programming and running your first example

Now that we have all we need installed, we will go through our first example. In this example, we will test the installation and then see a glimpse of OGR's capabilities.

To do this, we will open a vector file containing the boundaries of all the countries in the world and make a list of country names. The objective of this simple example is to present the logic behind OGR objects and functions and give an understanding of how geospatial files are represented. Here's how:

1. First, you need to copy the sample data provided with the book to your project folder. You can do this by dragging and dropping the data folder into the geopy folder. Make sure that the data folder is named data and that it's inside the geopy folder.

2. Now, create a new directory for this chapter code, inside PyCharm. With your geopy project opened, right-click on the project folder and select **New | Directory**. Name it Chapter1.

3. Create a new Python file. To do this, right-click on the Chapter1 folder and select **New | Python File**. Name it world_borders.py, and PyCharm will automatically open the file for editing.

4. Type the following code in this file:

   ```
   import ogr
   # Open the shapefile and get the first layer.
   datasource = ogr.Open("../data/world_borders_simple.shp")
   layer = datasource.GetLayerByIndex(0)
   print("Number of features: {}".format(layer.GetFeatureCount()))
   ```

5. Now, run the code; in the menu bar, navigate to **Run | Run**, and in the dialog, choose world_borders. An output console will open at the bottom of the screen, and if everything goes fine, you should see this output:

   ```
   C:\Python27\python.exe C:/geopy/world_borders.py
   Number of features: 246

   Process finished with exit code 0
   ```

Congratulations! You successfully opened a Shapefile and counted the number of features inside it. Now, let's understand what this code does.

The first line imports the ogr package. From this point on, all the functions are available as ogr.FunctionName(). Note that ogr doesn't follow the Python naming conventions for functions.

Preparing the Work Environment

The line after the comment opens the OGR datasource (this opens the shapefile containing the data) and assigns the object to the `datasource` variable. Note that the path, even on Windows, uses a forward slash (/) and not a backslash.

The next line gets the first layer of the data source by its index (0). Some data sources can have many layers, but this is not the case of a Shapefile, which has only one layer. So, when working with Shapefiles, we always know that the layer of interest is layer 0.

In the final line, the print statement prints the number of features returned by `layer.GetFeatureCount()`. Here, we will use Python's string formatting, where the curly braces are replaced by the argument passed to `format()`.

Now, perform the following steps:

1. In the same file, let's type the next part of our program:

   ```
   # Inspect the fields available in the layer.
   feature_definition = layer.GetLayerDefn()
   for field_index in range(feature_definition.GetFieldCount()):
       field_definition = feature_definition.GetFieldDefn(field_index)
       print("\t{}\t{}\t{}".format(field_index,
                                   field_definition.GetTypeName(),
                                   field_definition.GetName()))
   ```

2. Rerun the code; you can use the *Shift + F10* shortcut for this. Now, you should see the number of features as before plus a pretty table showing information on all the fields in the shapefile, as follows:

   ```
   Number of features: 246
       0 String   FIPS
       1 String   ISO2
       2 String   ISO3
       3 Integer  UN
       4 String   NAME
       5 Integer  POP2005
       6 Integer  REGION
       7 Integer  SUBREGION
   
   Process finished with exit code 0
   ```

What happens in this piece of code is that `feature_definition = layer.GetLayerDefn()` gets the object that contains the definition of the features. This object contains the definition for each field and the type of geometry.

In the `for` loop, we will get each field definition and print its index, name, and type. Note that the object returned by `layer.GetLayerDefn()` is not iterable, and we can't use `for` directly with it. So first, we will get the number of fields and use it in the `range()` function so that we can iterate through the indexes of the fields:

3. Now, type the last part, as follows:

    ```
    # Print a list of country names.
    layer.ResetReading()
    for feature in layer:
        print(feature.GetFieldAsString(4))
    ```

4. Run the code again and check the results in the output:

    ```
    Number of features: 246
     0 String FIPS
     1 String ISO2
     2 String ISO3
     3 Integer UN
     4 String NAME
     5 Integer POP2005
     6 Integer REGION
     7 Integer SUBREGION
    Antigua and Barbuda
    Algeria
    Azerbaijan
    Albania
    Armenia
    Angola
    ...
    Saint Barthelemy
    Guernsey
    Jersey
    South Georgia South Sandwich Islands
    Taiwan

    Process finished with exit code 0
    ```

The layer is iterable, but first, we need to ensure that we are at the beginning of the layer list with `layer.ResetReading()` (this is one of OGR's "gotcha" points).

The `feature.GetFieldAsString(4)` method returns the value of field 4 as a Python string. There are two ways of knowing whether the country names are in field 4:

- Looking at the data's DBF file (by opening it with LibreOffice or Excel)
- Looking at the table that we printed in the first part of the code

Your complete code should look similar to the following:

```
import ogr


# Open the shapefile and get the first layer.
datasource = ogr.Open("../data/world_borders_simple.shp")
layer = datasource.GetLayerByIndex(0)
print("Number of features: {}".format(layer.GetFeatureCount()))

# Inspect the fields available in the layer.
feature_definition = layer.GetLayerDefn()
for field_index in range(feature_definition.GetFieldCount()):
    field_definition = feature_definition.GetFieldDefn(field_index)
    print("\t{}\t{}\t{}".format(field_index,
                                field_definition.GetTypeName(),
                                field_definition.GetName()))

# Print a list of country names.
layer.ResetReading()
for feature in layer:
    print(feature.GetFieldAsString(4))
```

Transforming the coordinate system and calculating the area of all countries

Now, the objective is to know how much area is occupied by each country. However, the coordinates of country borders are expressed in latitude and longitude, and we can't calculate areas in this coordinate system. We want the area to be in the metric system, so first we need to convert the spatial reference system of the geometries.

Let's also take a step further in the programming techniques and start using functions to avoid the repetition of code. Perform the following steps:

1. Create a new file in the `Chapter1` directory, name this file `world_areas.py`, and program this first function:

   ```
   import ogr


   def open_shapefile(file_path):
       """Open the shapefile, get the first layer and returns
       the ogr datasource.
       """
       datasource = ogr.Open(file_path)
       layer = datasource.GetLayerByIndex(0)
       print("Opening {}".format(file_path))
       print("Number of features: {}".format(
       layer.GetFeatureCount()))
       return datasource
   ```

2. Run the code, go to **Run | Run...** in the menu, and select `world_areas`. If everything is correct, nothing should happen. This is because we are not calling our function. Add this line of code at the end and outside the function:

   ```
   datasource = open_shapefile("../data/world_borders_simple.shp")
   ```

3. Now, run the code again with *Shift + F10* and check the output, as follows:

   ```
   Opening ../data/world_borders_simple.shp
   Number of features: 246

   Process finished with exit code 0
   ```

That's wonderful! You just created a piece of very useful and reusable code. You now have a function that can open any shapefile, print the number of features, and return the `ogr` datasource. From now on, you can reuse this function in any of your projects.

You are already familiar with how this code works, but there are a few novelties here that deserve an explanation. The `def` statement defines a function with the `def function_name(arguments):` syntax.

Remember when I told you that OGR doesn't follow Python's naming convention? Well, the convention is that function names should all be in lowercase with an underscore between words. A good hint for names is to follow the `verb_noun` rule.

> These conventions are described in a document called **PEP-8**, where **PEP** stands for **Python Enhancement Program**. You can find this document at https://www.python.org/dev/peps/pep-0008/.

Right after the function's definition, you can see a description between triple quotes; this is a docstring, and it is used to document the code. It's optional but very useful for you to know what the function does.

Now, let's get back to our code. The second important thing to point out is the `return` statement. This makes the function return the values of the variables listed after the statement—in this case, the datasource.

> It's very important that all pieces of the OGR objects flow together through the program. In this case, if we return only the layer, for example, we will get a runtime error later in our program. This happens because in OGR internals, the layer has a reference to the data source, and when you exit a Python function, all objects that don't exit the function are trashed, and this breaks the reference.

Now, the next step is to create a function that performs the transformation. In OGR, the transformation is made in the feature's geometry, so we need to iterate over the features, get the geometry, and transform its coordinates. We will do this using the following steps:

1. Add the following function to your `world_areas.py` file just after the `open_shapefile` function:

    ```
    def transform_geometries(datasource, src_epsg, dst_epsg):
        """Transform the coordinates of all geometries in the
    first layer.
    """
        # Part 1
        src_srs = osr.SpatialReference()
        src_srs.ImportFromEPSG(src_epsg)
        dst_srs = osr.SpatialReference()
        dst_srs.ImportFromEPSG(dst_epsg)
        transformation = osr.CoordinateTransformation(src_srs, dst_srs)
        layer = datasource.GetLayerByIndex(0)

        # Part 2
        geoms = []
    ```

```
    layer.ResetReading()
    for feature in layer:
        geom = feature.GetGeometryRef().Clone()
        geom.Transform(transformation)
        geoms.append(geom)
    return geoms
```

The function takes three arguments: the ogr layer, the EPSG code of the coordinate system of the file, and the EPSG code for the transformation output.

Here, it created an `osr.CoordinateTransformation` object; this object contains the instructions to perform the transformation.

Probably by now, Pycharm should be complaining that `osr` is an `unresolved reference`; `osr` is the part of GDAL that deals with coordinate systems.

2. Now, import the module by adding this line at the top of your code:

   import osr

   Here, the code iterates over all features, gets a reference to the geometry, and performs the transformation. As we don't want to change the original data, the geometry is cloned, and the transformation is made on the clone.

   Python lists are ordered; this means that the elements are in the same order in which they are appended to the list, and this order is always kept. This allows us to create a list of geometries in the same order of the features that are in the data source. This means that the geometries in the list and the features have the same index and can be related in the future by the index.

3. Now, let's test the code; add the following lines at the end of the file (the first line is the one that you already added before):

   ```
   datasource = open_shapefile("../data/world_borders_simple.shp")
   layer = datasource.GetLayerByIndex(0)
   feature = layer.GetFeature(0)
   print("Before transformation:")
   print(feature.GetGeometryRef())
   transformed_geoms = transform_geometries(datasource, 4326, 3395)
   print("After transformation:")
   print(transformed_geoms[0])
   ```

4. Finally, before you run the code, add one more `import` at the beginning of the program. It should be the first statement of your code, as follows:

   from __future__ import print_function

   This `import` allows us to use the `print()` function from Python 3 with the desired behavior, thus maintaining the compatibility.

[21]

Preparing the Work Environment

5. The complete code should look similar to this:
   ```
   from __future__ import print_function
   import ogr
   import osr


   def open_shapefile(file_path):
       ...

   def transform_geometries(datasource, src_epsg, dst_epsg):
       ...

   datasource = open_shapefile("../data/world_borders_simple.shp")
   layer = datasource.GetLayerByIndex(0)
   feature = layer.GetFeature(0)
   print("Before transformation:")
   print(feature.GetGeometryRef())
   transformed_geoms = transform_geometries(datasource, 4326, 3395)
   print("After transformation:")
   print(transformed_geoms[0])
   ```

6. Run your program again by pressing *Shift + F10*. In the output, note the difference in the coordinates before and after the transformation:
   ```
   Opening ../data/world_borders_simple.shp
   Number of features: 246
   Before transformation:
   MULTIPOLYGON (((-61.686668 17.024441000000138 ... )))
   After transformation:
   MULTIPOLYGON (((-6866928.4704937246 ... )))

   Process finished with exit code 0
   ```

7. Now, add another function. This function will calculate the area in square meters (because we will use the geometries that have coordinates in meters), convert the value (or not) to square kilometers or square miles, and store the values in another list with the same order as before. Execute the following code:
   ```
   def calculate_areas(geometries, unity='km2'):
       """Calculate the area for a list of ogr geometries."""
       # Part 1
       conversion_factor = {
           'sqmi': 2589988.11,
           'km2': 1000000,
   ```

[22]

```
        'm': 1}
# Part2
if unity not in conversion_factor:
    raise ValueError(
        "This unity is not defined: {}".format(unity))
# Part 3
areas = []
for geom in geometries:
    area = geom.Area()
    areas.append(area / conversion_factor[unity])
return areas
```

Firstly, note that in the function definition, we use `unity='km2'`; this is a keyword argument, and when you call the functions, this argument is optional.

In `Part 1`, a dictionary is used to define a few conversion factors for the area unit. Feel free to add more units if you wish. By the way, Python doesn't care if you use single or double quotes.

In `Part 2`, a verification is made to check whether the passed unity exists and whether it is defined in `conversion_factor`. Another way of doing this is catching the exception later; however, for now, let's opt for readability.

In `Part 3`, the code iterates the `ogr` geometries, calculates the area, converts the values, and puts it on a list.

8. Now, to test the code, edit your first line, including `division` to the future imports. This will ensure that all divisions return floating point numbers and not integers. Here's how it should look:

   ```
   from __future__ import print_function, division
   ```

9. Then, update the testing part of your code to the following:

   ```
   datasource = open_shapefile("../data/world_borders_simple.shp")
   transformed_geoms = transform_geometries(datasource, 4326, 3395)
   calculated_areas = calculate_areas(transformed_geoms, unity='sqmi')
   print(calculated_areas)
   ```

10. Run it, change the unity, then run again, and note how the results change.

Very well, unity conversion is another very important procedure in geoprocessing, and you just implemented it in your `calculate_areas` function.

However, having a list of numbers as the output is not very useful to us. So, it's time to combine everything that we did so far in order to extract valuable information.

Sort the countries by area size

You programmed three functions so far; now, let's add another one to our list by converting the code that generated a list of country names to a function and add this function to `world_areas.py`, as follows:

```
def get_country_names(datasource):
    """Returns a list of country names."""
    layer = datasource.GetLayerByIndex(0)
    country_names = []
    layer.ResetReading()
    for feature in layer:
        country_names.append(feature.GetFieldAsString(4))
    return country_names
```

Now, we have four functions, which are:

- `open_shapefile`
- `transform_geometries`
- `calculate_areas`
- `get_country_names`

All these functions return iterables, with each item sharing the same index on all of them, thus making it easy to combine the information.

So, let's take advantage of this feature to sort the countries by area size and return a list of the five biggest countries and their areas. For this, add another function, as follows:

```
def get_biggest_countries(countries, areas, elements=5):
    """Returns a list of n countries sorted by area size."""
    countries_list = [list(country)
                      for country in zip(areas, countries)]
    
    sorted_countries = sorted(countries_list,
                              key=itemgetter(0), reverse=True)
    return sorted_countries[:5]
```

In the first line, the two lists are zipped together, producing a list of country-area pairs. Then, we used the Python list's `sorted` method, but as we don't want the lists to be sorted by both values, we will define the key for sorting. Finally, the list is sliced, returning only the desired number of values.

1. In order to run this code, you need to import the `itemgetter` function and put it at the beginning of the code but after `from __future__` imports, as follows:

    ```
    from operator import itemgetter
    ```

2. Now, edit the testing part of your code to look similar to the following:
   ```
   datasource = open_shapefile("../data/world_borders_simple.shp")
   transformed_geoms = transform_geometries(datasource, 4326, 3395)
   country_names = get_country_names(datasource)
   country_areas = calculate_areas(transformed_geoms)
   biggest_countries = get_biggest_countries(country_names,
                                             country_areas)
   for item in biggest_countries:
       print("{}\t{}".format(item[0], item[1]))
   ```

3. Now, run the code and take a look at the results, as follows:
   ```
   Opening ../data/world_borders_simple.shp
   Number of features: 246
   82820725.1423  Russia
   51163710.3726  Canada
   35224817.514   Greenland
   21674429.8403  United States
   14851905.8596  China

   Process finished with exit code 0
   ```

Summary

In this chapter, we had a brief introduction to the libraries and packages that we will use in this book. By installing these libraries, you also learned the general procedure of how to search and install Python packages. You can use this procedure in other cases whenever you feel the need for other libraries in your applications.

Then, we wrote code that made use of the OGR library to open a shapefile and perform area calculation and sorting. These simple procedures showed a little bit of the internal organization of OGR, how it handles geographic data, and how it is possible to extract information from them. In the next chapter, we will use some of the techniques learned here to read data and process vector points.

2
The Geocaching App

In this chapter, we will build a geocaching app that will initially get geocache points from the Internet and return the coordinates and information on the point closest to a user's location.

We will go through some of the most important steps in every geoprocessing application: we will discuss opening files, reading information, preparing data for analysis, and performing calculations with each object in your data. To achieve this, you will learn how to organize your code with Python and use the resources provided by the language to write consistent applications.

In this chapter, we will start to make use of classes, methods, functions, decorators, and exception handling, which will help us build an application with reusable components and clean code. Don't worry if these terms are new to you; they will be explained in the examples. In short, here's what we will cover:

- Programming the basic application structures
- Downloading geocaching data
- Opening geocaching files and getting their contents
- Combining functions into an application
- Setting your current location
- Handling exceptions
- Finding the closest point

The Geocaching App

Building the basic application structure

There are two main reasons to define a good basic structure for our application:

- It keeps our code organized
- It allows us to reuse pieces of code in later applications

Python is a flexible language in terms of code organization, and although users are allowed to write the whole application in a single file, it's preferable to separate the functionalities into modules and packages.

Modules are Python files that contain classes and functions that can be imported into another file with the import statement. Packages are special directories (folders) that contain modules. This leads to organized and well-structured code that is less prone to having bugs and is easier to maintain.

The proposed structure is to have a folder for each chapter. Inside it, we can create packages or files for each application; we will create a package for a common utility code that can be imported and reused and a directory to perform experiments.

Creating the application tree structure

Here are the steps that you need to perform:

- If you went through *Chapter 1*, *Preparing the Work Environment*, you should now have a PyCharm project named geopy with the Chapter1 and data directories located at C:\geopy in Windows or ~/geopy in Linux. Start PyCharm and open your project.
- In the project root (the uppermost folder named geopy), right-click, select **New** | **Directory**, and name it Chapter2.
- Right-click on Chapter2, select **New** | **Directory**, and name it experiments.
- Again, right-click inside the Chapter2 directory; this time, select **New** | **Python Package** and name it utils.

Now, you should have a tree structure similar to this:

```
\geopy
+---Chapter1
|       world_areas.py
|       world_borders.py
|
+---Chapter2
|   |
```

```
|   \---experiments
|   \---utils
|
|
+---data
```

> **Python Packages**
>
> Packages are special folders that contain another packages and modules. They are directories with a special file called __init__.py. This file may be empty and is used to denote that the package can be imported with the import statement.
>
> For example, if we have a directory called foo (with a __init__.py file) and we create a bar.py file inside it, we can later use import foo.bar or from foo import bar in our code.

Functions and methods

Functions and methods (which are functions inside classes) should be concise so that when you call them, you can trust that you will get the desired results or appropriate exceptions. The programmer doesn't want to check the function's contents every time they use it; they want to call it and get the anticipated results, which is called taking *the leap of faith*. For example, in this book, we use many external packages; when we use a given function of a package, we trust that this function will do what it's supposed to do or raise an error telling us that something went wrong. Anything besides this is called *unexpected behavior*, and this is the most dangerous type of bug that an application can have because it is passed silently but has consequences later in code.

> So far, we saw a module that may have this kind of unexpected behavior: GDAL/OGR. The ogr.Open() function is passed silently even if the file doesn't exist, unless we specifically tell OGR that we want it to raise exceptions for us.

Documenting your code

As the application starts to gain scale, it's very important to keep track of what each piece of code does. This prevents the programmer from repeating code and saves a lot of time later trying to find out what is going on. Also, it allows other people to use and improve your code. There are two crucial tools that can be used to document the code, and we had a glimpse of it in the first chapter:

- **Code comments**: These are the comments inserted in code with the # symbol. Everything from this symbol to the next line is a comment and will be ignored when the program runs. The Python syntax is intuitive, and a well-written code requires a few comments. Here are two tips to concisely comment your code:
    - Place a comment before each logical block of code telling what it's doing
    - Comment pieces of code that are hard to read or understand

- **Docstrings**: Docstrings are texts placed in special locations in document classes, functions, and methods. They have a special meaning because they can be interpreted by some programs and used to provide the user with help and automatically generate documentation. Docstrings can also be used to test your code, but this will not be covered in this book. In PyCharm, docstrings have a special purpose and provide hints for automatic code inspection. Within docstrings, you can specify parameters and return types (for example, strings, list, and dictionary). PyCharm uses this to make auto-complete suggestions and warn you about possible mistakes.

> In this book, we will use the reStructuredText type of markup for docstrings; you can find more information at http://docutils.sourceforge.net/rst.html.

In the following example, you can note a class and method documented with docstrings (you don't need to type this code):

```
class MyClass:
    """This is an example of a docstring of a class."""

    def __init__(self):
        """You can also put docstrings in the __init__ method."""
        pass

    def sum_values(self, arg1, arg2):
        """This is the docstring for a method, you can describe
```

```
        the arguments and specify its types.
        If you do so, PyCharm will use that information
        for autocomplete and to check your code.

        :param float arg1: The first argument.
        :param float arg2: The second argument.
        :returns float: The sum of the arguments.
        """
        return arg1 + arg2
```

Creating the application entry point

The entry point of an application is the first thing executed when you run the program. In Python, it's the first line of code. We can write an application that runs top-down, mixing function and class declarations along with other statements, but this would make the code harder to develop and debug, especially when it starts to grow more complex. It would be a better idea if we explicitly show where the program starts, and from this point, different parts of the program will be called as needed.

Let's do an experiment to understand some points on how the code is executed and modules are imported:

1. Inside your `Chapter2/experiments` folder, create two new files named `import_test.py` and `module_test.py`. To do this, right-click inside the `experiments` folder and choose **New | Python file**.

2. Double-click on `module_test.py` to open it for editing.

3. Now, type the following code:
   ```
   # coding=utf-8


   print "I'm module_test.py and my name is: " + __name__


   def function1():
       print "Hi, I'm inside function1."


   print "Calling function1..."
   function1()
   ```

   Every module contains a `__name__` attribute, and we will print its value in the first line of the code of this test.

Next, we will declare a function that, when called, prints `"Hi, I'm inside function1."` to the output.

Finally, we will print that the function will be called, and then we will call `function1`.

4. Run the code, press *Alt + Shift + F10* and choose `module_test` from the list. Take a look at the output:

   ```
   I'm module_test.py and my name is:  __main__
   Calling function1...
   Hi, I'm inside function1.

   Process finished with exit code 0
   ```

   > Note here that the `__name__` attribute is equal to `__main__`; this is a special condition in Python. The module (the file) that is run is always called `__main__`.

5. To understand more about this mechanism, create a new Python file inside the `experiments` folder, name it `import_test.py`, and open it for editing. Now, type the following code:

   ```
   # coding=utf-8


   print "I'm import_test.py and my name is: " + __name__


   print "Importing module_test"
   import module_test


   print "Calling function1 from within import_test"
   module_test.function1()
   ```

6. Now, run `import_test.py` (press *Alt + Shift + F10* and select it from the list) and take a look the following output:

   ```
   I'm import_test.py and my name is:  __main__
   Importing module_test
   I'm module_test.py and my name is: module_test
   Calling function1...
   Hi, I'm inside function1.
   Calling function1 from within import_test
   Hi, I'm inside function1.

   Process finished with exit code 0
   ```

This time it is import_test that is called __main__ because it is the file that is executed. Next, when we import module_test, the code in it is executed. Note that module_test is not called __main__ anymore; it's called module_test.

The behavior of this special __name__ attribute allows us to implement a technique in Python, which in turn allows us to execute some code when a file is run directly and avoid this code's execution when this same file is imported. Let's see how this works:

7. Edit module_test.py and change its code, as follows:

```
# coding=utf-8


print "I'm module_test.py and my name is: " + __name__


def function1():
    print "Hi, I'm inside function1."


if __name__ == '__main__':
    print "Calling function1 - only if i'm __main__..."
    function1()
```

So, if __name__ is equal to '__main__', the code inside this block is executed, and we know that __name__ is __main__ only when the file is executed directly. Therefore, the code inside this block is executed only when the file is run and not when it's imported.

8. Next, run import_test.py again (to rerun the last file, press *Shift + F10*), and take a look at what happens:

```
I'm import_test.py and my name is: __main__
Importing module_test
I'm module_test.py and my name is: module_test
Calling function1 from within import_test
Hi, I'm inside function1.

Process finished with exit code 0
```

9. Now, run module_test.py (to choose the file to run, press *Alt + Shift + F10*) and look at the output:

```
I'm module_test.py and my name is: __main__
Calling function1 - only if i'm __main__...
Hi, I'm inside function1.

Process finished with exit code 0
```

As expected, the code inside the `if __name__ == '__main__':` block ran only when `module_test.py` was run directly and not when it was imported.

Now that we know how to make an entry point explicit in Python, let's create our first file for the application and make an entry point.

10. Create a new file inside your `Chapter2` folder and name it `geocaching_app.py`.
11. Then, open the file to edit and insert the following piece of code:

```
# coding=utf-8

def main():
    print("Hello geocaching APP!")


if __name__ == "__main__":
    main()
```

The purpose of the `main()` function is to receive the initial parameters and then take actions so that the program executes and produces the desired results. The content of the `main` function should be minimal and should try to express a clear sequence of actions. This makes the application's logic very easy to debug.

> For Windows users, the `if __name__ == '__main__'` technique is also required in order for parallel processing to work; we will discuss this in *Chapter 10, Parallel Processing*.

Downloading geocaching data

We now have the basic application structure with an entry point; next, we will start writing modules that execute the tasks that the application needs to produce the desired results.

The first thing that we need is to obtain some geocaching data from the Internet, and we want our application to do this for us. There are two common ways of doing this, and they are not restricted only to geocaching data. Many geographical data repositories can be accessed by these methods:

- **Direct download**: This is a download similar to what you do in a browser. There is a link, a request is made to this link, and the download starts.

- **REST API**: Many services offer this kind of data access. **REST (Representational State Transfer)** is a way of serving data where a client makes requests with a series of constraints, and the server responds with the result. It's particularly useful because it allows the user to customize the data of interest.

Geocaching data sources

There are many sources of geocaching data on the Internet; some are commercial, and some are community driven. In the following table, you can note the summary of some of the sources available:

Site	REST		Region
`http://www.opencaching.us/`	Y (OKAPI)	Open	USA
`http://opencaching.pl/`	Y (OKAPI)	Open	Poland
`http://www.opencaching.de/`	Y (OKAPI)	Open	Denmark
`http://www.opencaching.nl/`	Y (OKAPI)	Open	Netherlands
`http://www.opencaching.ro/`	Y (OKAPI)	Open	Romania
`http://www.opencaching.it/`	N	Open	Italy
`http://www.opencachingspain.es/`	N	Open	Spain
`http://www.opencaching.org.uk/`	N	Open	United Kingdom
`http://www.opencaching.cz/`	N	Open	Czech Republic
`https://www.geocaching.com/play`	Y	Commercial	Global

> OKAPI is a public API project for National Opencaching sites (also known as **Opencaching Nodes**).
>
> It provides OC sites with a set of useful, well-documented API methods, allows external developers to easily read public Opencaching data, allows us to read and write private (that is, user-related) data with OAuth 3-legged authentication. The project aims to become a standard API for all National `Opencaching.xx` sites. (`http://opencaching.pl/okapi/introduction.html`)

[35]

Fetching information from a REST API

We will make a simple test to fetch data from a geocaching REST API. We won't go deep into communicating with REST APIs this time because all geocaching sites require a user key so that users can access the data; this is in order to avoid abuses and misuse. For now, we will have a glimpse at how this works and request a method that doesn't require a key. If you are interested in accessing the download functions, you can contact the site and request a key. Here's how you can do this:

1. Create a new file inside your `Chapter2/utils` directory and name it `data_transfer.py`.

2. Type this code in the file:

   ```
   # coding=utf-8


   from pprint import pprint
   import requests


   def request_api_methods():
       result = requests.get(
      "http://www.opencaching.us/okapi/services/apiref/method_index")
       pprint(result.json())


   if __name__ == "__main__":
       request_api_methods()
   ```

3. Run this file, press *Alt* + *Shift* + *F10*, and select `rest_api` on the list. Now, take a look at the results:

   ```
   [{u'brief_description': u'Retrieve information on given issue',
     u'name': u'services/apiref/issue'},
    {u'brief_description': u'Get information on a given OKAPI service method',
     u'name': u'services/apiref/method'},
    {u'brief_description': u'Get a list of OKAPI methods with brief descriptions',
     u'name': u'services/apiref/method_index'},
    {u'brief_description': u'Get information on this OKAPI installation',
     u'name': u'services/apisrv/installation'},
   ...
   ```

```
    {u'brief_description': u'Retrieve information on a single user',
     u'name': u'services/users/user'},
    {u'brief_description': u'Retrieve information on multiple users',
     u'name': u'services/users/users'}]

Process finished with exit code 0
```

The URL that you see is meant to retrieve a list containing the description of all methods exposed by the API. The module `requests` makes everything much easier for us, and the `result.json()` method converts the result of our request to a Python object (a list of dictionaries) and `pprint` (that is, pretty print) prints the list one item per line. Note that we made use of `if __name__ == 'main':` here so that we can test our function; later, when this function is imported by other modules, all the code following `if name == 'main':` won't run, so we can safely put all our tests there.

Downloading data from a URL

To avoid the API key restriction in the geocaching sites and give continuity to our examples, we prepared some sample data that can be downloaded directly from a link. The function that you write downloads a file from a given URL and saves it to the disk. This function will be generalized and may be used by other applications in the future. We want to pass the following as parameters (that is, arguments):

- The URL or link to the file
- A path to the destination folder
- An override to the name of the file.

Perform the following steps:

1. In the `data_transfer.py` file, add the `download_data` function and edit the `if __name__ == '__main__'` block. Your code should look similar to this:

   ```
   # coding=utf-8


   from pprint import pprint
   import requests
   from os import path


   def request_api_methods():
       result = requests.get(
           "http://www.opencaching.us/okapi/services/apiref/method_index")
   ```

The Geocaching App

```
        pprint(result.json())


def download_data(base_url, data_path, data_filename):
    save_file_path = path.join(data_path, data_filename)
    request = requests.get(base_url, stream=True)

    # Save the download to the disk.
    with open(save_file_path, 'wb') as save_file:
        for chunk in request.iter_content(1024):
            save_file.write(chunk)


if __name__ == "__main__":
    download_data('https://s3.amazonaws.com/geopy/geocaching.gpx',
                  '../../data',
                  'geocaching_test.gpx')
```

2. Now, run the code and check your data directory; there should be a new file there named `geocaching_test.gpx`.

What happens in the function is that first, we prepare the `save_file_path` variable using the `os.path` function; this function takes care of concatenating paths and ensuring that the result is correct for every operating system. Whenever we handle paths in our application, we prefer using `os.path`.

Using the `requests` library, we can make a request to the desired URL. The optional `stream=True` parameter tells it that we want the download to happen in chunks, as we request, as opposed to downloading the whole file to the memory once. This is important because some files may be large in size and occupy a lot of memory.

Finally, a file is opened and the chunks of data are read and written to the disk. The `with` statement is also called a **context manager** because it makes a given resource (a file, in this case) available only inside the block. Then, chunks of 1024 bytes each are read and written in the file. When the program exits the `with` block, the file is automatically closed and the `save_file` variable is deleted.

We don't want the application to download the file every time we run it; this would be a waste of time. So, in the next part, we need to implement a verification to make the program skip the download if there is already a file with the chosen name.

Edit the `download_data` function, as follows:

```
def download_data(base_url, data_path, data_filename):
    save_file_path = path.join(data_path, data_filename)
    request = requests.get(base_url, stream=True)
```

```
    # Check if the file exists.
    if path.isfile(save_file_path):
        print('File already available.')

    # Save the download to the disk.
    with open(save_file_path, 'wb') as save_file:
        for chunk in request.iter_content(1024):
            save_file.write(chunk)
```

Now, run your application again, and you should see the following output warning you that the file was already downloaded:

```
File already available.

Process finished with exit code 0
```

Downloading data manually

Now, you may want to choose the data specifically for your region; to do this, you need to go to a geocaching site, filter the data, and download the file manually.

As an example, we will go through the process to download data from the site `http://www.opencaching.us/`. You don't need an account; just follow these steps:

1. Open the website. In the left-hand side menu, click on **Seek A Cache**:

The Geocaching App

2. This will open a page containing various fields. First, select the limiting factors for your search using the fields shown in the following image:

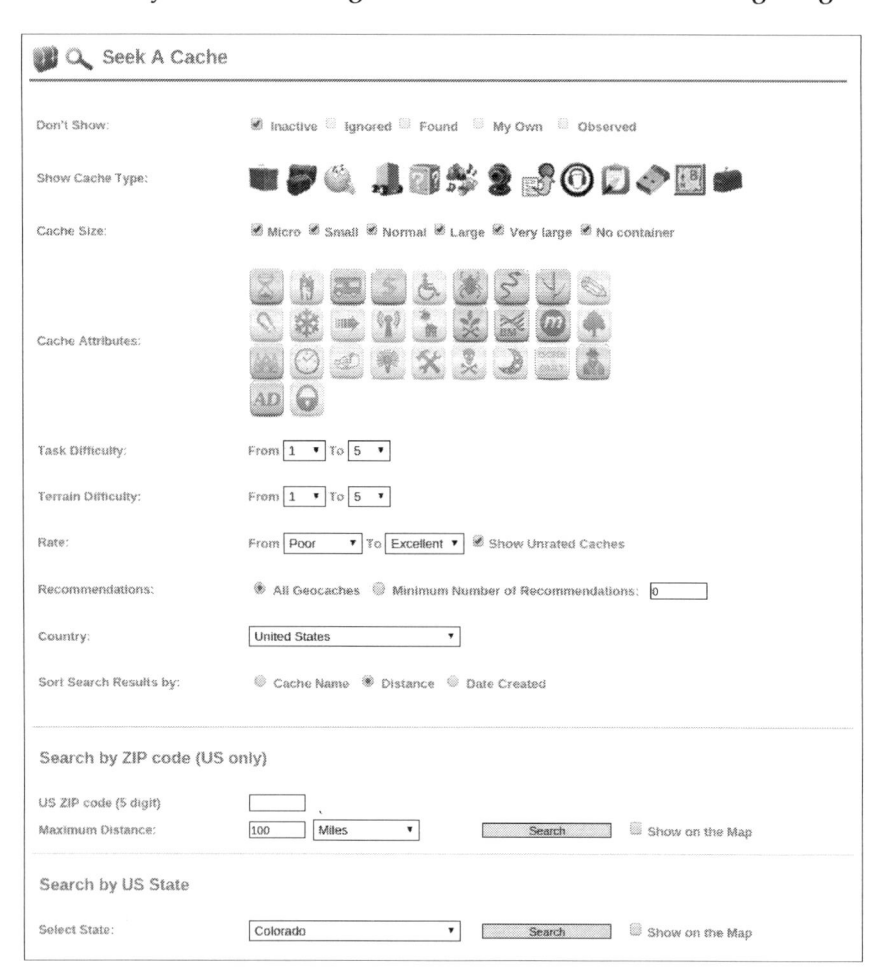

3. Next, you need to specify a region or criteria to search for the geocaches. There are many alternatives to choose from, so scroll through the page and take a look. You can use a zip code, coordinates, a state, and others. Let's search by state; select **New York** and click on **Search**.

[40]

4. A list with the results will appear. Scroll to the end of the page, and you will note the links to download data. Choose to download **Caches From All Pages** in the **GPX** format:

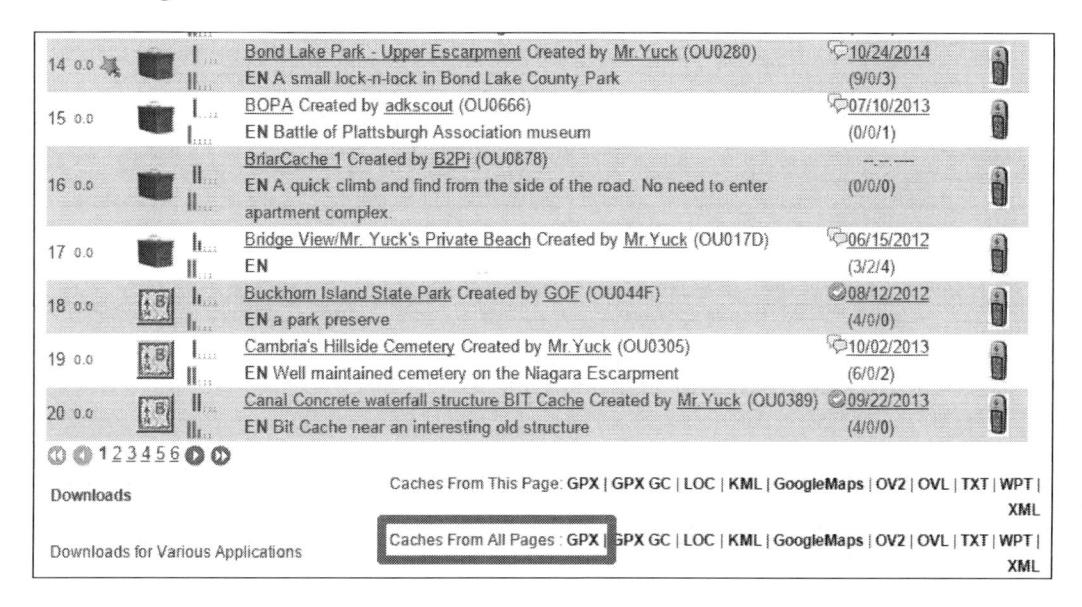

Opening the file and getting its contents

Now, we will open the downloaded file and prepare it for processing. This is something that we already did in *Chapter 1, Preparing the Work Environment*, so we will copy our function and improve it so that we can reuse it in this application and the ones to come. Here are the steps that we will perform:

1. Create a new file named `geo_functions.py` inside the `utils` directory.

2. Open the `world_areas.py` file from *Chapter 1, Preparing the Work Environment*, and copy the `open_shapefile` function. Then, paste it into the created file.

3. Now, change the name of the function to `open_vector_file` so that it makes more sense as we will use this function to open many kinds of file. The geocaching file isn't a shapefile—it's a GPX, and to open it, we don't need to change anything. OGR will handle this for us.

4. Now, to keep the code well documented, change the docstring to reflect the function's capabilities. Change it to something similar to `"Opens a vector file compatible with OGR, gets the first layer, and returns the OGR data source"`.

5. Finally, don't forget to import the required packages. Your code should look similar to this:

```
# coding=utf-8


import ogr
import osr


def open_vector_file(file_path):
    """Opens an vector file compatible with OGR, get the first layer
    and returns the ogr datasource.

    :param str file_path: The full path to the file.
    :return: The ogr datasource.
    """
    datasource = ogr.Open(file_path)
    layer = datasource.GetLayerByIndex(0)
    print("Opening {}".format(file_path))
    print("Number of features: {}".format(
        layer.GetFeatureCount()))
    return datasource


if __name__ == "__main__":
    open_vector_file("../../data/geocaching.gpx")
```

6. Run the code again, and you should see the following output (don't worry about the warnings):

```
Opening ../data/geocaching.gpx
Warning 1: Could not parse {2010-10-01T00:00:00Z} as a valid dateTime
Warning 1: Could not parse {2011-04-10T00:00:00Z} as a valid dateTime
Warning 1: Could not parse {2010-11-21T00:00:00Z} as a valid dateTime
Number of features: 130
Warning 1: Could not parse {2010-11-22T00:00:00Z} as a valid dateTime
```

Preparing the content for analysis

This application makes use of distances such as meters or miles, so we do not want our measurements to be in degrees. Most geocaching coordinates and point data come in degrees, so we need to convert the coordinate system into the metric system.

To do this, we will start by using a function from *Chapter 1, Preparing the Work Environment*: `transform_geometries`. Perform the following:

1. Copy this function and paste it into the `geo_functions.py` file. This function will iterate over the features in the data to get its geometry and then convert the coordinate system, returning a list with all of the converted geometries. The function should look similar to this:

```python
def transform_geometries(datasource, src_epsg, dst_epsg):
    """Transform the coordinates of all geometries in
    the first layer.
    """

    # Part 1
    src_srs = osr.SpatialReference()
    src_srs.ImportFromEPSG(src_epsg)
    dst_srs = osr.SpatialReference()
    dst_srs.ImportFromEPSG(dst_epsg)
    transformation = osr.CoordinateTransformation(src_srs, dst_srs)
    layer = datasource.GetLayerByIndex(0)

    # Part 2
    geoms = []
    layer.ResetReading()
    for feature in layer:
        geom = feature.GetGeometryRef().Clone()
        geom.Transform(transformation)
        geoms.append(geom)
    return geoms
```

Combining functions into an application

So far, we looked at very useful utility functions that perform specific tasks; however, to form an application, we need to combine these functions by calling them in an ordered manner to achieve our objectives. We need code that orchestrates the calls and results—one that will make the application run.

The Geocaching App

For this, we will dive into one of the most beautiful and powerful parts of Python programming: classes and methods.

Python is an object-oriented programming language (but it is not strict). If you are not familiar with the concept of object-oriented programming, don't worry; the best way to understand what this is about is by examples, so I won't go into theories now but teach by example instead. Perform the following steps now:

1. Remember the application's entry point? It's in the Chapter2 folder, in the geochaching_app.py file. Open it for editing, and you should have this:

    ```
    # coding=utf-8

    def main():
        print "Hello geocaching APP!"


    if __name__ == "__main__":
        main()
    ```

2. Now, let's import the modules that we have written so far so that we can use them in our application. Also, let's import the other modules that we will need. Insert the import statements after the encoding declaration (# coding=utf-8). Your code should now be similar to this:

    ```
    # coding=utf-8


    from utils.geo_functions import open_vector_file
    from utils.geo_functions import transform_geometries


    import numpy as np
    import math


    def main():
        print "Hello geocaching APP!"


    if __name__ == "__main__":
        main()
    ```

3. Now, remove the `main()` function, and right after the imports, add the class that will represent our application:

```
class GeocachingApp(object):
    def __init__(self, data_file=None):
        """Application class.

        :param data_file: An OGR compatible file
        with geocaching points.
        """
        # Part 1.
        self._datasource = None
        self._transformed_geoms = None

        # Part 2.
        if data_file:
            self.open_file(data_file)

    def open_file(self, file_path):
        """Open a file containing geocaching data and prepare it
for use.

        :param file_path:
        """
        self._datasource = open_vector_file(file_path)
        self._transformed_geoms = transform_geometries(
            self._datasource, 4326, 3395)
```

Here, we created a class representing our application. Inside the class, there is a special method called `__init__`. This method is called when the class is instantiated, which means when a new instance of the class is created. Here, we can see a parameter named `self`; this parameter is passed by the class to all instance methods, and `self` is the class instance itself. Again, don't worry if these terms are strange to you, we will discuss more on them soon.

In the first part, we defined two properties that any instance of this class may have; note that the underscore before the name denotes that a given property is for internal use only and should not be called from outside the class. This notation is only a convention, and it doesn't really prevent the property from being used from outside the method. In second part, if the user passes the optional file, the application calls the `open_file` method, which in turn opens the file and prepares the data using the functions that we already developed. The way it's coded allows us to change the file that we work on at any time.

The Geocaching App

Note that as we reached this point, we have achieved a higher level of abstraction. First, you had the OGR library with basic functions, where many lines of code were needed to be written to perform a given task. Then, you have the `utils` package, which wraps `ogr` functions into utility functions that perform simple tasks with a single line of code. Now, you have the application class that combines utility functions into methods that automate the processes by calling each one of them in the right order and with the right parameters.

At this point, you need to perform the following steps:

1. Edit your `if __name__ == '__main__':` block with the following code:

   ```
   if __name__ == "__main__":
       my_app = GeocachingApp()
       my_app.open_file('../data/geocaching.gpx')
   ```

2. Run the application, and take a look at the results.

Setting your current location

So far, the application can open a file. The next step is to define your location so that we can find the closest geocache. To do this, we will change the `GeocachingApp` class so that it can keep track of the current location through a property. We will also create methods to change the location (similar to the geometries), transform its coordinates, and prepare it for processing.

Here are the steps that need to be performed:

1. Edit the GeocachingApp class `init` method using the following code:

   ```
   #..
       def __init__(self, data_file=None, my_location=None):
           """Application class.

           :param data_file: An OGR compatible file
            with geocaching points.
           """
           self._datasource = None
           self._transformed_geoms = None
           self._my_location = None
           self.distances = None

           if data_file:
               self.open_file(data_file)

           if my_location:
               self.my_location = my_location
   ```

2. Now, add these two methods to the class:

```
@property
def my_location(self):
    return self._my_location

@my_location.setter
def my_location(self, coordinates):
    self._my_location = transform_points([coordinates])[0]
```

The logic here is that the class instance should have a `my_location` property, and we want the program to automatically convert its coordinate system, as it does with geocaching data.

There are many ways to achieve this kind of behavior. If you have experience with other programming languages, you may have come across the concept of getters and setters. Getters and setters are methods designed to retrieve and set a given property of a class. The use of methods instead of direct access to the properties allows the programmer, among other things, to modify values or perform complex procedures when retrieving or changing a property.

We can have a getter and setter method for this property—`get_my_location()` and `set_my_location()`, for example—but Python provides an elegant way of intervening in the processes of setting and getting a given property with the `@property` decorator.

As can be noted in the preceding code, the actual value of `my_location` is stored in the `_my_location` property and defined in the `__init__` method (the underscore before the name denotes that the property shouldn't be accessed outside the class).

Then, there are two methods with the same name, which is the name of the property that we want to expose. These functions are decorated so that the first one becomes a getter and the second one a setter. In the setter, we will call the functions that transform the coordinates of the point before storing it (we will get to this function in the next steps).

As we did with the data, the location can be passed as an initial parameter to the class and changed at any time. Here's how we can do this:

1. Now, your complete class should be similar to this:

```
class GeocachingApp(object):
    def __init__(self, data_file=None, my_location=None):
        """Application class.

        :param data_file: An OGR compatible file
          with geocaching points.
```

The Geocaching App

```python
        :param my_location: Coordinates of your location.
        """
        self._datasource = None
        self._transformed_geoms = None
        self._my_location = None
        self.distances = None

        if data_file:
            self.open_file(data_file)

        if my_location:
            self.my_location = my_location

    def open_file(self, file_path):
        """Open a file containing geocaching data
        and prepare it for use.

        :param file_path:
        """
        self._datasource = open_vector_file(file_path)
        self._transformed_geoms = transform_geometries(
            self._datasource, 4326, 3395)

    @property
    def my_location(self):
        return self._my_location

    @my_location.setter
    def my_location(self, coordinates):
        self._my_location = transform_points([coordinates])[0]
```

2. As we don't have a `transform_points` function, you should notice that PyCharm underlines `transform_points` in red. So, let's create one in the `geo_functions.py` file. Also, we will avoid boilerplate code by creating another function that creates the OSR transformation:

> **Boilerplate code**
>
> Boilerplate code, or boilerplate, are pieces of code that repeated in many places with little or no alteration.

```python
def create_transform(src_epsg, dst_epsg):
    """Creates an OSR tranformation.

    :param src_epsg: EPSG code for the source geometry.
```

```
        :param dst_epsg: EPSG code for the destination geometry.
        :return: osr.CoordinateTransformation
        """
        src_srs = osr.SpatialReference()
        src_srs.ImportFromEPSG(src_epsg)
        dst_srs = osr.SpatialReference()
        dst_srs.ImportFromEPSG(dst_epsg)
        return osr.CoordinateTransformation(src_srs, dst_srs)

    def transform_points(points, src_epsg=4326, dst_epsg=3395):
        """Transform the coordinate reference system of a list of
    coordinates (a list of points)

        :param src_epsg: EPSG code for the source geometry.
        :param dst_epsg: EPSG code for the destination geometry.
        """
        transform = create_transform(src_epsg, dst_srs)
        points = transform.TransformPoints(points)
        return points
```

The `transform_points` function uses an OSR function with the same name that performs the transformation over an array. This function is incredibly efficient and can transform pairs of coordinates in an order of a magnitude of millions per second in an ordinary home computer. The reason that we will wrap it in our function is that we want to avoid repeating code and add default parameters.

Note that in the `my_location` setter, we put the coordinates inside a list and then got the first element of the returning value (`self.mylocation = transform_points([coordinates])[0]`).

Finding the closest point

To find the closest point, we need to first calculate the distance between the current location (my location) and all points. Then, we need to find the point that has the smallest distance from my location.

So, for each of the points, we must apply an equation that returns the distance to my location and stores these results in the same order as the points in the following table:

Point index	x	y	Distance to my location
0	35	44	?
1	20	92	?
2	11	77	?

The distance between two points is given by the following equation:

$$d = \sqrt{(x_2 - x_1)^2 + (y_2 - y_1)^2}$$

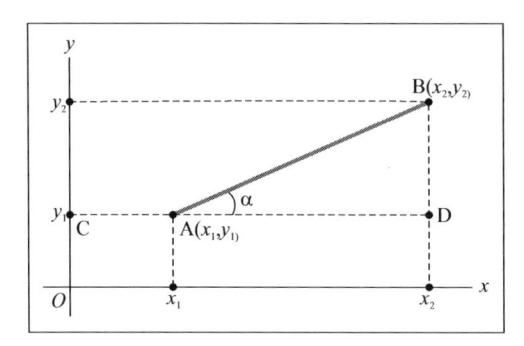

Translating this equation to Python, we have the following code:

```
distance = math.sqrt((xb-xa)**2 + (yb-ya)**2)
```

The following table illustrates the basic Python math operators

Syntax	Mathematical Expression	Operation Name
a + b	$a + b$	Addition
a - b	$a - b$	Subtraction
a * b	$a \times b$	Multiplication
a / b	$a \div b$	Division
a ** b	a^b	Exponent
math.sqrt(a)	$\sqrt{a}$	Square root

Now, insert the preceding method inside the GeocachingApp class by executing the following code:

```
#...
    def calculate_distances(self):
        """Calculates the distance between a
        set of points and a given location.

        :return: A list of distances in the same order as
        the points.
        """
```

```
xa = self.my_location[0]
ya = self.my_location[1]
points = self._transformed_geoms
distances = []
for geom in points:
    point_distance = math.sqrt(
        (geom.GetX() - xa)**2 + (geom.GetY() - ya))
    distances.append(point_distance)
return distances
```

> **Gradual optimization of code**
>
> Some equations or operations may be very complex, and they sometimes become hard to write, or you may need to see the results for the intermediary steps to debug. The tip for these situations is to not worry about writing optimized and fast code right away.
>
> Start by writing readable and clear code, separating each intermediary step into variables. For example, consider the following equation for distance:
>
> ```
> distance = math.sqr((xb-xa)**2 + (yb-ya)**2)
> ```
>
> This can be broken into intermediary steps:
>
> ```
> vertical_distance = yb - ya
> horizontal_distance = xb - xa
> distance = math.sqrt(horizontal_distance**2 +
> vertical_distance**2)
> ```

Now, debug and check the results; when you are sure that the logic is correct and the result is what you expect, you can gradually optimize the code by replacing parts and trying alternative paths to improve the performance by checking whether the results match.

The final part is to find the closest point in the list of distances, which means to find the index of the item that has the minimum value. Add this method to the class:

```
#...
    def find_closest_point(self):
        """Find the closest point to a given location and
        return the cache that's on that point.

        :return: OGR feature containing the point.
        """
        # Part 1.
        distances = self.calculate_distances()
```

The Geocaching App

```
        index = np.argmin(distances)
        # Part 2.
        layer = self._datasource.GetLayerByIndex(0)
        feature = layer.GetFeature(index)
        print "Closest point at: {}m".format(distances[index])
        return feature
```

There is a possibility that the data contains repeated values, which will result in the same distance, or a remote possibility that two points have the same distance.

So, in the first part, the `np.argmin` function returns the index or indexes with a minimum value among all points. In the second part, the program gets the feature at this index. Perform the following steps:

1. Now, let's test our application and edit the `if __name__ == '__main__'` block, as follows:

   ```
   if __name__ == "__main__":
       my_app = GeocachingApp('../data/geocaching.gpx', [-73.0, 43.0])
       my_app.find_closest_point()
   ```

2. Now, your `geocaching_app.py` should look similar to this:

   ```
   # coding=utf-8

   from utils.geo_functions import open_vector_file
   from utils.geo_functions import transform_geometries
   from utils.geo_functions import transform_points

   import numpy as np
   import math


   class GeocachingApp(object):
       def __init__(self, data_file=None, my_location=None):
           """Application class.

           :param data_file: An OGR compatible file
             with geocaching points.
           :param my_location: Coordinates of your location.
           """
           self._datasource = None
           self._transformed_geoms = None
           self._my_location = None
           self.distances = None
   ```

```python
        if data_file:
            self.open_file(data_file)

        if my_location:
            self.my_location = my_location

    def open_file(self, file_path):
        """Open a file containing geocaching data and
        prepare it for use.

        :param file_path:
        """
        self._datasource = open_vector_file(file_path)
        self._transformed_geoms = transform_geometries(
            self._datasource, 4326, 3395)

    @property
    def my_location(self):
        return self._my_location

    @my_location.setter
    def my_location(self, coordinates):
        self._my_location = transform_points([coordinates])[0]

    def calculate_distances(self):
        """Calculates the distance between a
        set of points and a given location.

        :return: A list of distances in the same order as
         the points.
        """
        xa = self.my_location[0]
        ya = self.my_location[1]
        points = self._transformed_geoms
        distances = []
        for geom in points:
            point_distance = math.sqrt(
                (geom.GetX() - xa)**2 + (geom.GetY() - ya))
            distances.append(point_distance)
        return distances

    def find_closest_point(self):
        """Find the closest point to a given location and
        return the cache that's on that point.

        :return: OGR feature containing the point.
        """
```

```
            # Part 1.
            distances = self.calculate_distances()
            index = np.argmin(distances)
            # Part 2.
            layer = self._datasource.GetLayerByIndex(0)
            feature = layer.GetFeature(index)
            print "Closest point at: {}m".format(distances[index])
            return feature


    if __name__ == "__main__":
        my_app = GeocachingApp('../data/geocaching.gpx', [-73.0,
    43.0])
        my_app.find_closest_point()
```

3. Run the code, press *Alt* + *Shift* + *F10*, and select `geocaching_app`. Take a look at the result in the output:

```
Closest point at: 49653.3244095m

Process finished with exit code 0
```

Summary

In this chapter, we discussed important concepts related to code organization and data manipulation. This was accomplished by writing code with an increasing level of abstraction until we had a class with high-level functionality.

First, we wrote utility functions in order to automate tasks and prepare the data to be processed. Some of these functions were simple abstractions over the OGR library, which were made to avoid unnecessary code repetition.

Then, we wrote methods in a class representing the application. These methods take care of performing sequences of operations to make an application work.

Finally, we presented the foundation of how to perform mathematical operations over the elements of data. We wrote a very efficient method that calculates the distance for a list of elements.

In the next chapter, we will improve our data abstraction and make it possible for the application to combine multiple sources of data.

3
Combining Multiple Data Sources

Geographic data tends to be heterogeneous. Just to cite a few factors that contribute to this heterogeneity, it may come from different sources, have been produced at different times, or even have different languages. Given this fact, writing programs that can combine multiple sources of data is a fundamental topic in geoprocessing.

Data sources may come in different formats, such as shapefiles, text files, Google KML files, GPX files from GPS, and so on. They may also vary in their contents; for example, they may have different types of geometries, coordinate systems, and attributes.

In this chapter, we will enhance our application by adding the capability to combine multiple sources of data from both different sites and different file formats. In order to achieve this, we will write code capable of identifying the type of data, and depending on this, we will make transformations to obtain a homogeneous set of data.

By extending OGR capabilities and including our own functions, we can represent the data in Python classes and add some smart capabilities to them that would make the process of combining many sources very easy for this application and others.

In order to achieve these objectives, we will cover the following topics in this chapter:

- The structure of geographic data files
- How geometries are represented
- How to transform data into Python objects
- How to combine multiple sources of data
- Using class inheritance in Python to write better code

Combining Multiple Data Sources

Representing geographic data

Most file formats that contain geographic data are made of a common simple structure consisting of a number of features, each containing a geometry and innumerous named properties.

Here, you can take a look at a sample of the contents of a GeoJSON file. This type of geographic file has the advantage of being human readable, allowing us to see exactly the structure that is being described. You don't need to type this example; just take a good look at it.

Its structure is very similar to a Python dictionary. At the uppermost level, there is `FeatureCollection`, which contains a list of features. Each feature has a geometry, whose type may vary, and a *dictionary* of properties that may contain any arbitrary property defined by the user. In brief, it follows exactly the described schema of data representation as shown in the following code:

```
{"type": "FeatureCollection",
 "features": [
   {"type": "Feature",
     "geometry": {
       "type": "Point",
       "coordinates": [102.0, 0.5]},
     "properties": {"prop0": "value0"}
   },
   {"type": "Feature",
     "geometry": {
       "type": "LineString",
       "coordinates": [[102.0, 0.0], [103.0, 1.0], [104.0, 0.0]]
     },
     "properties": {
       "prop0": "value0",
       "prop1": 0.0
     }
   },
   {"type": "Feature",
     "geometry": {
       "type": "Polygon",
       "coordinates": [
         [ [100.0, 0.0], [101.0, 0.0], [101.0, 1.0],
           [100.0, 1.0], [100.0, 0.0] ]
       ]
     },
     "properties": {
       "prop0": "value0",
```

```
            "prop1": {"this": "that"}
        }
      }
   ]
}
```

JSON stands for **JavaScript Object Notation** and is a format that can be easily read and written in a number of programming languages. Specifically in Python, a JSON object can be transformed into a dictionary and vice versa.

There a number of other formats that implement the same structure; some of them add extra functionality and some have characteristics that are very specific for a given purpose.

For example, the **ESRI** shapefile has indexing capabilities, the **GPX** format is made to work with GPS devices to store waypoints and tracks, and **SpatiLite** is a single file spatial database at the top of SQLite that allows objects to have relations with each other.

In the following table, there are some common file formats and a brief description of each:

Format	Description
Cartesian coordinate system	This is a simple point cloud.
Digital Line Graph (DLG)	This is a USGS format for vector data.
Geography Markup Language	This is an XML-based open standard (by OpenGIS) for GIS data exchange.
GeoJSON	This is a lightweight format based on JSON and is used by many open source GIS packages.
Spatialite	This is a spatial extension to SQLite that provides vector geodatabase functionality. It is similar to PostGIS, Oracle Spatial, and SQL Server with spatial extensions.
Shapefile	This is a popular vector data GIS format developed by Esri.

Representing geometries

As we saw before, in geographic data, each feature contains a geometry. A geometry is the spatial representation of a given object. For example, a point can represent a tree, a place of interest, or, as in our case, a geocache. A line can be a road, a river, and so on. Countries, cities, states, or any other type of areas can be represented by polygons.

In this book, we will follow the geometry representation described by the simple features specifications standardized in ISO 19125. It consists of two-dimensional geographic data made of points, lines, polygons, and aggregations or collections of them, as shown in the following image:

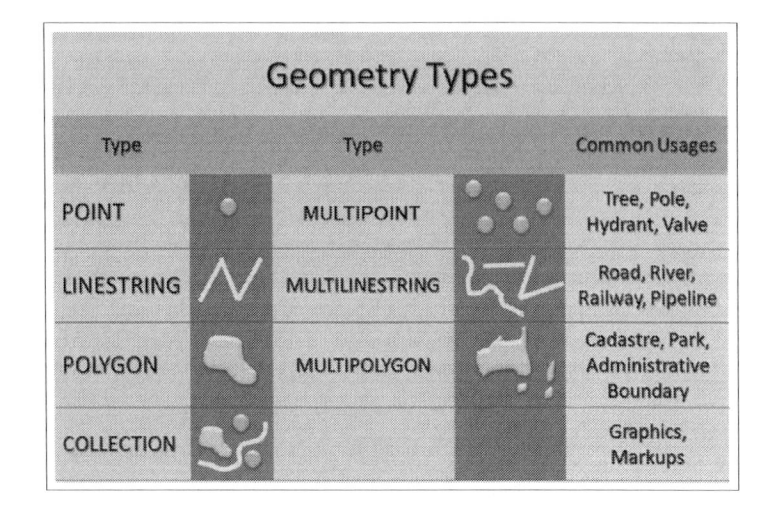

Geometry Types

Type		Type		Common Usages
POINT	•	MULTIPOINT	•••	Tree, Pole, Hydrant, Valve
LINESTRING	∧	MULTILINESTRING		Road, River, Railway, Pipeline
POLYGON		MULTIPOLYGON		Cadastre, Park, Administrative Boundary
COLLECTION				Graphics, Markups

Any geometry in this format is represented by points and a linear interpolation between them. An example of this would be two points that form a line.

This type of geometry is simple, very common, and easy to use. Nevertheless, there are noticeable flaws, and the most important one is the lack of topological representation.

For example, we may have two features representing two neighbor countries—for example, Canada and USA. For each feature (that is, each country) there is a polygon representing the whole limit of the country. By consequence, the borders shared by the two countries will overlap.

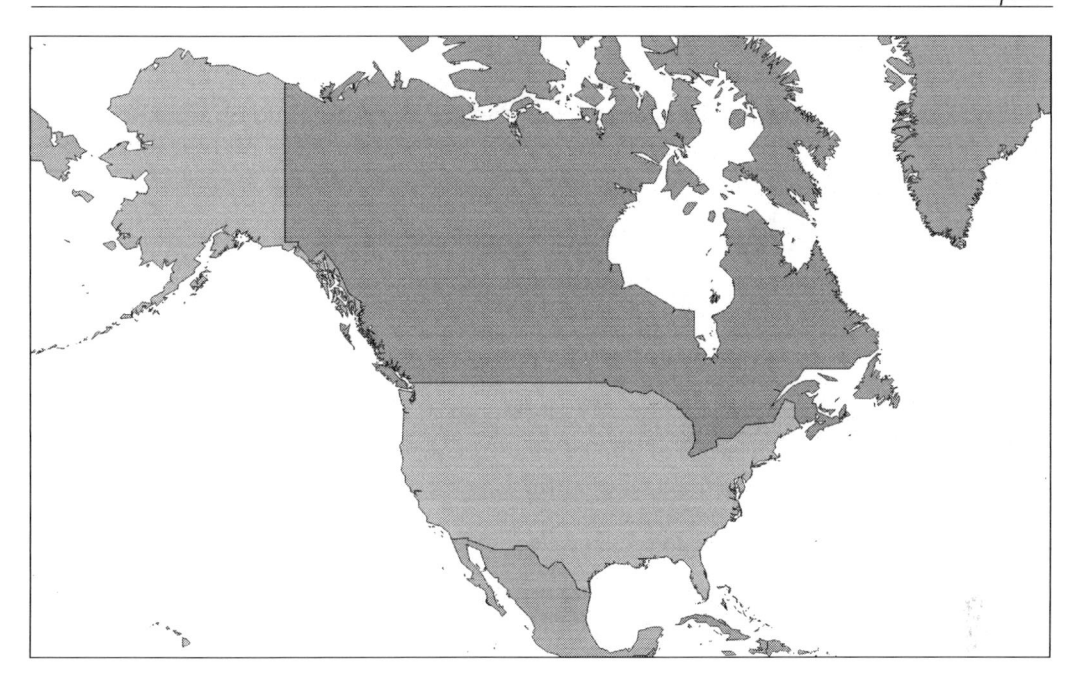

Now, think about the states in the USA and the provinces of Canada; each will be a polygon, their borders will also overlap, and they will, in turn, overlap the countries' borders. So, we will end up with the following:

- States/provinces
- Country border
- Other country border
- Other states/provinces

This makes four overlapping lines; if we want to represent cities, districts, and so on, the number of overlapping geometries would increase. With this, we would have a higher probability of errors and require more space for storage.

This is why this type of geometry representation is also called **spaghetti data**; it ends with a juxtaposition of a lot of lines (similar to spaghetti).

This flaw can be solved through the topological representation of the geometries. The big difference is that, in this example, it wouldn't store polygons; it would store the relationships between objects. You have a set of boundaries that relate to each other and represent an area, and two areas can have the same boundary. **OpenStreetMap** is a good example of a topological representation of geographic features.

Although topological representation is more advanced, it is much harder to work with, and the vast majority of geographic analysis can be done with a simple representation.

Making data homogeneous

What relates the representation of data to real-life objects is the simple combination of geometry with the properties of a feature.

A line for example, can be a road, river, fence, and so on. The only difference may be the `type` property that tells us what it is. Alternatively, we may have a file named `roads` that lets us know that it contains roads.

However, the computer doesn't know about this as it doesn't know what the other properties represent or what the file is. Because of this, we need to make transformations in the data in order to have a common format that can be analyzed.

This common format is the subject of this topic; it is how data can be represented in Python in an optimal way and in which the objects can be manipulated and analyzed to produce the expected results.

The objective is to transform the basic data representation of features, geometries, and properties into a representation of real-life objects and hide the details of the functionality under the hood in this process. In computer science, this is called **abstraction**.

Instead of just writing some prepared code and magically performing the transformation, we will go step by step through the process of deduction of how the transformation needs to be done. This is very important because it's the foundation of developing code to perform any kind of transformation on any type of geographic data that you can put to use in the future.

The concept of abstraction

Now that we have a clear understanding of how data is represented, let's get back to our geocaching application.

Abstraction is a programming technique intended to reduce the complexity of code for the programmer. It's done by encapsulating complex code under progressive layers of more human-friendly solutions. The lower the level of abstraction, the closer to the machine language and the harder to maintain it is. The higher the level of abstraction, the more the code tries to mimic the behavior of real things or the more it resembles a natural language, thus becoming more intuitive and easier to maintain and extend.

Going back to the examples that we saw so far, we may notice many levels of abstraction—for example, when we use the OGR library in the function we use to open shapefiles. Take a look at the following code:

```python
def open_vector_file(file_path):
    """Opens an vector file compatible with OGR, get the first layer
    and returns the ogr datasource.

    :param str file_path: The full path to the file.
    :return: The ogr datasource.
    """
    datasource = ogr.Open(file_path)
    layer = datasource.GetLayerByIndex(0)
    print("Opening {}".format(file_path))
    print("Number of features: {}".format(layer.GetFeatureCount()))
    return datasource
```

Just at the uppermost layers of abstraction, we have the function itself that hides the functionality of OGR. Then, we have the OGR Python bindings that abstract the OGR C API, which in turn handles memory allocation, all the mathematics, and so on.

Abstracting the geocache point

So, we need to handle multiple sources of data in a smart way so that:

- We don't need to change the code for each type of data
- It's possible to combine data from multiple sources
- If we add extra functionality to our program, we don't need to worry about file formats and data types

Combining Multiple Data Sources

How will we do this? The answer is simple: we will abstract our data and hide the process of format and type handling in the internal functionality.

The objective is that after this point in the app, we won't need to deal with OGR, layers, features, and so on. We will have one and only one type of object that we will use to represent our data, and all the interaction will be done with this object. The geocache object will represent a single geocaching point with the properties and methods that can be used to manipulate this object.

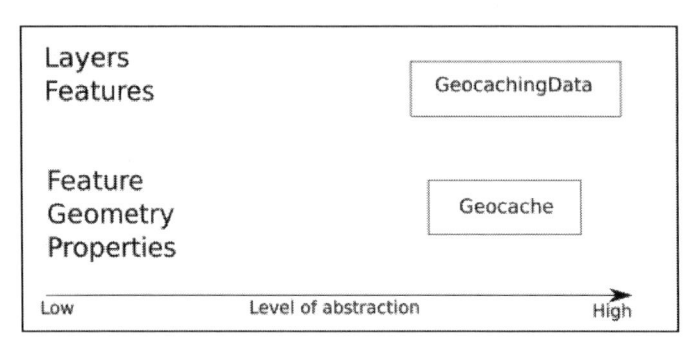

```
Layers
Features                          GeocachingData


Feature
Geometry                              Geocache
Properties


Low           Level of abstraction           High
```

Now, perform the following steps:

1. First, let's organize the project structure. Open your geopy project in PyCharm and create a directory named `Chapter3`.

2. Copy all the files and directories from `Chapter2` to `Chapter3`. You should end up with a structure similar to the following:

   ```
   +---Chapter3
   |   |   geocaching_app.py
   |   |   __init__.py
   |   |
   |   +---experiments
   |   |       import_test.py
   |   |       module_test.py
   |   |
   |   \---utils
   |           data_transfer.py
   |           geo_functions.py
   |           __init__.py
   ```

3. Inside `Chapter3`, create a new file named `models.py` (from this point on, we will work inside the `Chapter3` directory).

4. Now, add this code to the file:

   ```
   class Geocache(object):
       """This class represents a single geocaching point."""

       def __init__(self, x, y):
           self.x = x
           self.y = y

       @property
       def coordinates(self):
           return self.x, self.y
   ```

5. Now, we have a geocache class with its first properties: the coordinates for the geocache. To test our class, we can write the following code:

   ```
   if __name__ == '__main__':
       one_geocaching_point = Geocache(20, 40)
       print(one_geocaching_point.coordinates)
   ```

6. Run your code, press *Alt + Shift + F10*, and select the models files. You should get this output in the console:

   ```
   (20, 40)

   Process finished with exit code 0
   ```

Abstracting geocaching data

As we have a single point, we also need to have a collection of points. We will call this `PointCollection`. Continuing the process of abstraction, the objective is to hide the operations of importing and converting the data. We will do this by creating a new class and encapsulating some of our utility functions inside it. Go to your `models.py` file and add the following class:

```
class PointCollection(object):
    def __init__(self):
        """This class represents a group of vector data."""
        Self.data = []
```

It's a simple class definition, and in the `__init__` method, we will define that each instance of this class will have a `data` property. Now that we have created our simple abstractions, let's add functionality to it.

Combining Multiple Data Sources

Importing geocaching data

In the previous chapter, we generalized our import function by adding the capability to import more types of data supported by OGR.

Now, we will improve it again, make it handle some errors, make it compatible with our objects, and add two new capabilities. We will also convert the data in order to produce uniform objects.

To achieve our goals, we will analyze what kind of information is stored in the files that we want to open. We will use OGR to inspect the files and return some information that may help us with the data conversion.

First, let's alter our `open_vector_file` function, allowing it to handle incorrect paths and filenames, which is a very a common error. Perform the following steps:

1. Go to the `utils` folder and open the `geo_functions.py` file.
2. Add the following `import` statements at the beginning of the file:

   ```
   # coding=utf-8

   import ogr
   import osr
   import gdal
   import os
   from pprint import pprint
   ```

3. Now, edit the `open_vector_file` function via the following code:

   ```
   def open_vector_file(file_path):
       """Opens an vector file compatible with OGR,
       get the first layer and returns the ogr datasource.

       :param str file_path: The full path to the file.
       :return: The ogr datasource.
       """
       datasource = ogr.Open(file_path)
       # Check if the file was opened.
       if not datasource:
           if not os.path.isfile(file_path):
               message = "Wrong path."
           else:
               message = "File format is invalid."
           raise IOError(
               'Error opening the file {}\n{}'.format(
                   file_path, message))
   ```

```
layer = datasource.GetLayerByIndex(0)
print("Opening {}".format(file_path))
print("Number of features: {}".format(
    layer.GetFeatureCount()))
return datasource
```

In this step, we added a verification to check whether the file was correctly opened. If the file doesn't exist or if there are any other problems, OGR will be silent and the datasource will be empty. So, if the datasource is empty (None), we will know that something went wrong and perform another verification to see whether there was a mistake with the file path or something else happened. In either case, the program will raise an exception, preventing it from continuing with bad data.

4. Now, we will add another function to print some information about the datasource for us. After the open_vector_file function, add the get_datasource_information function with the following code:

```
def get_datasource_information(datasource, print_results=False):
    """Get informations about the first layer in the datasource.

    :param datasource: An OGR datasource.
    :param bool print_results: True to print the results on
      the screen.
    """
    info = {}
    layer = datasource.GetLayerByIndex(0)
    bbox = layer.GetExtent()
    info['bbox'] = dict(xmin=bbox[0], xmax=bbox[1],
                        ymin=bbox[2], ymax=bbox[3])
    srs = layer.GetSpatialRef()
    if srs:
        info['epsg'] = srs.GetAttrValue('authority', 1)
    else:
        info['epsg'] = 'not available'
    info['type'] = ogr.GeometryTypeToName(layer.GetGeomType())
    # Get the attributes names.
    info['attributes'] = []
    layer_definition = layer.GetLayerDefn()
    for index in range(layer_definition.GetFieldCount()):
        info['attributes'].append(
            layer_definition.GetFieldDefn(index).GetName())
    # Print the results.
    if print_results:
        pprint(info)
    return info
```

Combining Multiple Data Sources

Here, we will use a number of OGR's methods and functions to get information from the datasource and layer on it. This information is put in a dictionary, which is returned by the function. If we have `print_results = True`, the dictionary is printed with the `pprint` function (pretty print). This function tries to print Python objects in a more human-friendly way.

5. Now, to test our code, edit the `if __name__ == '__main__':` block at the end of the file, as follows:

   ```
   if __name__ == "__main__":
       gdal.PushErrorHandler('CPLQuietErrorHandler')
       datasource = open_vector_file("../../data/geocaching.gpx")
       info = get_datasource_information(
           datasource, print_results=True)
   ```

   There is a new element here: `gdal.PushErrorHandler('CPLQuietErrorHandler')`. Geocaching files normally contain features with empty date fields. When OGR finds this situation, it prints a warning message. This could get pretty annoying when we have a lot of features. This command tells OGR/GDAL to suppress these messages so that we can have a clean output with only what we want to see.

6. Run the code, press *Alt* + *Shift* + *F10*, and select **geo_functions**. You should get the following output showing the information that is collected:

   ```
   Opening ../../data/geocaching.gpx
   Number of features: 130
   {'attributes': ['ele',
                   'time',
                   'magvar',
                   'geoidheight',
                   'name',
                   'cmt',
                   'desc',
                   'src',
                   'url',
                   'urlname',
                   'sym',
                   'type',
                   'fix',
                   'sat',
                   'hdop',
                   'vdop',
                   'pdop',
                   'ageofdgpsdata',
                   'dgpsid'],
   ```

```
            'bbox': {'xmax': -73.44602,
                     'xmin': -79.3536,
                     'ymax': 44.7475,
                     'ymin': 40.70558},
            'epsg': '4326',
            'type': 'Point'}

Process finished with exit code 0
```

> The `attributes` key of the dictionary contains the field names that could be read from the data. Every feature on our GPX file (that is, every point) contains this set of attributes. The `bbox` code is the bounding box of the data, which are the coordinates of the upper-left and lower-right corners of the rectangle that comprises the geographical extent of the data. The `epsg` code contains the code for the coordinate system of the data. Finally, `type` is the type of geometry identified by OGR.

Reading GPX attributes

Take a look at the attributes (field names) found by OGR in the previous example; we have a name, a description, and the time. We have some technical data about the GPS solution (pdop, hdop, sat, fix, and many more) and some other fields, but none of them contains in-depth information about the geocache.

In order to take a look at what information the GPX file contains that OGR is not displaying, let's open it in PyCharm:

1. In your `geopy` project, go to the `data` folder.
2. Locate `geocaching.gpx`. To open it, either drag and drop it in the editor area or double-click on the filename.

   PyCharm will open it for editing but won't recognize the file format and will display it in a single color; so, let's inform it that this is an XML file.

3. Right-click on the `geocaching.gpx` file. In the menu, select **Associate with File Type**, and a window with a list will pop up. Select **XML Files** and then click on the **OK** button.

Combining Multiple Data Sources

Now, the contents of the GPX file should appear with colors differentiating the various elements of the extended markup language. PyCharm is also capable of recognizing the file structure, as it does with Python. Let's take a look via the following steps:

1. Press *Alt + 7* or navigate to the **View | Tool Windows | Structure** menu.

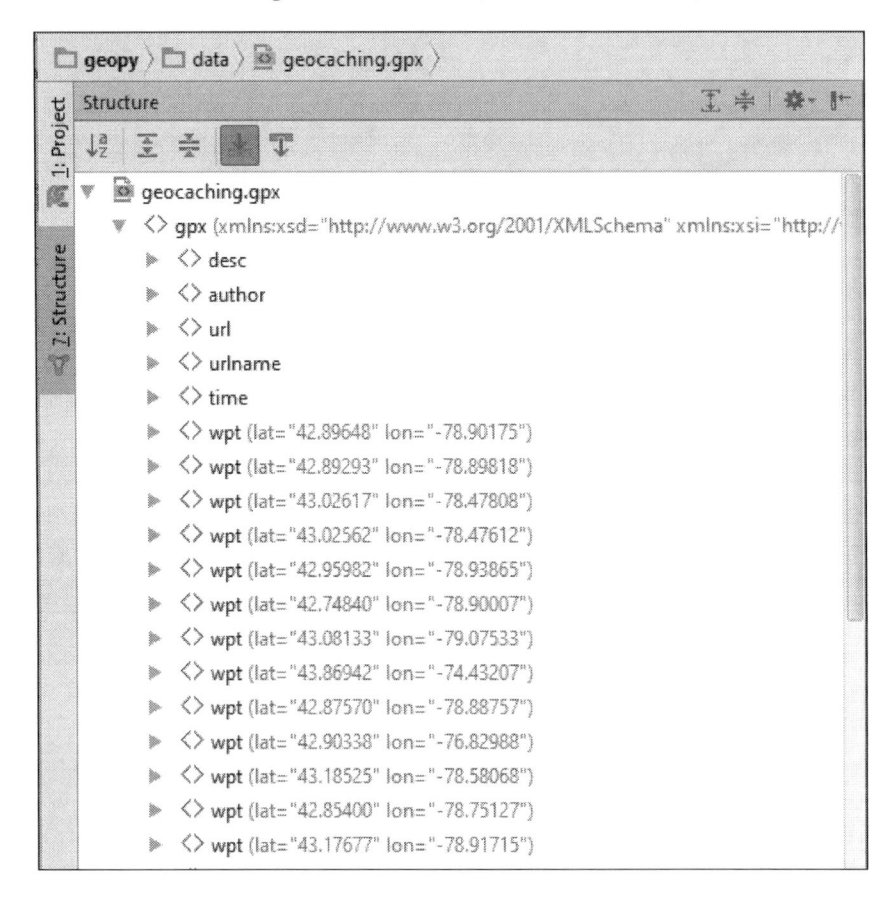

```
geopy > data > geocaching.gpx
Structure
  geocaching.gpx
    gpx (xmlns:xsd="http://www.w3.org/2001/XMLSchema" xmlns:xsi="http://
      desc
      author
      url
      urlname
      time
      wpt (lat="42.89648" lon="-78.90175")
      wpt (lat="42.89293" lon="-78.89818")
      wpt (lat="43.02617" lon="-78.47808")
      wpt (lat="43.02562" lon="-78.47612")
      wpt (lat="42.95982" lon="-78.93865")
      wpt (lat="42.74840" lon="-78.90007")
      wpt (lat="43.08133" lon="-79.07533")
      wpt (lat="43.86942" lon="-74.43207")
      wpt (lat="42.87570" lon="-78.88757")
      wpt (lat="42.90338" lon="-76.82988")
      wpt (lat="43.18525" lon="-78.58068")
      wpt (lat="42.85400" lon="-78.75127")
      wpt (lat="43.17677" lon="-78.91715")
```

2. This is the GPX file structure. Note that after some initial tags, it contains all the waypoints. Click on the arrow to the left of any waypoint to expand it. Then, locate the waypoint's geocache tag and expand it too.

Chapter 3

```
▼ <> wpt (lat="42.89648" lon="-78.90175")
    ▶ <> time
    ▶ <> name
    ▶ <> desc
    ▶ <> src
    ▶ <> url
    ▶ <> urlname
    ▶ <> sym
      <> type
    ▼ <> geocache (status="Available" xmlns="http://geocaching.com.au/ge
        ▶ <> name
        ▶ <> owner
        ▶ <> locale
        ▶ <> state
        ▶ <> country
        ▶ <> type
        ▶ <> container
        ▶ <> difficulty
        ▶ <> terrain
        ▶ <> summary (html="false")
        ▶ <> description (html="true")
        ▶ <> hints
        ▶ <> licence
        ▶ <> logs
        ▶ <> geokrety
```

3. As you can note, the geocaching point contains much more information than OGR is capable of reading, including the status attribute of the geocache tag.
4. Before we proceed, explore the file to get familiar with its notation. Click on some of the tags and look at the code editor to see the contents.

Combining Multiple Data Sources

Since we can't access these attributes directly with OGR, we will program an alternative. The objective is to read this information and flatten it in a single level of key/value pairs in a dictionary. GPX files are XML files, so we can use an XML parser to read them. The choice here is the `xmltodict` package; it will simply convert the XML file into a Python dictionary, making it easier to manipulate as we are very familiar with dictionaries. Now, perform the following steps:

1. Add the import of `xmltodict` at the beginning of the `geo_functions.py` file by executing the following code:

    ```
    # coding=utf-8

    import xmltodict
    import ogr
    import osr
    import gdal
    import os
    from pprint import pprint
    ```

2. Create a new function before `open_vector_file` and add the following code:

    ```
    def read_gpx_file(file_path):
        """Reads a GPX file containing geocaching points.

        :param str file_path: The full path to the file.
        """
        with open(file_path) as gpx_file:
            gpx_dict = xmltodict.parse(gpx_file.read())
        print("Waypoint:")
        print(gpx_dict['gpx']['wpt'][0].keys())
        print("Geocache:")
        print(gpx_dict['gpx']['wpt'][0]['geocache'].keys())
    ```

3. Now, edit the `if __name__ == '__main__':` block to test the code:

    ```
    if __name__ == "__main__":
        gdal.PushErrorHandler('CPLQuietErrorHandler')
        read_gpx_file("../../data/geocaching.gpx")
    ```

4. Run the code again with *Shift* + *F10* and look at the results:

    ```
    Waypoint:
    [u'@lat', u'@lon', u'time', u'name', u'desc', u'src', u'url',
    u'urlname', u'sym', u'type', u'geocache']
    Geocache:
    ```

[70]

```
[u'@status', u'@xmlns', u'name', u'owner', u'locale', u'state',
u'country', u'type', u'container', u'difficulty', u'terrain',
u'summary', u'description', u'hints', u'licence', u'logs',
u'geokrety']

Process finished with exit code 0
```

With the `print(gpx_dict['gpx']['wpt'][0].keys())` statement, we obtained the value of gpx and then that of wpt, which is a list. Then, we got the keys of the first element on this list and printed it.

Next, through `print(gpx_dict['gpx']['wpt'][0]['geocache'].keys())`, we got the value of geocache and also printed its keys.

Look at the output and note that it's the same thing that we did when we were exploring the GPX file structure in PyCharm. The structure is now available as a dictionary, including the tag's properties, which are represented in the dictionary with an @ symbol.

Now that we have a nice and easy way to handle the dictionary of the GPX file, let's extract and flatten the relevant information and make the function return it. Edit the read_gpx_file function, as follows:

```
def read_gpx_file(file_path):
    """Reads a GPX file containing geocaching points.

    :param str file_path: The full path to the file.
    """
    with open(file_path) as gpx_file:
        gpx_dict = xmltodict.parse(gpx_file.read())
    output = []
    for wpt in gpx_dict['gpx']['wpt']:
        geometry = [wpt.pop('@lat'), wpt.pop('@lon')]
        # If geocache is not on the dict, skip this wpt.
        try:
            geocache = wpt.pop('geocache')
        except KeyError:
            continue
        attributes = {'status': geocache.pop('@status')}
        # Merge the dictionaries.
        attributes.update(wpt)
        attributes.update(geocache)
        # Construct a GeoJSON feature and append to the list.
        feature = {
            "type": "Feature",
            "geometry": {
```

Combining Multiple Data Sources

```
            "type": "Point",
            "coordinates": geometry},
        "properties": attributes}
    output.append(feature)
return output
```

Note that here, we used the dictionary's `pop` method; this method returns the value of a given key and removes the key from the dictionary. The objective is to have two dictionaries only with attributes (properties) that can be merged into a single dictionary of attributes; the merging is done with the `update` method.

Some waypoints doesn't have the geocache key, when this happens, we catch the exception and skip this point.

Finally, the information is combined in a dictionary with a GeoJSON-like structure. You can do this as follows:

1. Edit the `if __name__ == '__main__':` block using the following code:

   ```
   if __name__ == "__main__":
       gdal.PushErrorHandler('CPLQuietErrorHandler')
       points = read_gpx_file("../../data/geocaching.gpx")
       print points[0]['properties'].keys()
   ```

2. Run the code, and you will see the following output:

   ```
   ['status', u'logs', u'locale', u'terrain', u'sym', u'geokrety',
   u'difficulty', u'licence', u'owner', u'urlname', u'desc', u'@
   xmlns', u'src', u'container', u'name', u'url', u'country',
   u'description', u'summary', u'state', u'time', u'hints', u'type']

   Process finished with exit code 0
   ```

That's great! Now, all the geocache attributes are contained inside the *properties* of the feature.

Returning the homogeneous data

We have a `read_gpx_file` function that returns a list of features in a dictionary and an `open_vector_file` function that returns an OGR datasource. We also have a `get_datasource_information` function that returns the information that we need about the file.

[72]

Now, it's time to combine these functions in order to be able to read multiple types of data (GPX, Shapefiles, and many more). To do this, we will change the `open_vector_file` function so that it can make decisions depending on the file format and convert the data in order to always return the same structure. Perform the following steps:

1. First, make sure that the functions inside `geo_function.py` are in the correct order; if not, rearrange them to be in this order:

    ```
    def read_gpx_file(file_path):

    def get_datasource_information(datasource, print_results=False):

    def open_vector_file(file_path):

    def create_transform(src_epsg, dst_epsg):

    def transform_geometries(datasource, src_epsg, dst_epsg):

    def transform_points(points, src_epsg=4326, dst_epsg=3395):
    ```

2. Now, add a new function to transform OGR features into dictionaries as we did with the GPX file. This function can be inserted anywhere before `open_vector_file`, as follows:

    ```
    def read_ogr_features(layer):
        """Convert OGR features from a layer into dictionaries.

        :param layer: OGR layer.
        """
        features = []
        layer_defn = layer.GetLayerDefn()
        layer.ResetReading()
        type = ogr.GeometryTypeToName(layer.GetGeomType())
        for item in layer:
            attributes = {}
            for index in range(layer_defn.GetFieldCount()):
                field_defn = layer_defn.GetFieldDefn(index)
                key = field_defn.GetName()
                value = item.GetFieldAsString(index)
                attributes[key] = value
            feature = {
                "type": "Feature",
                "geometry": {
                    "type": type,
    ```

Combining Multiple Data Sources

```
                "coordinates": item.GetGeometryRef().
ExportToWkt()},
            "properties": attributes}
        features.append(feature)
    return features
```

3. Now, edit the `open_vector_file` function via the following code:

   ```
   def open_vector_file(file_path):
       """Opens an vector file compatible with OGR or a GPX file.
       Returns a list of features and informations about the file.

       :param str file_path: The full path to the file.
       """
       datasource = ogr.Open(file_path)
       # Check if the file was opened.
       if not datasource:
           if not os.path.isfile(file_path):
               message = "Wrong path."
           else:
               message = "File format is invalid."
           raise IOError('Error opening the file {}\n{}'.format(
               file_path, message))
       metadata = get_datasource_information(datasource)
       file_name, file_extension = os.path.splitext(file_path)
       # Check if it's a GPX and read it if so.
       if file_extension in ['.gpx', '.GPX']:
           features = read_gpx_file(file_path)
       # If not, use OGR to get the features.
       else:
           features = read_ogr_features(
               datasource.GetLayerByIndex(0))
       return features, metadata
   ```

4. Just to make sure that everything is fine, let's test the code by opening two different file types. Edit the `if __name__ == '__main__':` block, as follows:

   ```
   if __name__ == "__main__":
       gdal.PushErrorHandler('CPLQuietErrorHandler')
       points, metadata = open_vector_file(
       "../../data/geocaching.shp")
       print points[0]['properties'].keys()
       points, metadata = open_vector_file(
       "../../data/geocaching.gpx")
       print points[0]['properties'].keys()
   ```

5. Run the code and take a look at the following output:

```
['src', 'dgpsid', 'vdop', 'sat', 'name', 'hdop', 'url', 'fix',
'pdop', 'sym', 'ele', 'ageofdgpsd', 'time', 'urlname', 'magvar',
'cmt', 'type', 'geoidheigh', 'desc']
['status', u'logs', u'locale', u'terrain', u'sym', u'geokrety',
u'difficulty', u'licence', u'owner', u'urlname', u'desc', u'@
xmlns', u'src', u'container', u'name', u'url', u'country',
u'description', u'summary', u'state', u'time', u'hints', u'type']

Process finished with exit code 0
```

Converting the data into Geocache objects

So far, we have defined the Geocache class; it has the latitude and longitude properties and a method to return this pair of coordinates. `PointCollection` is a collection of geocaches. We also have the `open_vector_file` function that returns a list of dictionaries representing features.

Now, we will reach a higher level of abstraction by implementing the process of importing data into the `PointCollection` class by making use of the `open_vector_file` function. Perform the following steps:

1. Open your `models.py` file and edit the imports at the beginning of the file by executing the following code:

   ```
   # coding=utf-8
   
   Import gdal
   import os
   from pprint import pprint
   from utils.geo_functions import open_vector_file
   ```

2. Now, let's make `PointCollection` automatically import a file when it's instantiated. Go to the `models.py` file, change your class `__init__` method, and add the `import_data` and `_parse_data` methods. Run this script:

   ```
   class PointCollection(object):
       def __init__(self, file_path=None):
           """This class represents a group of vector data."""
           self.data = []
           self.epsg = None
           
           if file_path:
               self.import_data(file_path)
       
       def import_data(self, file_path):
   ```

Combining Multiple Data Sources

```
        """Opens an vector file compatible with OGR and parses
           the data.

        :param str file_path: The full path to the file.
        """
        features, metadata = open_vector_file(file_path)
        self._parse_data(features)
        self.epsg = metadata['epsg']
        print("File imported: {}".format(file_path))

    def _parse_data(self, features):
        """Transforms the data into Geocache objects.

        :param features: A list of features.
        """
        for feature in features:
            geom = feature['geometry']['coordinates']
            attributes = feature['properties']
            cache_point = Geocache(geom[0], geom[1],
                                   attributes=attributes)
            self.data.append(cache_point)
```

3. Now, we will just need to adapt the `Geocache` class to receive and store the attributes. Replace it with the following code:

```
class Geocache(object):
    """This class represents a single geocaching point."""

    def __init__(self, lat, lon, attributes=None):
        self.lat = lat
        self.lon = lon
        self.attributes = attributes

    @property
    def coordinates(self):
        return self.lat, self.lon
```

The attribute arguments are called **keyword arguments**. Keyword arguments are optional, and the default value is the value defined after the equal symbol.

As at this moment there is no standardization in data format for geocaching, we will store all the attributes that are read from the source file unchanged.

In Python, you are not obliged to define which properties a class instance will have in advance; the properties can be added during the code's execution. However, it's good practice to define them in the __init__ method because it avoids mistakes, such as trying to access undefined properties. PyCharm can track these properties and warn you about typos. It also serves as documentation.

1. Before we test the code, edit the `PointCollection` class and add a method that shows some information for us, as follows:

    ```
    #...
        def describe(self):
            print("SRS EPSG code: {}".format(self.epsg))
            print("Number of features: {}".format(len(self.data)))
    ```

2. In order to test your code, edit the `if __name__ == '__main__'` block via the following lines of code:

    ```
    if __name__ == '__main__':
        gdal.PushErrorHandler('CPLQuietErrorHandler')
        vector_data = PointCollection("../data/geocaching.gpx")
        vector_data.print_information()
    ```

3. Now, run the code. You should see the following output:

    ```
    File imported: ../data/geocaching.gpx
    SRS EPSG code: 4326
    Number of features: 112

    Process finished with exit code 0
    ```

Merging multiple sources of data

Now that our data is in the form of `PointCollection` containing Geocache objects, merging data from multiple files or multiple `PointCollection` data should be easy. Perform the following steps:

1. Make another test. First, we will see whether we can import multiple files and edit the `if __name__ == '__main__'` block of the `models.py` file. Execute the following code:

    ```
    if __name__ == '__main__':
        gdal.PushErrorHandler('CPLQuietErrorHandler')
        vector_data = PointCollection("../data/geocaching.gpx")
        vector_data.describe()
        vector_data.import_data("../data/geocaching.shp")
        vector_data.describe()
    ```

Combining Multiple Data Sources

2. Run the code again. Now, you should see the number of features double after you import another file, as follows:

   ```
   File imported: ../data/geocaching.gpx
   SRS EPSG code: 4326
   Number of features: 112
   File imported: ../data/geocaching.shp
   SRS EPSG code: None
   Number of features: 242

   Process finished with exit code 0
   ```

3. Let's implement something very elegant. We will add a magic method to our `PointCollection` class so that we can merge the content of two instances.

4. Edit the `PointCollection` class and add the `__add__` method just after the `__init__` method via the following code:

   ```
   class PointCollection(object):
       def __init__(self, file_path=None):
           """This class represents a group of vector data."""
           self.data = []
           self.epsg = None

           if file_path:
               self.import_data(file_path)

       def __add__(self, other):
           self.data += other.data
           return self
   ```

Similar to the `__init__` method, the `__add__` method is one of Python's *magic methods*. These methods are not called directly; they are automatically called when something specific happens. The `__init__` method is called when the class is instantiated, and the `__add__` method is called when the plus (+) operator is used. So, to merge the data of two `PointCollection` instances, we just need to sum them. Here's what we need to do for this:

1. Edit the `if __name__ == '__main__':` block, as follows:

   ```
   if __name__ == '__main__':
       gdal.PushErrorHandler('CPLQuietErrorHandler')

       my_data = PointCollection("../data/geocaching.gpx")
       my_other_data = PointCollection("../data/geocaching.shp")
       merged_data = my_data + my_other_data
       merged_data.describe()
   ```

2. Then, run the code and take a look at the results:

   ```
   File imported: ../data/geocaching.gpx
   File imported: ../data/geocaching.shp
   SRS EPSG code: 4326
   Number of features: 242

   Process finished with exit code 0
   ```

Integrating new functionality into the application

In *Chapter 2, The Geocaching App*, we developed the application so that it could find points close to your location. However, the data was organized differently inside the application; although it was a very efficient way of handling data, it became very hard for us to understand how to perform operations on this data.

Through abstraction, we implemented a new form of data representation—one that is very intuitive and easy to use.

Now, we will change the application so that it can use this new type of data to perform its functions and also to aggregate the new capability of combining multiple sources of data.

Take a look at the `GeocachingApp` and `PointCollection` classes; you may notice that they have some parts that look similar to each other. Both of them store data and have methods to open data.

At this point, with little modification, if we transfer methods from one class to another, we could end up with a functional application, and that's what we will do. However, instead of copying and pasting, we will use Python's class inheritance. We will take the `GeocachingApp` class and make it inherit all the functionality of the `PointCollection` class.

For a complete understanding, we will go through the processes one method at a time. Open your `geocaching_app.py` file, and now, let's focus on the class declarations and `__init__` method. Make the following changes on the imports section, and in the class, you can keep the other methods as they are; don't delete them:

```
# coding=utf-8

from pprint import pprint
import gdal
import numpy as np
```

Combining Multiple Data Sources

```python
import math
from utils.geo_functions import transform_geometries
from utils.geo_functions import transform_points
from models import Geocache, PointCollection


class GeocachingApp(PointCollection):
    def __init__(self, data_file=None, my_location=None):
        """Application class.

        :param data_file: An OGR compatible file
         with geocaching points.
        :param my_location: Coordinates of your location.
        """
        super(GeocachingApp, self).__init__(file_path=data_file)

        self._datasource = None
        self._transformed_geoms = None
        self._my_location = None
        self.distances = None

        #Delete the code containing "if data_file..."

        if my_location:
            self.my_location = my_location
```

In the class declaration (`class GeocachingApp(PointCollection)`), we added `GeocachingClass`, which tells Python that the `GeocachingApp` class should inherit methods and properties from `PointCollection`. However, as both classes have an `__init__` method, unless we do something, the Geocaching app's `__init__` method will completely overwrite the `PointCollection` method.

We want both of the `__init__` methods called, so we will use the `super()` function. This tells Python to call the `__init__` method of the inherited class. Also, as the `PointCollection` class handles the files importing now, we will pass the `data_file` argument to it. Perform the following steps:

1. Let's test it and check whether the inheritance works. Go to the `if __name__ == "__main__":` block at the end of the file and edit it as follows:

   ```python
   if __name__ == "__main__":
       gdal.PushErrorHandler('CPLQuietErrorHandler')
       # Create the application:
       my_app = GeocachingApp()
       # Now we will call a method from the PointCollection class:
       my_app.import_data("../data/geocaching.gpx")
   ```

[80]

2. In fact, as you type the code, you may notice that PyCharm's auto-completion feature now includes methods and properties from the inherited class.
3. Run the code, and you should see this output:

```
File imported: ../data/geocaching.gpx

Process finished with exit code 0
```

Congratulations! You have just used class inheritance with success. This is a very powerful and handy feature of Python.

Summary

In this chapter, the challenge was to find a way to combine data from multiple sources. The solution for this is to make code that can take different types of data and transform it into a common type of object.

In order to achieve this, we first created two new Python classes. The first was the `Geocache` class, which represents a single geocache location and contains its coordinates, a name, and a description. The second was the `PointCollection` class, which represents a collection of Geocache objects. This class has the ability to import and convert the information from as many files as needed.

This technique that we used is called **abstraction**; its foundations reside in hiding complex procedures behind objects that can be easily understood by humans.

Finally, we integrated this new layer of abstraction into the application using class inheritance. The `GeocachingApp` class inherited the `PointCollection`, and in the end, it could behave similarly to any and both of them at the same time.

In the next chapter, while we will improve the application's capability to search for points, you will also learn other ways of combining classes.

4
Improving the App Search Capabilities

So far, our app is capable of simply searching points that are close to a defined location. In this chapter, we are going to make a huge steep and make our app filter the data by geographic boundaries and by any field in the data.

By the end of this chapter, you will be able to search geocaching points that are inside a given city, state, country, or any boundary defined by you. In addition, you will be able to search points by any of its properties such as difficult levels, name, user, and so on. It will also be possible to combine multiple filters.

In the process, we will see how to work with polygons and how the relations between geometries can be analyzed in a geoprocessing application.

To achieve these goals, we will go through the following topics:

- How to describe polygons using well-known text
- Using the Shapely package to handle geometries
- Importing polygon data
- Importing line data
- The use of base classes and inheritance
- The types of geometry relationships
- Filtering by multiple properties and method chaining

Working with polygons

Supposing we want to filter our data by a given region, it's possible to assume that this region is represented by a polygon.

For example, the following image represents the world counties' borders, it was rendered from a Shapefile where each feature is a country and it's geometry is a polygon.

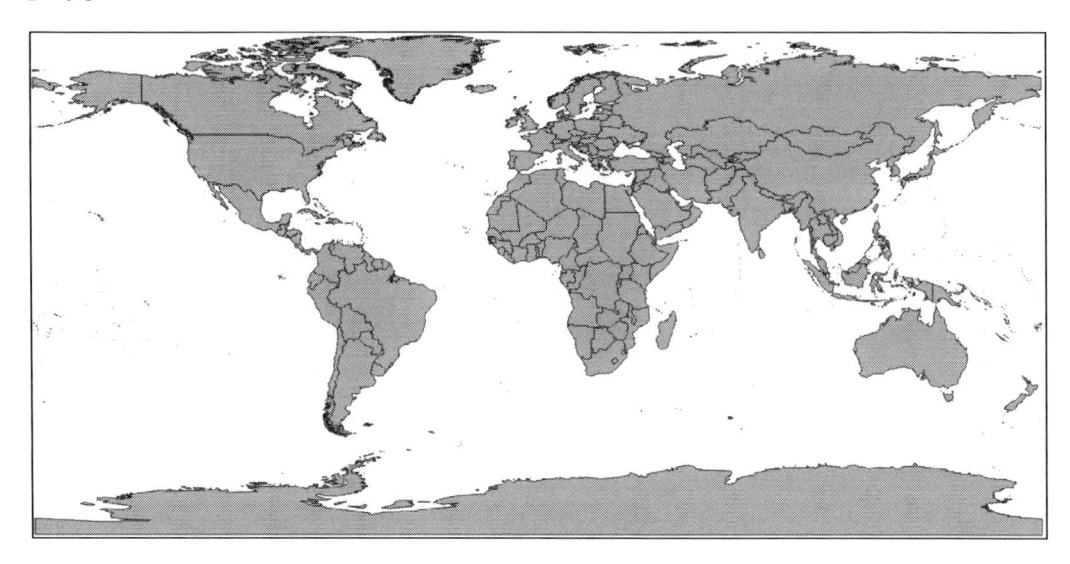

Differently from the geocaching point, whose geometries are only a pair of coordinates, a polygon is a sequence of at least three-point coordinates beginning and ending at the same point.

By now, you can assume that we won't be able to store the polygon's coordinates with the same structure that we had with the geocaching point. We will need to store the whole OGR geometry or store something that can be transformed from or to it.

How these polygons are represented is an important subject, because mastering it allows you to manipulate them any way you need to do any kind of work. It also allows you to build polygons from point coordinates (from a GPS for example) or form shapes such as a rectangle.

Knowing well-known text

Well-known text (**WKT**) is a human readable markup language to represent geometries in a spatial application. It was originally defined by the **Open Geospatial Consortium** (**OGC**) and is accepted by many software as a form of data exchange. The WKT has a binary equivalent called **well-known binary** (**WKB**). It is used for data storage and transfer where human readability is not required.

Let's go through some examples to see how WKT works. First, we will create an OGR geometry of the polygon shown in the following image:

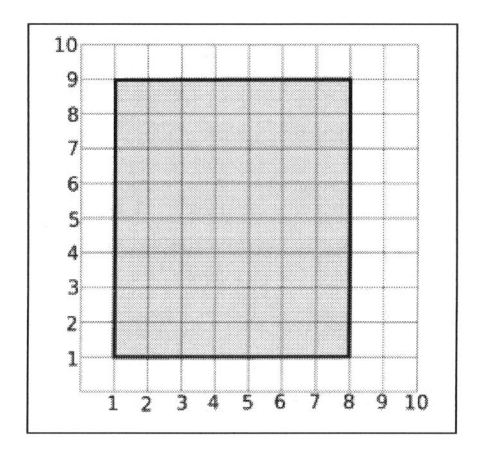

1. Make a copy of your `Chapter3` folder inside the geopy project and rename it to `Chapter4`.
2. Locate the `Chapter4\experiments` directory and delete the files inside it. If you don't have this directory, create it.
3. Inside the `Chapter4\experiments` folder, create a new Python file. To do this in PyCharm, right-click on the folder and choose **New** | **Python File**. Name this file `wkt_experiments.py`.
4. Type the following code:

    ```
    # coding=utf-8

    import ogr

    wkt_rectangle = "POLYGON ((1 1, 1 9, 8 9, 8 1, 1 1))"
    geometry = ogr.CreateGeometryFromWkt(wkt_rectangle)

    print(geometry.__class__)
    print(geometry.Area())
    print(8*7)
    ```

Improving the App Search Capabilities

5. Now run it (*Alt* + *Shift* + *F10* and choose `wkt_experiments`). You should see the following output:

    ```
    <class 'osgeo.ogr.Geometry'>
    56.0
    56

    Process finished with exit code 0
    ```

    What we did here was to define the WKT representation of a polygon in a Python string. Note that it started from coordinate `1.1` and listed all the coordinates clockwise ending at `1.1` again (the direction is not important; it could also be counter clockwise).

    In the next line, we called OGR's `CreateGeometryFromWkt` function that passed the string as a parameter. Internally, it converted the string into a OGR geometry object.

    To make sure that everything went fine in the next three lines, we printed the class name of the object, the area calculated by OGR, and the manually calculated area.

    Now, a more complicated polygon, one with a hole in the middle or an *island*.

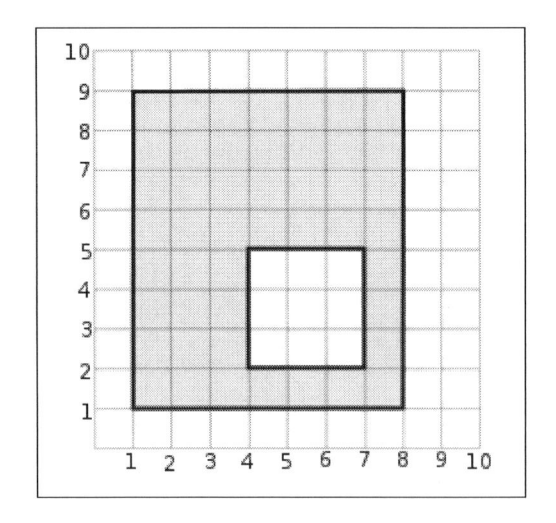

6. Edit your code:

    ```
    # coding=utf-8

    import ogr

    wkt_rectangle = "POLYGON ((1 1, 1 9, 8 9, 8 1, 1 1))"
    geometry = ogr.CreateGeometryFromWkt(wkt_rectangle)
    ```

```
print(geometry.__class__)
print(geometry.Area())
print(8*7)

wkt_rectangle2 = "POLYGON ((1 1, 8 1, 8 9, 1 9, 1 1)," \
                 "(4 2, 4 5, 7 5, 7 2, 4 2))"
geometry2 = ogr.CreateGeometryFromWkt(wkt_rectangle2)
print(geometry.__class__)
print(geometry2.Area())
print((8*7) - (3*3))
```

7. Now run it again (*Shift* + *F10*). You should see the following output:

```
<class 'osgeo.ogr.Geometry'>
56.0
56
<class 'osgeo.ogr.Geometry'>
47.0
47
```

Every polygon ring comes inside the parenthesis separated by commas. The exterior ring should be described first, then all the interior rings.

Managing geometries with WKT gets complicated as the complexity and the number of coordinates increase. To solve this and other problems, we will use another package that will make things a lot easier for us.

Using Shapely to handle geometries

Shapely is a Python package for the analysis of planar features. It uses functions from the GEOS library and a port of the **Java Topology Suite (JTS)**.

It has mainly the same classes and functions as OGR while dealing with geometries. Although it's not a replacement for OGR, it has a more *pythonic* and a very intuitive interface, it is better optimized, and it has a well-developed documentation.

To make things clear, Shapely is intended to analyze geometries and only geometries. It does not handle features' attributes, neither is it capable of reading and writing geospatial files.

For a direct comparison of Shapely and OGR, we are going to rewrite the previous examples:

1. Add the following lines to the `wkt_experiments.py` file (you can keep or remove the previous code, it's up to you):

```
from shapely.geometry import Polygon

print('Examples with Shapely')
polygon1 = Polygon([(1, 1), (1, 9), (8, 9), (8, 1), (1, 1)])
print(polygon1.__class__)
print(polygon1.area)

polygon2 = Polygon([(1, 1), (1, 9), (8, 9), (8, 1), (1, 1)],
                  [[(4, 2), (4, 5),(7, 5), (7, 2), (4, 2)]])
print(polygon2.__class__)
print(polygon2.area)
```

2. Now run the code again and look at the output:

```
Examples with Shapely
<class 'shapely.geometry.polygon.Polygon'>
56.0
<class 'shapely.geometry.polygon.Polygon'>
47.0

Process finished with exit code 0
```

Everything worked as expected, but you may notice a few differences. First, in order to create the polygon, we passed a list of tuples (it could be a list of lists) where each tuple is a point coordinate. This small change makes a big difference; lists are much easier to manipulate than strings.

Secondly, when we print the name of the class of the object created by Shapely, we see that it's a Polygon class and not a Geometry as it was with OGR. This represents a higher level of abstraction as explained in *Chapter 3, Combining Multiple Data Sources*. With it comes all the goodies of abstraction and less worries about the internal functionality.

As you typed the code, specifically `print(polygon1.area)`, PyCharm showed you a list of methods for the `Polygon` class. This is another feature of Shapely, it is a well-written and IDE-friendly Python package. The consequence is that it allows you to take autocompletion, code inspections, refactoring, and a lot of the other features that come with modern IDEs.

Importing polygons

Now that we have the basics on how to work with polygons and we know how to represent and store them, we will go back to our app and add the ability to import geospatial files containing polygons. As we did with the points, we will abstract the features into the Python objects and we will also use class inheritance.

First, let's look at the code we already wrote. In the `models.py` file, we have the `PointCollection` class:

```
class PointCollection(object):
    def __init__(self, file_path=None):
        """This class represents a group of vector data."""
        self.data = []
        self.epsg = None

        if file_path:
            self.import_data(file_path)

    def __add__(self, other):
        self.data += other.data
        return self

    def import_data(self, file_path):
        """Opens an vector file compatible with OGR and parses
         the data.

        :param str file_path: The full path to the file.
        """
        features, metadata = open_vector_file(file_path)
        self._parse_data(features)
        self.epsg = metadata['epsg']
        print("File imported: {}".format(file_path))

    def _parse_data(self, features):
        """Transforms the data into Geocache objects.

        :param features: A list of features.
        """
        for feature in features:
            geom = feature['geometry']['coordinates']
            attributes = feature['properties']
            cache_point = Geocache(geom[0], geom[1],
                               attributes = attributes)
```

Improving the App Search Capabilities

```
            self.data.append(cache_point)

    def describe(self):
        print("SRS EPSG code: {}".format(self.epsg))
        print("Number of features: {}".format(len(self.data)))
```

This class represents a collection of geocaching points and is responsible for importing these points and converting and storing them. These are exactly the same functionality that we want to implement to import polygons.

In the previous chapter, you saw how it's possible, through inheritance, to make a class inherit functionalities from other classes. We will use this same technique to use what we already have to import the polygons.

Since the processing of geocaching points and polygons may have its particularities, it will need some of the things to be specific for each one. A specific example is the `_parse_data` method that, for now, converts features into geocaching points.

So, it's not a good idea to make the class that represents polygons to inherit directly from the `PointCollection` class. Instead, the idea is to have two base classes, one that represents a single object and other that represents a collection of that object. These base classes will contain methods that are common to the points and the polygons, then the child classes will contain methods specific for each case.

The polygons that we will import could be countries, boundaries, states, or provinces of a country, city, district regions, and so on. Since it's not clear yet, let's call it *boundaries*. This is explained in the following steps:

1. We will start creating the `BaseGeoObject` object and adapting from the `Geocache` class. Open the `models.py` file in the `Chapter4` folder.
2. Make a copy of the `Geocache` class with all its methods (copy and paste).
3. Rename the first copy to `BaseGeoObject` and change `docstring` to something like `"Base class for single geo objects."`. You should have this:

```
class BaseGeoObject(object):
    """Base class for a single geo object."""
    def __init__(self, lat, lon, attributes=None):
        self.lat = lat
        self.lon = lon
        self.attributes = attributes

    @property
    def coordinates(self):
        return self.lat, self.lon
```

```
class Geocache(object):
    """This class represents a single geocaching point."""
    def __init__(self, lat, lon, attributes=None):
        self.lat = lat
        self.lon = lon
        self.attributes = attributes

    @property
    def coordinates(self):
        return self.lat, self.lon
```

Now try to think, looking at both of the classes, what is specific for the Geocache, what doesn't belong to a generic GeoObject or what belongs to it, and what properties and methods every type of geospatial object could have.

This separation could lead to some debate, and sometimes, depending on the complexity of the project and the nature of what you are dealing with, it may be hard to reach a final state in the first iteration through the code. In your projects, you may need to come back and change how the classes are organized more than once.

For now, I'm going to propose the following logic:

- **Lat, lon**: These properties are for the Geocache only. As we saw, we may have other types of geometries and we want to generalize how the geometries are stored.
- **Attributes**: All the objects should have this property.
- **A __repr__ method**: This is another *magic method* like __init__ and __add__ that we had in the previous chapter. __repr__ is called when you use the print() function on an object. We will add it and set it to not be implemented on the base class, because every type of object should have its own representation.
- **Coordinates property**: All geo objects should have coordinates, but how it is implemented here is specific to the Geocache. We will change that to a generic form: a geom property that will contain the object geometry.

Let's make the first changes to these classes. Edit your code to be as follows:

```
class BaseGeoObject(object):
    """Base class for a single geo object."""
    def __init__(self, geometry, attributes=None):
        self.geom = geometry
        self.attributes = attributes

    @property
```

```python
    def coordinates(self):
        raise NotImplementedError

    def __repr__(self):
        raise NotImplementedError


class Geocache(BaseGeoObject):
    """This class represents a single geocaching point."""
    def __init__(self, geometry, attributes=None):
        super(Geocache, self).__init__(geometry, attributes)

    def __repr__(self):
        name = self.attributes.get('name', 'Unnamed')
        return "{} {} - {}".format(self.geom.x,
                                    self.geom.y, name)
```

A `geom` property was added to the class as a required argument while instantiating it. In this property, we will store the Shapely object. The `lat` and `lon` properties were removed; they can be accessed directly from the Shapely object (`geom`) and we will adapt `PointCollection` to do this.

The `__repr__` method of the `Geocache` class returns a string containing the coordinates of the point and the `name` attribute when it's available or `Unnamed`.

Now add the Boundary class:

```python
class Boundary(BaseGeoObject):
    """Represents a single political Boundary."""
    def __repr__(self):
        return self.name
```

For now, the `Boundary` class is almost the same as the `BaseGeoObject` class, so we only change the `__repr__` method, so it returns only the name of the boundary.

The next step is to edit the collection classes. Our `PointCollection` class is almost compatible with the new organization. We only need to make a few changes to the `_parse_data` method, transform this class into a base class, and create the classes that will inherit from it:

1. First, like we did earlier, make a copy of the `PointCollection` class.
2. Now, rename the first occurrence of this class and change its docstring:

```python
class BaseGeoCollection(object):
    """This class represents a collection of spatial data."""
    ...
```

3. Go to the `_parse_data` method and alter it to be as follows:

    ```
    #...
        def _parse_data(self, features):
            raise NotImplementedError
    ```

What we did here was we explicitly told that this method is not implemented in the base class. This is a good practice for two reasons: first it is a hint for the programmer that this method needs to be implemented when this class is inherited and it also states the *signature* for the method (the arguments that it should receive). Secondly, if it is not implemented, Python will raise `NotImplementedError` instead of `AttributeError`, leading to a better debugging experience.

1. Before we continue, edit the imported modules at the beginning of the file to match the following code:

    ```
    # coding=utf-8

    from __future__ import print_function
    import gdal
    from shapely.geometry import Point
    from shapely import wkb, wkt
    from utils.geo_functions import open_vector_file
    ```

2. The base class is ready and now we are going to edit the `PointCollection` class. Firstly, you can remove all the methods from this class. Leave only the docstring and the `_parse_data` method.

3. Edit the class declaration and make it inherit from `BaseGeoCollection`.

4. Finally, edit the `_parse_data` method to be compliant with the geometry represented by Shapely objects. Your code should be as follows:

    ```
    class PointCollection(BaseGeoCollection):
        """This class represents a collection of
        geocaching points.
        """
        def _parse_data(self, features):
            """Transforms the data into Geocache objects.

            :param features: A list of features.
            """
            for feature in features:
                coords = feature['geometry']['coordinates']
                point = Point(float(coords[1]), float(coords[0]))
                attributes = feature['properties']
                cache_point = Geocache(point, attributes = attributes)
                self.data.append(cache_point)
    ```

Improving the App Search Capabilities

Note that the difference is that while instancing the Geocache, instead of passing the coordinates, we are now passing a `Point` object, which is an instance of the `Point` class provided by Shapely.

5. Next we are going to create the `BoundaryCollection` class. Insert this code anywhere after the base classes:

```
class BoundaryCollection(BaseGeoCollection):
    """This class represents a collection of
    geographic boundaries.
    """
    def _parse_data(self, features):
        for feature in features:
            geom = feature['geometry']['coordinates']
            attributes = feature['properties']
            polygon = wkt.loads(geom)
            boundary = Boundary(geometry=polygon,
                                attributes=attributes)
            self.data.append(boundary)
```

The difference from `PointCollection` is that we are now creating polygons and instances of the `Boundary` class. Note how the polygon is created with the statement `wkt.loads(geom)`.

6. We are almost done. Check whether everything is correct. The complete `models.py` file should contain the following code:

```
# coding=utf-8

from __future__ import print_function
import gdal
from shapely.geometry import Point
from shapely import wkb, wkt
from utils.geo_functions import open_vector_file

class BaseGeoObject(object):
    """Base class for a single geo object."""
    def __init__(self, geometry, attributes=None):
        self.geom = geometry
        self.attributes = attributes

    @property
    def coordinates(self):
        raise NotImplementedError

    def __repr__(self):
```

```python
            raise NotImplementedError


class Geocache(BaseGeoObject):
    """This class represents a single geocaching point."""
    def __init__(self, geometry, attributes=None):
        super(Geocache, self).__init__(geometry, attributes)

    def __repr__(self):
        name = self.attributes.get('name', 'Unnamed')
        return "{} {} - {}".format(self.geom.x,
                                    self.geom.y, name)

class Boundary(BaseGeoObject):
    """Represents a single geographic boundary."""
    def __repr__(self):
        return self.attributes.get('name', 'Unnamed')

class BaseGeoCollection(object):
    """This class represents a collection of spatial data."""
    def __init__(self, file_path=None):
        self.data = []
        self.epsg = None

        if file_path:
            self.import_data(file_path)

    def __add__(self, other):
        self.data += other.data
        return self

    def import_data(self, file_path):
        """Opens an vector file compatible with OGR and parses
         the data.

        :param str file_path: The full path to the file.
        """
        features, metadata = open_vector_file(file_path)
        self._parse_data(features)
        self.epsg = metadata['epsg']
        print("File imported: {}".format(file_path))

    def _parse_data(self, features):
```

```
        raise NotImplementedError

    def describe(self):
        print("SRS EPSG code: {}".format(self.epsg))
        print("Number of features: {}".format(len(self.data)))


class PointCollection(BaseGeoCollection):
    """This class represents a collection of
    geocaching points.
    """
    def _parse_data(self, features):
        """Transforms the data into Geocache objects.

        :param features: A list of features.
        """
        for feature in features:
            coords = feature['geometry']['coordinates']
            point = Point(coords)
            attributes = feature['properties']
            cache_point = Geocache(point, attributes=attributes)
            self.data.append(cache_point)


class BoundaryCollection(BaseGeoCollection):
    """This class represents a collection of
    geographic boundaries.
    """
    def _parse_data(self, features):
        for feature in features:
            geom = feature['geometry']['coordinates']
            attributes = feature['properties']
            polygon = wkt.loads(geom)
            boundary = Boundary(geometry=polygon,
                                attributes=attributes)
            self.data.append(boundary)
```

7. Now, in order to test it, go to the end of the file and edit the `if __name__ == '__main__':` block:

```
if __name__ == '__main__':
    world = BoundaryCollection("../data/world_borders_simple.shp")
    for item in world.data:
        print(item)
```

8. Now run it, press *Alt + Shift + F10*, and select `models`. If everything is OK, you should see a long list of the unnamed countries:

```
File imported: ../data/world_borders_simple.shp
Unnamed
Unnamed
Unnamed
Unnamed
...

Process finished with exit code 0
```

This is disappointing. We expected to see the names of the countries, but for some reason, the program failed to get it from the attributes. We will solve this problem in the next topic.

Getting the attributes' values

Let's explore the attributes of the world borders to find out why we were unable to get the names.

1. Edit the `if __name__ == '__main__':` block:

   ```
   if __name__ == '__main__':
       world = BoundaryCollection("../data/world_borders_simple.shp")
       print(world.data[0].attributes.keys())
   ```

2. Run the code and look at the output:

   ```
   File imported: ../data/world_borders_simple.shp
   ['SUBREGION', 'POP2005', 'REGION', 'ISO3', 'ISO2', 'FIPS', 'UN',
   'NAME']

   Process finished with exit code 0
   ```

   What we did was we got the first item in `world.data` and then printed its attribute keys. The list shown in the output has a `NAME` key, but it is all in the uppercase. This is very common for Shapefiles whose data is contained in the DBF files.

   Since we don't want to worry if the attributes' names are in the uppercase or lowercase, we have two possible solutions: convert the names at the moment of the import or convert the names on the fly when the attribute value is requested. Depending on your application, you may achieve better performance with one or the other method. Here, for didactic purposes, we will opt for the on-the-fly conversion and add a little spice to it.

Improving the App Search Capabilities

3. Instead of accessing the attributes directly, let's make a method that will do it for us. Edit the `BaseGeoObject` class' `__init__` method and also add a `get_attribute` method:

```
class BaseGeoObject(object):
    """Base class for a single geo object."""
    def __init__(self, geometry, attributes=None):
        self.geom = geometry
        self.attributes = attributes

        # Makes a lookup table of case insensitive attributes.
        self._attributes_lowercase = {}
        for key in self.attributes.keys():
            self._attributes_lowercase[key.lower()] = key

    @property
    def coordinates(self):
        raise NotImplementedError

    def get_attribute(self, attr_name, case_sensitive=False):
        """Gets an attribute by its name.

        :param attr_name: The name of the attribute.
        :param case_sensitive: True or False.
        """
        if not case_sensitive:
            attr_name = attr_name.lower()
            attr_name = self._attributes_lowercase[attr_name]
        return self.attributes[attr_name]

    def __repr__(self):
        raise NotImplementedError
```

In the `__init__` method, we made a dictionary that contains the equivalence between lowercase attribute names and the original names. If you search the Internet, there is a number of techniques to implement case-insensitive dictionaries. But the one we implemented here allows us to preserve the original names, giving the user the option to choose whether he wants the search to be case-sensitive or not.

4. Now, edit the `Boundary` class to use the new method:

```
class Boundary(BaseGeoObject):
    """Represents a single geographic boundary."""
    def __repr__(self):
        return self.get_attribute('name')
```

5. Edit the `if __name__ == '__main__':` block:
   ```
   if __name__ == '__main__':
       world = BoundaryCollection("../data/world_borders_simple.shp")
       for item in world.data:
           print(item)
   ```

6. Run the code again. Now, you should have a beautiful list of country names:
   ```
   File imported: ../data/world_borders_simple.shp
   Antigua and Barbuda
   Algeria
   Azerbaijan
   Albania
   Armenia
   ...
   Process finished with exit code 0
   ```

Importing lines

As we did with the geocaching points and political boundaries, we will implement the ability of the program to import lines (that is, linestrings). These lines can represent roads, rivers, power lines, and so on. With this kind of features, we will be able to search for points that are close to a given road for example.

The lines and the collection of lines will also be the subclasses of `BaseGeoObject` and `BaseGeoCollection`. Let's start by making a `LineString` and a `LineStringCollection` class, as follows:

1. Insert this new class into the `models.py` file. It could be anywhere after the base classes' definition:
   ```
   class LineString(BaseGeoObject):
       """Represents a single linestring."""
       def __repr__(self):
           return self.get_attribute('name')
   ```

   Again, we only implement the `__repr__` method. The other functionalities are inherited from the `BaseGeoObject` class.

2. Now, add the class representing a collection of linestrings and its `_parse_data` method:
   ```
   class LineStringCollection(BaseGeoCollection):
       """Represents a collection of linestrings."""
       def _parse_data(self, features):
           for feature in features:
   ```

Improving the App Search Capabilities

```
geom = feature['geometry']['coordinates']
attributes = feature['properties']
line = wkt.loads(geom)
linestring = LineString(geometry=line,
                        attributes=attributes)
self.data.append(linestring)
```

In order to test our new classes, we are going to use a shapefile containing USA's main roads.

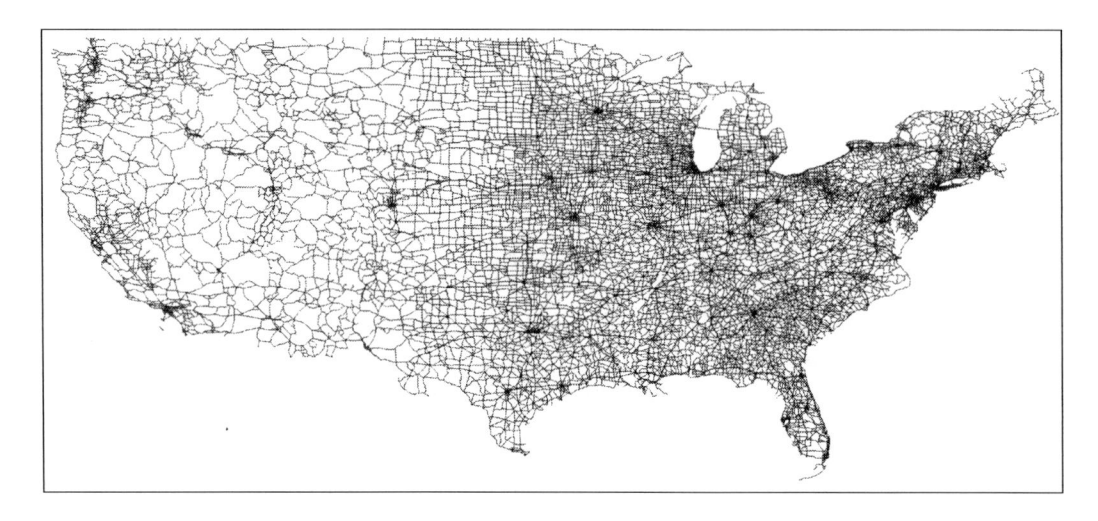

3. Edit the `if __name__ == '__main__':` block at the end of the file. You can comment the previous code if you wish instead of deleting it:

    ```
    if __name__ == '__main__':
        usa_roads = LineStringCollection('../data/roads.shp')
        for item in usa_roads.data:
            print(item)
    ```

4. Run the code. You should get a big list of the road names in the output console:

    ```
    File imported: ../data/roads.shp

    State Route 131
    State Route 3
    State Route 3
    State Route 3
    State Route 411
    State Route 3
    State Route 3
    State Route 5, State Route 786
    ...
    Process finished with exit code 0
    ```

In order to make our output more meaningful, we can change how each `LineString` class is printed. Remember that the special method named `__repr__` is called when you use the `print()` function on an object, and it should return a string to be printed. Let's return more information when `LineString` is printed.

5. Edit your `LineString` class and change the `__repr__` method, so it returns the road name and length:

   ```
   class LineString(BaseGeoObject):
       """Represents a single linestring."""
       def __repr__(self):
           length = self.geom.length
           return "{} - {}".format(self.get_attribute('name'),
                                   length)
   ```

   Here, we used Python's string formatting to compose a string that can be returned by this method.

6. Run the code and see the new output:

   ```
   File imported: ../data/roads.shp

   US Route 395-0.16619770512
   US Route 30-0.0432070790491
   State Route 84-0.0256320861143
   US Route 6-0.336460513878
   US Route 40-0.107844768871
   State Route 272-0.0264889614357
   ...
   Process finished with exit code 0
   ```

Although it's much better than before, it still has a problem. The length is in degrees, and it means little or nothing to us because we are used to meters, miles, or any other linear unity. So, we need to convert the unity before we print the length.

Converting the spatial reference system and units

Fortunately, we already did this kind of operation before and now we are going to adapt it to our data model.

Improving the App Search Capabilities

We will transform the coordinates of the geometries only when they are needed. To perform the transformation, we will create a new utility function, as follows:

1. Open `geo_functions.py` in our `utils` folder and create a new function:

    ```
    def transform_geometry(geom, src_epsg=4326, dst_epsg=3395):
        """Transforms a single wkb geometry.

        :param geom: wkb geom.
        :param src_epsg: EPSG code for the source geometry.
        :param dst_epsg: EPSG code for the destination geometry.
        """
        ogr_geom = ogr.CreateGeometryFromWkb(geom)
        ogr_transformation = create_transform(src_epsg, dst_epsg)
        ogr_geom.Transform(ogr_transformation)
        return ogr_geom.ExportToWkb()
    ```

    It takes as arguments geometries in the WKB format, its EPSG code, and the EPSG code for the desired coordinate system for the output. It performs the transformation and returns a WKB geometry again.

    Now back to the models; let's import this function and use it.

2. Edit the import at the beginning of the `models.py` file:

    ```
    # coding=utf-8

    from __future__ import print_function
    import gdal
    from shapely.geometry import Point
    from shapely import wkb, wkt
    from utils.geo_functions import open_vector_file
    from utils.geo_functions import transform_geometry
    ```

3. Now, edit `BaseGeoObject`, so our classes can inherit this new functionality:

    ```
    class BaseGeoObject(object):
        """Base class for a single geo object."""
        def __init__(self, geometry, attributes=None):
            self.geom = geometry
            self.attributes = attributes
            self.wm_geom = None

            # Makes a lookup table of case insensitive attributes.
            self._attributes_lowercase = {}
            for key in self.attributes.keys():
                self._attributes_lowercase[key.lower()] = key
    ```

```python
def transformed_geom(self):
    """Returns the geometry transformed into WorldMercator
    coordinate system.
    """
    if not self.wm_geom:
        geom = transform_geometry(self.geom.wkb)
        self.wm_geom = wkb.loads(geom)
    return self.wm_geom

def get_attribute(self, attr_name, case_sensitive=False):
    """Gets an attribute by its name.

    :param attr_name: The name of the attribute.
    :param case_sensitive: True or False.
    """
    if not case_sensitive:
        attr_name = attr_name.lower()
        attr_name = self._attributes_lowercase[attr_name]
    return self.attributes[attr_name]

def __repr__(self):
    raise NotImplementedError
```

Note that we opted to keep the geometries in both the coordinate systems. The geometry in `WorldMercator` is stored in the `wm_geom` property the first time the transformation occurs. The next time `transformed_geom` is called, it will only get the `property` value. This is called **memorization** and we will see more of this technique later in the book.

Depending on your application, this may be a good practice because you may want to use different coordinate systems for specific purposes. For example, to draw a map, you may want to use `lat/lon` and, to perform calculation, you would need the coordinates in meters. The downside is that the memory consumption is higher, because you will be storing two sets of geometry.

4. Finally, we go back to the `LineString` class and change its `__repr__` method to use `transformed_geom` to calculate the length:

```
class LineString(BaseGeoObject):
    """Represents a single linestring."""
    def __repr__(self):
        return "{}-{}".format(self.get_attribute('name'),
                              self.transformed_geom().length)
```

Improving the App Search Capabilities

5. Run the code and see the new output:

   ```
   File imported: ../data/roads.shp
   State Route 3-100928.690515
   State Route 411-3262.29448315
   State Route 3-331878.76971
   State Route 3-56013.8246795.73
   ...
   Process finished with exit code 0
   ```

It's much better now as we can see the road lengths in meters. But it is still not perfect because, normally, we would want the lengths in kilometres or miles. So, we need to convert the unit.

In *Chapter 1*, *Preparing the Work Environment*, we made a beautiful function capable of performing these transformations; we used it to convert area units. Using it as a template, we are going to implement it to convert length units.

Since it's a function that can be used in other parts of any application, we are going to put it into the geo_functions.py module in the utils package (that is, directory).

1. Edit the geo_functions.py files and copy and paste the function that we used in *Chapter 1*, *Preparing the Work Environment*, to calculate and transform area units. We will keep it there for later use:

   ```
   def calculate_areas(geometries, unity='km2'):
       """Calculate the area for a list of ogr geometries."""
       conversion_factor = {
           'sqmi': 2589988.11,
           'km2': 1000000,
           'm': 1}
       if unity not in conversion_factor:
           raise ValueError(
               "This unity is not defined: {}".format(unity))
       areas = []
       for geom in geometries:
           area = geom.Area()
           areas.append(area / conversion_factor[unity])
       return areas
   ```

2. Duplicate this function (copy and paste) and edit it to make it like the following code:

   ```
   def convert_length_unit(value, unit='km', decimal_places=2):
       """Convert the leng unit of a given value.
       The input is in meters and the output is set by the unity
           argument.
   ```

```
    :param value: Input value in meters.
    :param unit: The desired output unit.
    :param decimal_places: Number of decimal places of the output.
    """
    conversion_factor = {
        'mi': 0.000621371192,
        'km': 0.001,
        'm': 1.0}

    if unit not in conversion_factor:
        raise ValueError(
            "This unit is not defined: {}".format(unit))
    return round(value * conversion_factor[unit], decimal_places)
```

Again, it's a very versatile function because you can easily change its code to add more conversion factors to it. Here, we also introduced the `round()` function, so we can see a more readable result. By default, it will round the result to two decimal places, which in most cases, is enough for a good representation of length.

3. Go back to the models and import this new function after the other imports:

```
# coding=utf-8

from __future__ import print_function
import gdal
from shapely.geometry import Point
from shapely import wkb, wkt
from utils.geo_functions import open_vector_file
from utils.geo_functions import transform_geometry
from utils.geo_functions import convert_length_unit
```

4. Now edit the `LineString` class. We will add a *convenience method* (we will see more about this later in the chapter) that will return the length in a converted unit, change the `__repr__` value to use it, and also improve the string formatting to display the unit and get a better output:

```
class LineString(BaseGeoObject):
    """Represents a single linestring."""
    def __repr__(self):
        unit = 'km'
        return "{} ({}{})".format(self.get_attribute('name'),
                                  self.length(unit), unit)

    def length(self, unit='km'):
        """Convenience method that returns the length of the
```

```
        linestring in a given unit.

        :param unit: The desired output unit.
        """
        return convert_length_unit(self.transformed_geom().length,
                                   unit)
```

5. Run the code again and see what we have accomplished:

```
File imported: ../data/roads.shp

State Route 146    (10.77km)
US Route 7, US Route 20   (5.81km)
State Route 295    (13.67km)
Interstate Route 90   (3.55km)
State Route 152    (18.22km)
State Route 73    (65.19km)
State Route 20    (53.89km)
State Route 95    (10.38km)
...
Process finished with exit code 0
```

Geometry relationships

We want to filter the geocaching points that fall inside a given boundary (a country, state, city, and so on.). In order to perform this kind of filtering, we need to verify every point and see whether it's inside the polygon representing the boundary.

In geoprocessing, the relations between the two geometries are described by a set of known predicates. These relationships are very important because they allow conditions to be made, so one can perform operations and calculations.

Shapely comes with a complete set of predicates that analyze the relation of the two geometries. Before we go further in our app, let's take a look at the possible relation checks.

Touches

This is true if the geometries have one or more points in common without their interiors intersecting.

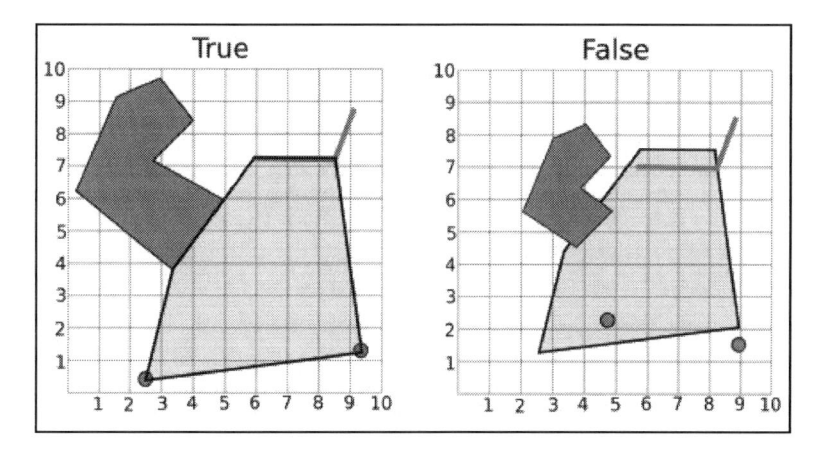

Crosses

This is true if there is an intersection between the two objects without one containing the other.

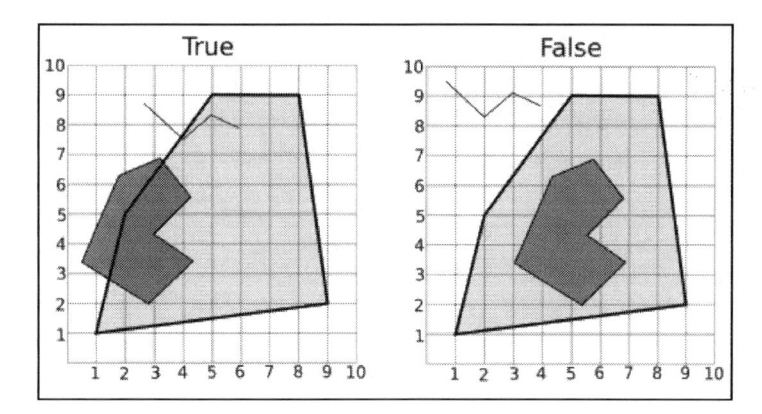

Contains

This indicates if one object completely contains the other object; all the boundaries, lines, or points must be inside the first object.

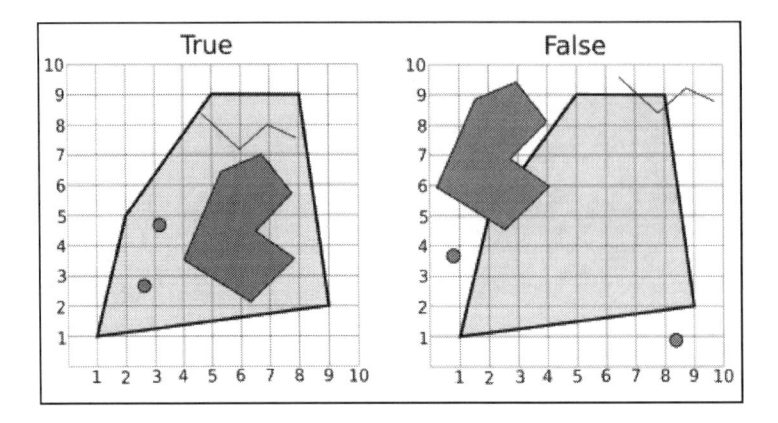

Within

This is true if one geometry is contained in another geometry. It's the same as *Contains*, but if you switch the two geometries.

Equals or almost equals

This is true if the two objects have the same boundary and interior. Almost equals allows a configurable tolerance in the precision of the test.

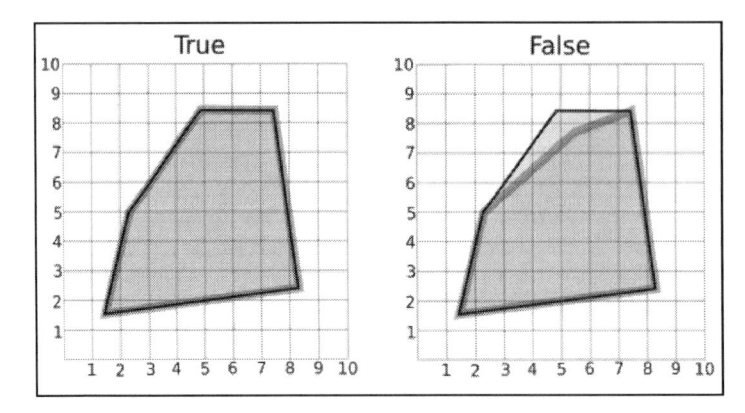

Intersects

This indicates that one geometry intersects the other in any way. It is true if any of these relations are true: contains, crosses, equals, touches, and within.

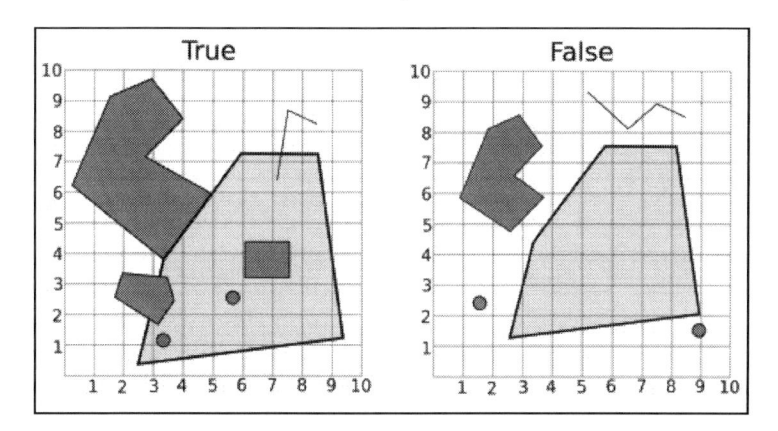

Disjoint

This returns true if the two geometries have no relation between them.

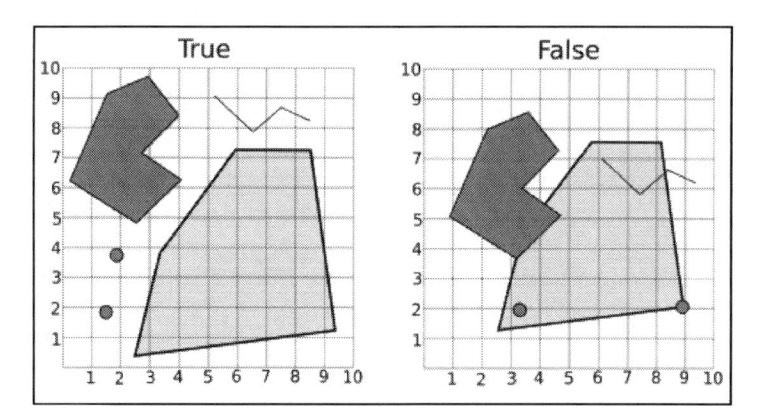

Filtering by attributes and relations

Now that we know how geometries relate to each other, we can search points using these relations. We already have the means for importing the points and the polygons that represent any kind of boundaries that may be of our interest.

Improving the App Search Capabilities

The data that comes with the book files contains examples of world countries' boundaries, but you are free to search the Internet for any data that is significant to you. Remember only that the data coordinates should be in latitudes and longitudes, and they need to have a `name` field.

For our tests, I prepared a special set of geocaching points that spans the whole globe, and as an exercise, we will filter these points by a country.

The proposed workflow is as follows:

- Import the points and boundaries
- Find the boundary that we want to use
- Filter the points by that boundary
- Return the points to the user

To find the points that we want, we will iterate over the data until it hits a match. Iterations can be costly in terms of processing depending on the amount of data and on the operations that are performed on each loop. Let's keep this in mind.

The first step in the workflow is already done, so let's write the code to find the boundary of our interest. If you are using the data provided, we can find the boundary of your country as follows:

1. Go to the `BoundaryCollection` class and add a new method `get_by_name`:

```python
class BoundaryCollection(BaseGeoCollection):
    """This class represents a collection of
    geographic boundaries.
    """
    def _parse_data(self, features):
        for feature in features:
            geom = feature['geometry']['coordinates']
            attributes = feature['properties']
            polygon = wkt.loads(geom)
            boundary = Boundary(geometry=polygon,
                                attributes=attributes)
            self.data.append(boundary)

    def get_by_name(self, name):
        """Find an object by its name attribute and returns it."""
        for item in self.data:
            if item.get_attribute('name') == name:
                return item
        raise LookupError(
            "Object not found with the name: {}".format(name))
```

This very simple method iterates over the data. When it finds the first boundary whose name property matches the name passed as an argument, the function execution stops and the object is returned. If nothing is found, `LookupError` will be raised.

2. Let's play with it. Go to the `if __name__ == '__main__':` block at the end of the file and edit it:

   ```
   if __name__ == '__main__':
       world = BoundaryCollection("../data/world_borders_simple.shp")
       print(world.get_by_name('Brazil'))
   ```

3. Try the different countries' names and see the results. If it's found, you should have an output similar to this:

   ```
   File imported: ../data/world_borders_simple.shp
   Brazil

   Process finished with exit code 0
   ```

4. If it's not found, you should get a nice exception:

   ```
   Traceback (most recent call last):
     File "Chapter 4/code/models.py", line 153, in <module>
       print(world_Boundarys.get_by_name('Foo'))
     File "Chapter 4/code/models.py", line 148, in get_by_name
       'Object not found with the name: {}'.format(name))
   LookupError: Object not found with the name: Foo

   Process finished with exit code 1
   ```

   Very well, our method works nice and with an additional (almost) unexpected feature: it's not specific for the boundaries; it can be used to find any type of GeoObject. Take a look and notice how it only uses properties that are available in our base classes.

5. Move the `get_by_name` method to the `BaseGeoCollection` class and test you code again. Remember that the order of the methods inside a class is irrelevant for the class' behavior, but the best practices recommend you to put the magic methods first, then the private ones, and then the others. Your complete `BaseGeoCollection` class should be as follows:

   ```
   class BaseGeoCollection(object):
       """This class represents a collection of spatial data."""
       def __init__(self, file_path=None):
           self.data = []
           self.epsg = None

           if file_path:
   ```

Improving the App Search Capabilities

```
            self.import_data(file_path)

    def __add__(self, other):
        self.data += other.data
        return self

    def _parse_data(self, features):
        raise NotImplementedError

    def import_data(self, file_path):
        """Opens an vector file compatible with OGR and parses
          the data.

        :param str file_path: The full path to the file.
        """
        features, metadata = open_vector_file(file_path)
        self._parse_data(features)
        self.epsg = metadata['epsg']
        print("File imported: {}".format(file_path))

    def describe(self):
        print("SRS EPSG code: {}".format(self.epsg))
        print("Number of features: {}".format(len(self.data)))

    def get_by_name(self, name):
        """Find an object by its name attribute and returns it."""
        for item in self.data:
            if item.get_attribute('name') == name:
                return item
        raise LookupError(
            "Object not found with the name: {}".format(name))
```

Now, in the next step, we will search for the points that are within the boundary that we found. This time, we will create a method directly inside the `BaseGeoCollection` class, so it becomes available to the `PointCollection` and the `BoundaryCollection` classes through inheritance. By doing this, we will get a bonus feature—we are able to filter the boundaries by another boundary.

6. Go to the `BaseGeoCollection` class and add the method `filter_by_boundary`:

```
#...
    def filter_by_boundary(self, boundary):
        """Filters the data by a given boundary"""
        result = []
        for item in self.data:
            if item.geom.within(boundary.geom):
```

```
            result.append(item)
    return result
```

Here, we created a variable `result` containing a list to store the objects that passes the test. The `within` predicate is used to test every item if it is inside the boundary that is passed as an argument. In this case, if nothing is found, no exception is raised and an empty list is returned.

7. Edit the testing code in the `if __name__ == '__main__':` block:

```
if __name__ == '__main__':
    gdal.PushErrorHandler('CPLQuietErrorHandler')
    world = BoundaryCollection("../data/world_borders_simple.shp")
    geocaching_points = PointCollection("../data/geocaching.gpx")
    usa_boundary = world.get_by_name('United States')
    result = geocaching_points.filter_by_boundary(usa_boundary)
    for item in result:
        print(item)
```

While testing, two instances are created, one from the `BoundaryCollection` class and one from the `PointCollection` class. The data files are passed as arguments. Then, the country of interest is found and stored in the `usa_boundary` variable. This variable is then passed to the `filter_by_boundary` method.

8. Run the code. You should see a long list of geocaches as follows:

```
-78.90175 42.89648   -   LaSalle Park No 1
-78.89818 42.89293   -   LaSalle Park No 2
-78.47808 43.02617   -   A Unique Walk in Akron
-78.93865 42.95982   -   A view of Strawberry Island
-78.90007 42.7484    -   A View to a Windmill
-79.07533 43.08133   -   A Virtual Made in the Mist
-74.43207 43.86942   -   Adirondack Museum Guestbook
...

Process finished with exit code 0
```

As expected, it prints a list of Geocache objects whose representation given by the `__repr__` method is their coordinates and names.

Filtering by multiple attributes

The next step is to search the geocaching points by their attributes. For example, we may want to filter the points by the author of the geocache, by the level of difficulty to find the geocache, and so on.

Improving the App Search Capabilities

We will borrow the techniques used in the methods that allowed us to get a GeoObject by its name property and the method that filtered by a polygon. The difference here is that we must allow the attribute that we want to filter by to be passed as a parameter, and we want to have the capability to combine multiple fields.

1. Let's start adding a simple filter method in the `BaseGeoCollection` class:

    ```
    #...
        def filter(self, attribute, value):
            """Filters the collection by an attribute.

            :param attribute: The name of the attribute to filter by.
            :param value: The filtering value.
            """
            result = []
            for item in self.data:
                if item.get_attribute(attribute) == value:
                    result.append(item)
            return result
    ```

    This method takes two arguments: the attribute name that we want to filter by and the value that this attribute needs to have to pass the filter. Different from `get_by_name`, this filtering function accumulates every object found into a list and returns this list.

2. To test the filtering method, edit the `if __name__ == '__main__':` block. We will filter the geocache points whose level of difficulty is 1:

    ```
    if __name__ == '__main__':
        gdal.PushErrorHandler('CPLQuietErrorHandler')
        points = PointCollection("../data/geocaching.gpx")
        result = points.filter('difficulty', '1')
        points.describe()
        print("Found {} points".format(len(result)))
    ```

3. Run the code. You should have this output:

    ```
    File imported: ../data/geocaching.gpx
    SRS EPSG code: 4326
    Number of features: 112
    Found 38 points

    Process finished with exit code 0
    ```

    From a total of 112 points, 38 match our criteria.

Chaining filters

This part deserves a topic because we are going to use a very handy Python technique that you will most certainly need more than once to solve your geoprocessing challenges.

So far, we can apply a single filter that will return a list of objects. If we want to apply more than one filter, we can simply make the filter function return another collection object with the results, instead of returning a list. This way, we can make it possible to take the results from one filtering and filter them again, thus narrowing the results.

Besides being surprisingly simple, this solution is also very efficient in terms of processing, because at each filtering pass, the results are smaller and the number of iterations reduces.

Python allows function calls to be chained. This means that we don't need to store each step into a variable. We can simply put each call one after another in a very elegant and intuitive pattern as exemplified here:

```
my_points = points.filter('difficulty', '1').filter('status',
'Available')
```

Note that this is an and condition. It will return the points that satisfy both the filters. But since we implemented the __add__ method to the BaseGeoCollection class, we can easily achieve an or type of filtering:

```
my_points = points.filter('difficulty', '1') + points.filter('difficulty', '2')
```

1. Let's make our method return a new instance to make this work. Edit the filter method in the BaseGeoCollection class:

    ```
    #...
        def filter(self, attribute, value):
            """Filters the collection by an attribute.

            :param attribute: The name of the attribute to filter by.
            :param value: The filtering value.
            """
            result = self.__class__()
            for item in self.data:
                if getattr(item, attribute) == value:
                    result.data.append(item)
            return result
    ```

Improving the App Search Capabilities

Now, the result is an instance of the same class that originated the instance where the method was called, because `__class__` is a property that contains the class that originated the instance. Since we are using inheritance, this ensures that we have the result in the same type and the data. Although this is a very simple solution, it works very well. Let's try it:

2. Edit the `if __name__ == '__main__':` block, so we can filter the points that match the two conditions (the and condition):

   ```
   if __name__ == '__main__':
       gdal.PushErrorHandler('CPLQuietErrorHandler')
       points = PointCollection("../data/geocaching.gpx")
       result = points.filter('difficulty', '1').filter('container',
                                                        'Virtual')
       points.describe()
       result.describe()
   ```

3. Run the following code:

   ```
   File imported: ../data/geocaching.gpx
   SRS EPSG code: 4326
   Number of features: 112
   SRS EPSG code: None
   Number of features: 34

   Process finished with exit code 0
   ```

   From the previous test, we know that 38 points are of difficulty 1, now we got 34 points because of those 38 points, four does not have a `container = Virtual`.

4. Try another test this time using an or condition:

   ```
   if __name__ == '__main__':
       gdal.PushErrorHandler('CPLQuietErrorHandler')
       points = PointCollection("../data/geocaching.gpx")
       result = points.filter('difficulty', '1') + points.filter(
           'difficulty', '2')
       points.describe()
       result.describe()
   ```

5. Run the code:

   ```
   File imported: ../data/geocaching.gpx
   SRS EPSG code: 4326
   Number of features: 112
   SRS EPSG code: None
   ```

[116]

```
Number of features: 50

Process finished with exit code 0
```

This time, these 38 points of difficulty 1 were combined with another 12 points of difficulty 2.

Integrating with the app

As we continue to work with increasing levels of abstraction, think of our app's organization. We have two types of data and we have the `GeocachingApp` class with high level functionality. At this point, what we want is to enable the app to filter like we did in the tests, but in a simple and straightforward way.

Take a look at the app as it is at this point:

```
class GeocachingApp(PointCollection):
    def __init__(self, data_file=None, my_location=None):
        """Application class.

        :param data_file: An OGR compatible file
         with geocaching points.
        :param my_location: Coordinates of your location.
        """
        super(GeocachingApp, self).__init__(file_path=data_file)

        self._datasource = None
        self._transformed_geoms = None
        self._my_location = None
        self.distances = None

        if my_location:
            self.my_location = my_location

    @property
    def my_location(self):
        return self._my_location

    @my_location.setter
    def my_location(self, coordinates):
        self._my_location = transform_points([coordinates])[0]

    def calculate_distances(self):
        """Calculates the distance between a
```

```python
        set of points and a given location.

        :return: A list of distances in the same order as
         the points.
        """
        xa = self.my_location[0]
        ya = self.my_location[1]
        points = self._transformed_geoms
        distances = []
        for geom in points:
            point_distance = math.sqrt(
                (geom.GetX() - xa)**2 + (geom.GetY() - ya))
            distances.append(point_distance)
        return distances

    def find_closest_point(self):
        """Find the closest point to a given location and
        return the cache that's on that point.

        :return: OGR feature containing the point.
        """
        # Part 1.
        distances = self.calculate_distances()
        index = np.argmin(distances)
        # Part 2.
        layer = self._datasource.GetLayerByIndex(0)
        feature = layer.GetFeature(index)
        print "Closest point at: {}m".format(distances[index])
        return feature
```

Inheritance was used to give the app the functionality contained in the `PointCollection` class. But this schema won't work anymore because we now have two types of data. We have to remove the inheritance and make a different approach.

What we will do is store instances of the collection classes (`PointCollection` and `BoundaryCollection`), and implement the methods that will relate them in the same way it was done in the tests of the chaining filters topic.

Let's start with the imports and the class' definition:

1. Open your `geocaching_app.py` file and edit the imports section at the beginning of the file to include new classes:

   ```
   # coding=utf-8

   import gdal
   ```

```
import numpy as np
import math
from utils.geo_functions import transform_points
from models import PointCollection, BoundaryCollection
```

2. Now, edit the `GeocachingApp` class definition and the `__init__` method to be as follows:

```
class GeocachingApp(object):
    def __init__(self,
                 geocaching_file=None,
                 boundary_file=None,
                 my_location=None):
        """Application class.

        :param geocaching_file: An OGR compatible file
         with geocaching points.
        :param boundary_file: A file with boundaries.
        :param my_location: Coordinates of your location.
        """
        self.geocaching_data = PointCollection(geocaching_file)
        self.boundaries = BoundaryCollection(boundary_file)
        self._my_location = None
        if my_location:
            self.my_location = my_location
```

The inheritance was removed and now the data is stored in the `geocaching_data` and `boundaries` properties. Optionally, if the user passes a file with geocaching data or with boundary data to the `GeocachingApp` class, these same files are passed as an argument to the `PointCollection` and `BoundaryCollection` creations.

With what you have now, you can already do any type of filtering. You just need to access `geocaching_data` and `boundaries` and do exactly what we did before. Let's try it.

3. Go to the end of the file where there is a line with `if __name__ == "__main__":` and edit the code:

```
if __name__ == "__main__":
    my_app = GeocachingApp("../data/geocaching.gpx",
                           "../data/world_borders_simple.shp")
    usa_boundary = my_app.boundaries.get_by_name('United States')
    result = my_app.geocaching_data.filter_by_boundary(
        usa_boundary)
    print(result)
```

4. Now run it. Remember that whenever you want to run a different file, you need to press *Alt + Shift + F10* and choose the file in the popup. You should see the output with the list of geocaching points again.

But let's suppose that there is a kind of filtering that is expected to be needed multiple times or, maybe, there is a filtering that you want to make explicit. Following the same example, suppose that we are filtering by a country name in this case.

We can use the `GeocachingApp` class, which stands in the highest level of abstraction in our code to implement this or any other high level filtering method.

5. Add this method to the `GeocachingApp` class:

```
#...
    def filter_by_country(self, name):
        """Filter by a country with a given name.

        :param name: The name of the boundary (ex. county name)
        :return: PointCollection
        """
        boundary = self.boundaries.get_by_name(name)
        return self.geocaching_data.filter_by_boundary(boundary)
```

In computer programming, this is also called **convenience method**. It's a method created for convenience in order to solve a more complex task or to avoid boilerplate code (that is, to avoid code repetition).

Summary

In this chapter, we saw that the different types of relationships between geometries can be tested, and that these tests can be used in the program to solve problems.

In order to filter by polygons, first we used the same code to import these polygons into the system like we did with the points, but this time we used Shapely to abstract the geometries of the polygons and points. Finally, we used geometry relationships to search for points inside the polygons.

Then, we implemented a way to filter the data by the name property and we made it filter the data by any property of the object or any combination of properties.

Finally, we adapted the app class to work with the new changes and saw that it's possible to add convenience methods to it in order to simplify some tasks.

In the next chapter, we will start working on the Map Maker App and create means to visualize our data.

5
Making Maps

In this chapter, we will start a new application and use it to produce nice maps from vector data.

In order to produce these maps, we will use Mapnik, one of the world's most used mapping packages. The objective is to understand how it works and adapt it to make an easy-to-use mapping application.

In the previous chapters, we produced some very functional classes that abstract geographic data; we will make this app capable of consuming this type of data.

We will cover the following topics:

- Getting to know Mapnik and see how it works
- Seeing the differences between pure Python and XML when defining a map
- Experimenting with different styles
- Using Python objects as a source of data for Mapnik
- Abstracting Mapnik into a high-level application

Making Maps

Knowing Mapnik

Mapnik is the tool that we will use to produce our maps. It's a very powerful mapping library used by many websites.

In this first topic, we will go through some experiments to get to know Mapnik's features.

Now we will perform a few experiments with Mapnik in order to know how it works. First, let's organize the code for this chapter:

1. Inside your `geopy` project, copy the `Chapter4` folder and rename it to `Chapter5`.
2. Inside the `Chapter5` folder, create a new folder named `mapnik_experiments`. To do that, right-click in your `Chapter5` folder and choose **New | Directory**.
3. Still in `Chapter5`, create another folder named `output`; we will place the maps and images we create into that folder.

Making a map with pure Python

Mapnik has two ways to define a map; one uses pure Python code, the other an XML file.

Mapnik's Python API is very extensive and wraps almost all of the package's functionalities. In the next steps we will experiment with making a map with Python code only.

1. Inside `mapnik_experiments`, create a Python file named `mapnik_python.py`.
2. Type the following code into `mapnik_python.py`:

    ```
    # coding=utf-8

    import mapnik


    # Create a Map
    map = mapnik.Map(800, 600)
    # Set the background color of the map.
    map.background = mapnik.Color('white')

    # Create a Style and a Rule.
    style = mapnik.Style()
    rule = mapnik.Rule()
    ```

```
# Create a PolygonSymbolizer to fill the polygons and
# add it to the rule.
polygon_symbolizer = mapnik.PolygonSymbolizer(
    mapnik.Color('#f2eff9'))
rule.symbols.append(polygon_symbolizer)
# Create a LineSymbolizer to style the polygons borders and
# add it to the rule.
line_symbolizer = mapnik.LineSymbolizer(
    mapnik.Color('rgb(50%,50%,50%)'), 0.1)
rule.symbols.append(line_symbolizer)

# Add the rule to the style.
style.rules.append(rule)

# Add the Style to the Map.
map.append_style('My Style', style)

# Create a data source from a shapefile.
data = mapnik.Shapefile(file='../../data/world_borders_simple.shp')

# Create a layer giving it the name 'world'.
layer = mapnik.Layer('world')
# Set the layer data source and add the style to the layer.
layer.datasource = data
layer.styles.append('My Style')
# Add the layer to the map.
map.layers.append(layer)

# Zoom the map to the extent of all layers.
map.zoom_all()
# Write the map to a image.
mapnik.render_to_file(map,'../output/world.png', 'png')
```

3. Now run the code; press *Alt + Shift + F10* and select `mapnik_python`.

Making Maps

4. There should be a new file named `world.png` inside your `output` folder. You can view this image in PyCharm; just double-click it. You should see this:

![world map](world.png)

Congratulations on creating this first beautiful map; note the superior quality of this rendering and how quickly Mapnik does its job.

Making a map with a style sheet

Instead of using only Python code, the map styles, layers, and other definitions can be put inside an XML file. Let's try this:

1. Inside the `mapnik_experiments` folder, create a new file named `map_style.xml`.

2. Type the following code:

```xml
<Map background-color="white">
  <Style name="My Style">
    <Rule>
      <PolygonSymbolizer fill="#f2eff9" />
```

```xml
            <LineSymbolizer stroke="rgb(50%,50%,50%)" stroke-width="0.1"
/>
        </Rule>
    </Style>

    <Layer name="world">
        <StyleName>My Style</StyleName>
        <Datasource>
            <Parameter name="file">
                    ../../data/world_borders_simple.shp
            </Parameter>
            <Parameter name="type">shape</Parameter>
        </Datasource>
    </Layer>
</Map>
```

This is the style definition of your map. Although PyCharm is a Python IDE, it's also capable of recognizing a lot of file types including XML; it should help you with the tags and should apply a nice coloring to the code.

Now you need the Python code to generate this map:

3. Create a Python file named `mapnik_xml.py` inside the `mapnik_experiments` folder and type this code:

    ```python
    # coding=utf-8

    import mapnik


    map = mapnik.Map(800, 600)
    mapnik.load_map(map, 'map_style.xml')
    map.zoom_all()
    mapnik.render_to_file(map, '../output/world2.png')
    ```

4. Run this file. Remember that, to run a different file from the previous one, you need to press *Alt + Shift + F10* and select it.

5. Open the generated image (`world2.png`) that is inside the `output` folder; you should see exactly the same result as before.

Styling maps in Python and XML has almost the same features. Except for a few very specific situations, you can obtain exactly the same results using either of them.

Making Maps

In those simple examples, there are two things to be noticed while using Python or XML: code readability and organization. Looking at the XML code, you should see that the map, styles, and rules have a tree-like organization; this is very clear here but in the pure Python definition this get confusing and can lead to mistakes.

This is a very simple map but, as you add more rules and symbolizers, things starts to get very confusing and hard to understand using pure Python.

Another important point is that it's a good idea to separate the map creation logic from the style. We will see how that helps to keep your code very clean and reusable in the next topic.

Creating utility functions to generate maps

Now we will create the first function that will compose our application.

1. Still in the `mapnik_experiments` folder, create a new file: `map_functions.py`.
2. Insert the code as follows into that file:

```
# coding=utf-8

import mapnik


def create_map(style_file, output_image, size=(800, 600)):
    """Creates a map from a XML file and writes it to an image.

    :param style_file: Mapnik XML file.
    :param output_image: Name of the output image file.
    :param size: Size of the map in pixels.
    """
    map = mapnik.Map(*size)
    mapnik.load_map(map, style_file)
    map.zoom_all()
    mapnik.render_to_file(map, output_image)


if __name__ == '__main__':
    create_map('map_style.xml', '../output/world3.png',
               size=(400, 400))
```

What we did here is pack the map generation code into a function that we can reuse in the future. It takes two required arguments: the XML style file and the name of the image file that Mapnik will write the results to.

The third optional parameter is the size of the map that will be created; you can pass a list or a tuple with the width and height of the map in pixels. This tuple or list is then unpacked with the * symbol into `mapnik.Map` arguments.

Finally, again we used the `if __name__ == '__main__':` technique to test the code. Remember that everything that is inside this `if` block is run only if the file is called directly. On the other hand, if this file is imported as a module, this code will be ignored. Look at the *Creating the application entry point* section in *Chapter 2*, *The Geocaching App*, if you need more information on that technique.

Changing the data source at runtime

This is a useful function; now we can create maps from XML files with a single line of code. But there is a flaw: the data source (the shapefile that will be used) is hardcoded inside the XML. Suppose that we want to generate maps for a bunch of shapefiles; for every file we would need to change the XML, impeding the execution of batch operations.

Fortunately, there are two ways that we can change the data source file that Mapnik will use without manually changing the XML. We can make code to edit the XML for us, or we can mix XML and Python in the map definition.

Mapnik's `Map` object has a couple of properties that can be accessed. At the moment, we are interested in accessing the layer, because the layer contains the data source that we want to define or change.

Every `Map` instance contains a `layers` property that returns a `Layers` object containing all the layers defined in the map. This object behaves like a list of `Layer` objects in which its items could be iterated or retrieved by an index. In turn, the `Layer` object contains the `name` and the `data source` properties. Let's take a look how this works:

> Check the Mapnik API documentation at: http://mapnik.org/docs/v2.2.0/api/python/. There you can find all the classes, methods, and properties that are available.

1. Change your function so we can inspect the properties of the `map` object:

    ```
    def create_map(style_file, output_image, size=(800, 600)):
        """Creates a map from a XML file and writes it to an image.

        :param style_file: Mapnik XML file.
    ```

Making Maps

```
    :param output_image: Name of the output image file.
    :param size: Size of the map in pixels.
    """
    map = mapnik.Map(*size)
    mapnik.load_map(map, style_file)

    layers = map.layers
    layer = layers[0]
    print(layer)
    print(layer.name)
    print(layer.datasource)

    map.zoom_all()
    mapnik.render_to_file(map, output_image)
```

The highlighted code gets the `layers` object and the first layer in it (at index 0), then prints it, its name, and the data source properties.

2. Just rerun the code and you should get this output:

```
<mapnik._mapnik.Layer object at 0x01E579F0>
world
<mapnik.Datasource object at 0x01F3E9F0>

Process finished with exit code 0
```

As you see in the output, the first layer is the `world` layer defined in the XML and it has a data source. This data source is what we want to set or modify during code execution.

3. Make another test. Open the `map_style.xml` file and remove the data source from the definition, like this:

```
<Map background-color="white">
  <Style name="My Style">
    <Rule>
      <PolygonSymbolizer fill="#f2eff9" />
      <LineSymbolizer stroke="rgb(50%,50%,50%)" stroke-width="0.1" />
    </Rule>
  </Style>

  <Layer name="world">
      <StyleName>My Style</StyleName>
  </Layer>
</Map>
```

Chapter 5

4. Run the code again and see the output:

   ```
   <mapnik._mapnik.Layer object at 0x01DD79F0>
   world
   None
   
   Process finished with exit code 0
   ```

   Now, when we print the `data source` property, it shows `None` because we removed it from the definition; also the image (`world3.png`) is empty because there is no data to display. Now we are going to define it in the Python code.

5. Edit the `map_functions.py` file:

   ```
   # coding=utf-8
   
   import mapnik
   
   
   def create_map(shapefile, style_file, output_image, size=(800,
   600)):
       """Creates a map from a XML file and writes it to an image.
   
       :param shapefile: Shapefile containing the data for the map.
       :param style_file: Mapnik XML file.
       :param output_image: Name of the output image file.
       :param size: Size of the map in pixels.
       """
       map = mapnik.Map(*size)
       mapnik.load_map(map, style_file)
   
       data source = mapnik.Shapefile(file=shapefile)
       layers = map.layers
       layer = layers[0]
       layer.datasource = data source
   
       map.zoom_all()
       mapnik.render_to_file(map, output_image)
   
   
   if __name__ == '__main__':
       create_map('../../data/world_borders_simple.shp',
                  'map_style.xml', '../output/world3.png',
                  size=(400, 400))
   ```

[129]

Making Maps

The new required argument in the function is the name of the shapefile containing the data. In the code we create a Mapnik data source from this file, get the first layer, and set its data source to the one that was created. Run the code and look at the output, you should see the rendered world map. Besides setting the data source, it is possible to combine XML and Python to change the map definition any way you want.

Automatically previewing the map

As we start to play with the map style, it could get a little boring to manually open the image every time we want to see the results. So we will write a function that will automatically open and display the image for us when we run the code. To do that we will use the **Open Computer Vision (OpenCV)** package.

1. Import the package at the beginning of the `map_functions.py` file:

    ```
    import mapnik
    import cv2
    ```

2. Create this new function before the `create_map` function:

    ```
    def display_map(image_file):
        """Opens and displays a map image file.

        :param image_file: Path to the image.
        """
        image = cv2.imread(image_file)
        cv2.imshow('image', image)
        cv2.waitKey(0)
        cv2.destroyAllWindows()
    ```

3. Now change our tests to call the function; to do that, edit the `if __name__ == '__main__':` block:

    ```
    if __name__ == '__main__':
        map_image = '../output/world3.png'
        create_map('../../data/world_borders_simple.shp',
                   'map_style.xml', map_image, size=(400, 400))
        display_map(map_image)
    ```

[130]

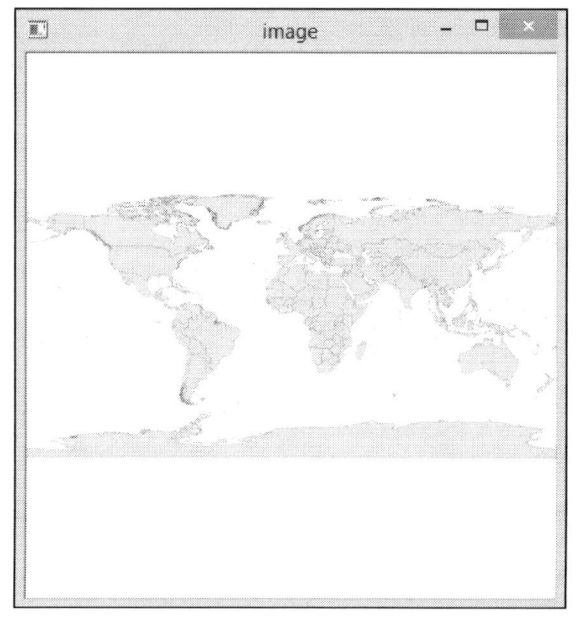

4. Run the code. Now you should see a window pop up with the map image:

We won't explore OpenCV functionality in depth now; just note that `cv2.waitKey(0)` halts code execution until any key is pressed or the window is closed.

Styling maps

Now that we have a function to generate the map and an easy way to preview them, we will experiment with the style options:

1. First, lets produce a bigger map so we can better see the changes. Edit the `if __name__ == '__main__':` block at the end of the `map_functions.py` file, changing the `size` argument of the `create_map` function call:

   ```
   if __name__ == '__main__':
       map_image = '../output/world3.png'
       create_map('../../data/world_borders_simple.shp',
                  'map_style.xml', map_image, size=(1024, 500))
       display_map(map_image)
   ```

Map style

The map is the canvas for the drawing; it is possible to change the background color or the background image, the coordinate reference system, and a few other options.

Making Maps

Let's try changing the background:

1. In the file `map_style.xml` edit the map tag to change the background color. You can use a hexadecimal value, a color name, or an RGB combination. Try this as an example:

   ```
   <Map background-color="#f8be78">
   ```

2. Run the code and see the changes.

3. Now try using an image as the background for the map. I provided one as an example that will resemble old paper; change the map tag again:

   ```
   <Map background-color="#f8be78"
        background-image="../../data/images/old-paper.png">
   ```

4. Run the code, you should see this output:

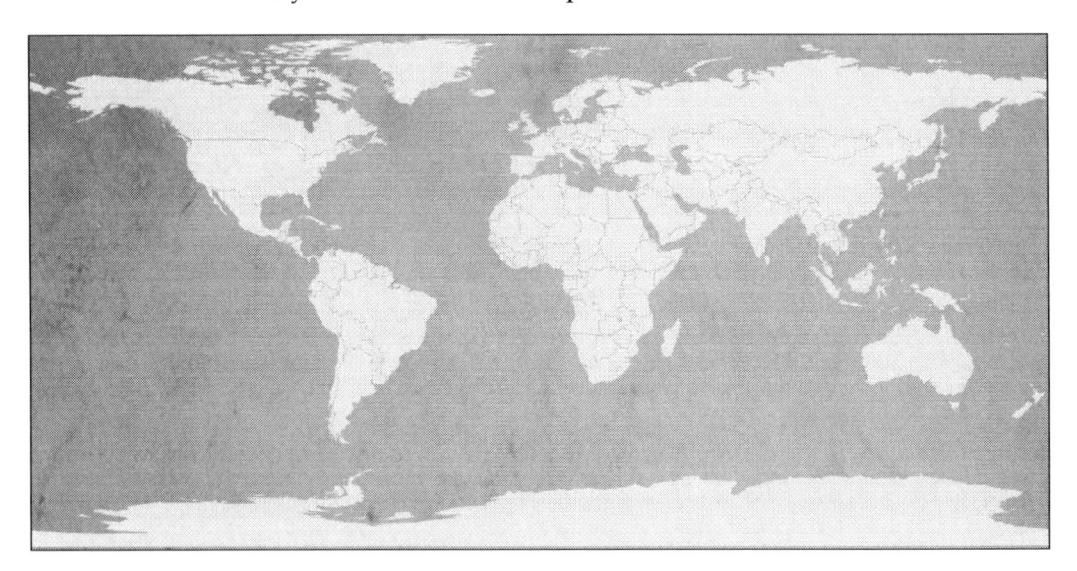

> Note that `background-image` **supersedes** `background-color` in order of importance when the map is generated.

Polygon style

In the XML tree that you have in your `map_style.xml` file, you should notice that, after the `<Map>` tag, you have the `<Style>` tag and then the `<Rule>` tag. We will explore them later; for now we will go directly to the symbolizers.

Each symbolizer is used to style a different type of geometry or part of the map. The first one that we used is the `PolygonSymbolizer` tag, which is used to style the internal area of the polygon with a solid color.

The polygon has also another possible symbolizer: the `PolygonPatternSymbolizer` tag, which fills the polygon with an image pattern. Let's see how it works:

1. Change the style again; let's include a pattern symbolizer after the `PolygonSymbolizer` tag:

   ```
   <Map background-color="#f8be78"
        background-image="../../data/images/old-paper.png">
     <Style name="My Style">
       <Rule>
         <PolygonSymbolizer fill="#f2eff9" />
         <PolygonPatternSymbolizer
                 file="../../data/images/tree_pattern.png"/>
         <LineSymbolizer stroke="rgb(50%,50%,50%)" stroke-width="0.1" />
       </Rule>
     </Style>
     <Layer name="world">
       <StyleName>My Style</StyleName>
     </Layer>
   </Map>
   ```

2. Run the code and see the results.

Making Maps

The style follows the **painter model**. This means that things are *painted* in the order that they are in the file, so the pattern was painted over the polygon fill.

Line styles

The lines (including polygon boundaries) are styled by the `LineSymbolizer` tag and the `LinePatternSymbolizer` tag. For the next examples, we will return the map to its initial style and zoom it so we can see better how the options influence the generated map, as follows:

1. Edit the style by removing the background image and the polygon pattern. Also, zoom in by changing `maximum-extent`:

   ```
   <Map background-color="white" maximum-extent="-21,68,66,28">
     <Style name="My Style">
       <Rule>
         <PolygonSymbolizer fill="#f2eff9" />
         <LineSymbolizer stroke="rgb(50%,50%,50%)" stroke-width="0.1" />
       </Rule>
     </Style>
     <Layer name="world">
       <StyleName>My Style</StyleName>
     </Layer>
   </Map>
   ```

2. Now change the `LineSymbolizer` tag:

   ```
   <LineSymbolizer stroke="red" stroke-width="3.0" />
   ```

3. Run the code and see how the lines got thicker and red.

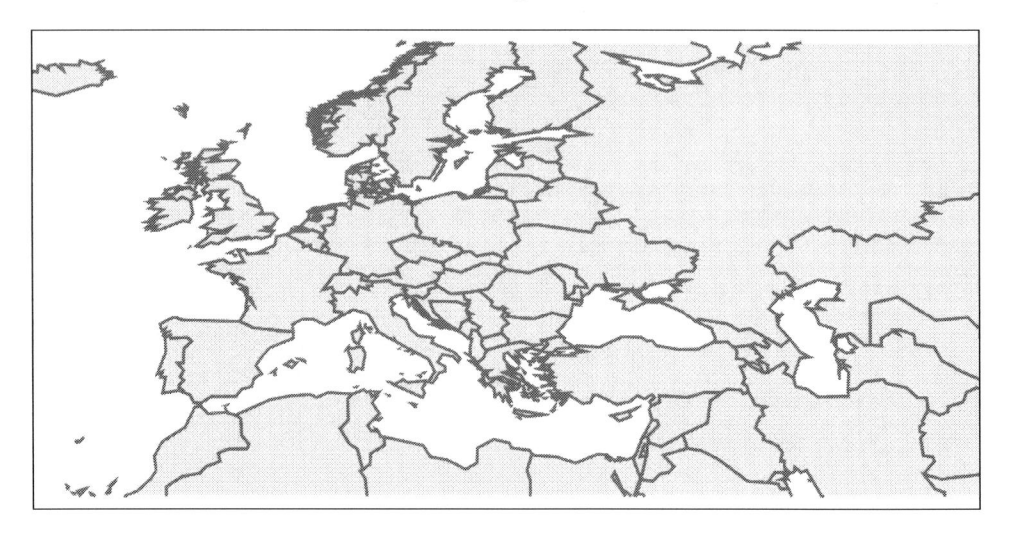

[134]

You may notice some strange edges and points because it's a low-resolution map of the world and the lines are too thick. We can improve this map by reducing the thickness and by using the `smooth` parameter.

4. Edit the `LineSymbolizer` tag again and run the code. Now you should have a much clearer map:

   ```
   <LineSymbolizer stroke="red" stroke-width="1.0" smooth="0.5" />
   ```

Text styles

Now, let's add the country names to our map. To do that, we will use the `TextSymbolizer` tag:

1. Change the `map_style.xml` file with the following code:

   ```
   <Map background-color="white" maximum-extent="-21,68,66,28">
     <Style name="My Style">
       <Rule>
         <PolygonSymbolizer fill="#f2eff9" />
         <LineSymbolizer stroke="red" stroke-width="1.0" smooth="0.5" />
         <TextSymbolizer face-name="DejaVu Sans Book" size="10"
                         fill="black" halo-fill= "white"
                         halo-radius="1" placement="interior"
                         allow-overlap="false">[NAME]
         </TextSymbolizer>
       </Rule>
     </Style>
   ```

Making Maps

```
    <Layer name="world">
        <StyleName>My Style</StyleName>
    </Layer>
</Map>
```

2. Run the code and see the results:

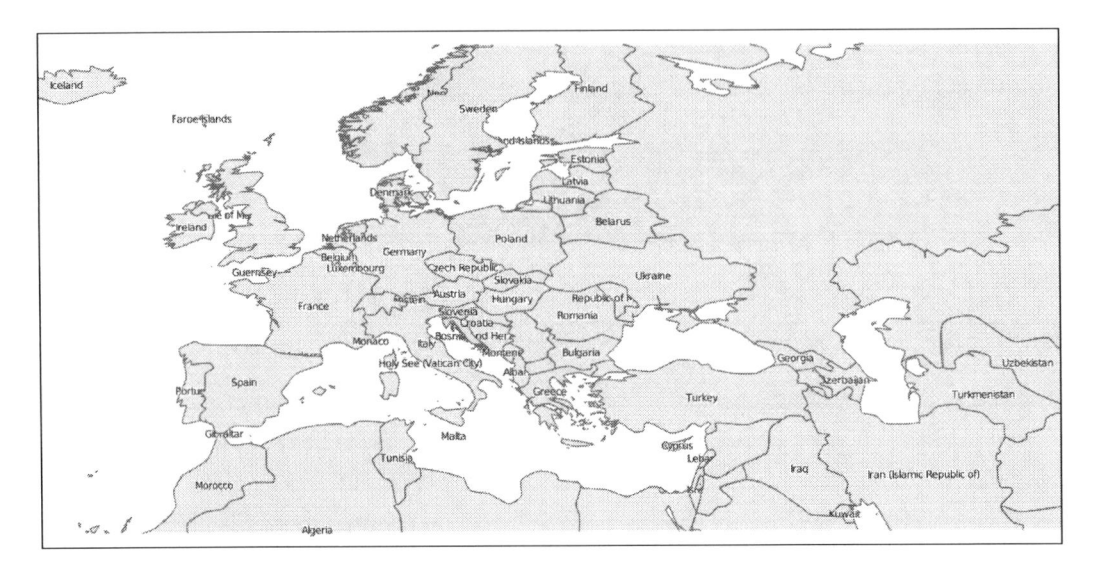

Adding layers to the map

We saw that it's possible to change the data source of the map with Python. In a Mapnik map, the data source resides inside a layer or inside the map; to keep it simple we will use only layers to hold the data sources.

If we want to add more than one data source (for example, points, lines, polygons, or images) we need to add more layers. As an example, we will add the geocaching points, which we saw in the previous chapters, to the map.

The first step is to completely remove the layer definition from the XML file. This will complete the separation of the code into two categories: the XML contains only the styling and the Python code handles the data and map creation.

Chapter 5

Secondly, we will change the `create_map` function so it adds layers to the map. This change will only be an experiment before we fully implement this functionality on the app:

1. In the `mapnik_xml.xml` file, remove the layer from the definition, change the style name to `style1`, and add a new style for the points. Also change the extent of the map to focus on the points. It should be like this:

    ```
    <Map background-color="white" maximum-extent="-81,45,-69,40">
      <Style name="style1">
        <Rule>
          <PolygonSymbolizer fill="#f2eff9" />
          <LineSymbolizer stroke="red" stroke-width="1.0" smooth="0.5" />
          <TextSymbolizer face-name="DejaVu Sans Book" size="10"
                          fill="black" halo-fill= "white"
                          halo-radius="1" placement="interior"
                          allow-overlap="false">[NAME]
          </TextSymbolizer>
        </Rule>
      </Style>
      <Style name="style2">
        <Rule>
          <PointSymbolizer/>
        </Rule>
      </Style>
    </Map>
    ```

2. In the `map_functions.py` file, change your `create_map` function and the `if __name__ == '__main__':` block. The complete code should look like this:

    ```
    # coding=utf-8

    import mapnik
    import cv2


    def display_map(image_file):
        """Opens and displays a map image file.

        :param image_file: Path to the image.
        """
        image = cv2.imread(image_file)
        cv2.imshow('image', image)
        cv2.waitKey(0)
    ```

[137]

Making Maps

```python
        cv2.destroyAllWindows()


def create_map(shapefile, gpx_file, style_file, output_image,
               size=(800, 600)):
    """Creates a map from a XML file and writes it to an image.

    :param shapefile: Shapefile containing the data for the map.
    :param style_file: Mapnik XML file.
    :param output_image: Name of the output image file.
    :param size: Size of the map in pixels.
    """
    map = mapnik.Map(*size)
    mapnik.load_map(map, style_file)
    layers = map.layers

    # Add the shapefile.
    world_datasource = mapnik.Shapefile(file=shapefile)
    world_layer = mapnik.Layer('world')
    world_layer.datasource = world_datasource
    world_layer.styles.append('style1')
    layers.append(world_layer)

    # Add the shapefile.
    points_datasource = mapnik.Ogr(file=gpx_file,
        layer='waypoints')
    points_layer = mapnik.Layer('geocaching_points')
    points_layer.datasource = points_datasource
    points_layer.styles.append('style2')
    layers.append(points_layer)

    map.zoom_all()
    mapnik.render_to_file(map, output_image)


if __name__ == '__main__':
    map_image = '../output/world3.png'
    create_map('../../data/world_borders_simple.shp',
               '../../data/geocaching.gpx',
               'map_style.xml', map_image, size=(1024, 500))
    display_map(map_image)
```

Now the function accepts two files: one shapefile with the world borders and one GPX file containing waypoints. For each file, a data source and a layer containing it are created and added to the map list of layers. We also define the styles for the layer using the style names defined in the XML.

3. Run the code; you should see the points rendered over the world borders with the default `PointSymbolizer` style:

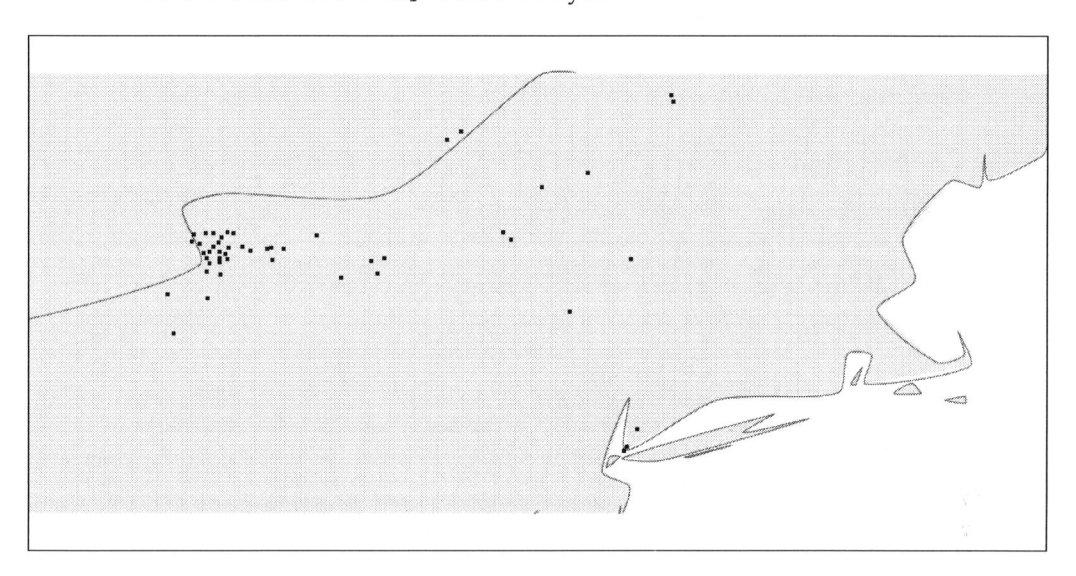

Point styles

Now we are going to improve the visual representation of the points:

1. Edit the `map_style.xml` file and change the point style:

```xml
<Map background-color="white" maximum-extent="-81,45,-69,40">
  <Style name="style1">
    <Rule>
      <PolygonSymbolizer fill="#f2eff9" />
      <LineSymbolizer stroke="red" stroke-width="1.0" smooth="0.5" />
      <TextSymbolizer face-name="DejaVu Sans Book" size="10"
                      fill="black" halo-fill= "white"
                      halo-radius="1" placement="interior"
                      allow-overlap="false">[NAME]
      </TextSymbolizer>
    </Rule>
  </Style>
  <Style name="style2">
    <Rule>
      <PointSymbolizer file="../../data/images/marker.svg"
                       transform="scale(0.3)"/>
    </Rule>
  </Style>
</Map>
```

Making Maps

We introduce the use of a **Scalable Vector Graphics (SVG)** file to represent the point; the advantage of this kind of file is that it can be scaled or zoomed without distortions because it is composed of vectors and not pixels.

Since the SVG that we used is too big for our map, it was used with the `transform` parameter to scale the image.

> You can find more about SVG transformations at http://www.w3.org/TR/SVG/coords.html.

2. Run your code and take a look at the results:

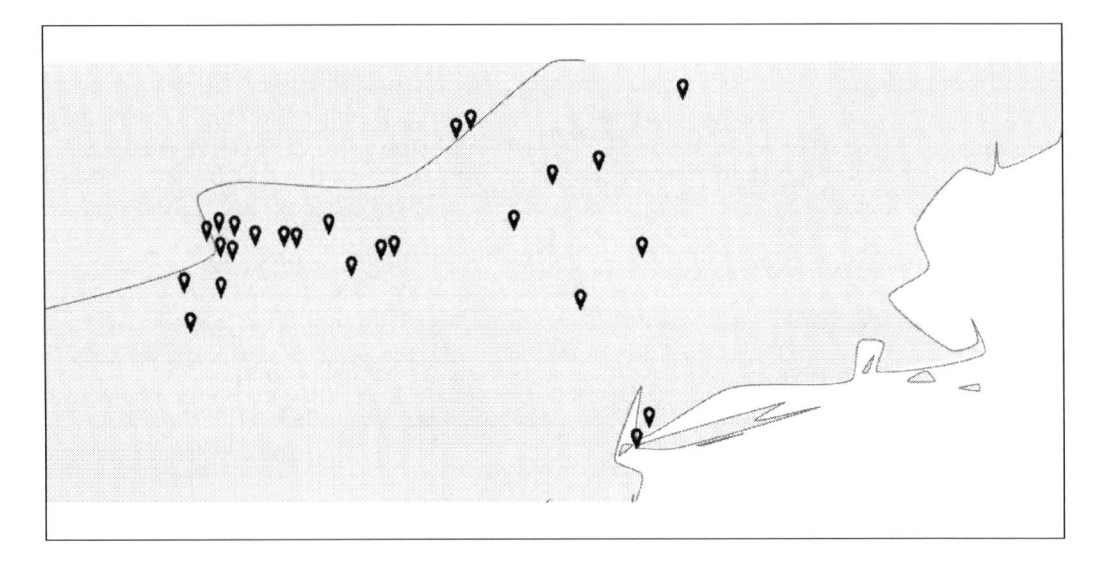

> If you need symbols for your projects, you can find a good collection in the **Noun Project**, which aggregates creations from the community around the world at https://thenounproject.com/.

We have a beautiful representation of the points, and now we are going to add more information on them.

[140]

Using Python objects as a source of data

> Mapnik for Windows does not come with the Python Datasource plugin and a workaround will be provided for Windows users; just follow the steps.

Data is represented internally on Mapnik by a `Datasource` object. This object is responsible for accessing the source of the data (for example, a file containing the data, a database, and so on) and transforming the features provided by this source of data into `Feature` objects. In turn, the `Feature` object contains a geometry and a number of properties (attributes). This organization is very similar to what we have seen in *Chapter 4, Improving the App Search Capabilities*, in the topic *How geographic data is represented*.

If we could hack into a Datasource and provide the features the way we want, we would be able to make Mapnik use Python objects that we provide as a source of data.

The advantage of using a Python object as a Datasource, instead of a file for example, is that we can perform any kind of transformation and analysis on the data and then feed it to Mapnik without needing to save it to disk. By doing that, we keep the data in memory, increase the performance of the application, and make it more versatile and easy-to-use.

Fortunately, Mapnik comes with a class already prepared for this kind of operation; as you may have guessed, it's called `PythonDatasource`.

As we prepare to build our application, in this step we will produce a class that inherits from `mapnik.PythonDatasource` and implements the required methods for it to work.

First, we are going to take a look at Mapnik's source code in order to understand the logic behind the `PythonDatasource` class.

1. Go to your `Chapter5` folder and create a file named `my_datasource.py`.
2. Insert this code in that file:

   ```
   # coding=utf-8

   import mapnik

   test_datasource = mapnik.PythonDatasource()
   ```

Making Maps

3. Now click anywhere on `PythonDatasource` to place your cursor on it and press *Ctrl* + *B*. Or, right-click anywhere on `PythonDatasource` then select **Go To | Declaration**. This will open and show the class declaration for you.

4. I will go through each part of the class, commenting the code. Don't worry if you are not near a computer. I'll place excerpts of the class before each explanation:

```
class PythonDatasource(object):
    """A base class for a Python data source.

    Optional arguments:
        envelope -- a mapnik.Box2d (minx, miny, maxx, maxy) envelope
          of the data source, default (-180,-90,180,90)
        geometry_type -- one of the DataGeometryType enumeration
          values, default Point
        data_type -- one of the DataType enumerations, default Vector
    """

    def __init__(self, envelope=None, geometry_type=None,
                 data_type=None):
        self.envelope = envelope or Box2d(-180, -90, 180, 90)
        self.geometry_type = geometry_type or DataGeometryType.Point
        self.data_type = data_type or DataType.Vector
```

This is the class declaration and the `__init__` method; the arguments to create the class are all optional but if we need to we can define the envelope (that is, the bounding box) and two important parameters:

- `geometry_type`: Can be `Collection`, `LineString`, `Point`, or `Polygon`
- `data_type`: Can be `Vector` or `Raster`

```
    def features(self, query):
        """Return an iterable which yields instances of Feature for
        features within the passed query.

        Required arguments:
            query -- a Query instance specifying the region for which
              features should be returned
        """
        return None
```

[142]

Chapter 5

This is the key method for `PythonDatasource` to work. This method should return an *iterable* containing the features.

An iterable is any Python object that can be used in a `for` loop or, as described in the Python glossary, any object capable of returning its members one at a time. It can be a list, a tuple, a dictionary, and so on.

Despite the description in the docstring, this method is empty and returns `None`. It's an indication that it should be implemented on the child classes and that how this iterable is created is entirely up to the programmer:

> Take a look at the Python glossary for information on new terms or terms that are still confusing for you: https://docs.python.org/2/glossary.html.

```
def features_at_point(self, point):
    """Rarely uses. Return an iterable which yields instances
    of Feature for the specified point."""
    return None
```

This is more of a convenience method, so we won't use it.

```
@classmethod
def wkb_features(cls, keys, features):
    """A convenience function to wrap an iterator yielding pairs
    of WKB format geometry and dictionaries of key-value pairs
    into mapnik features. Return this from
    PythonDatasource.features() passing it a sequence of keys
    to appear in the output and an iterator yielding features.

    For example. One might have a features() method in a derived
    class like the following:

    def features(self, query):
        # ... create WKB features feat1 and feat2

        return mapnik.PythonDatasource.wkb_features(
            keys = ( 'name', 'author' ),
            features = [
                (feat1, { 'name': 'feat1', 'author': 'alice' }),
                (feat2, { 'name': 'feat2', 'author': 'bob' }),
            ]
        )

    """
    ctx = Context()
```

```
        [ctx.push(x) for x in keys]

        def make_it(feat, idx):
            f = Feature(ctx, idx)
            geom, attrs = feat
            f.add_geometries_from_wkb(geom)
            for k, v in attrs.iteritems():
                f[k] = v
            return f

        return itertools.imap(make_it, features, itertools.count(1))

    @classmethod
    def wkt_features(cls, keys, features):
        """A convenience function to wrap an iterator yielding pairs
        of WKT format geometry and dictionaries of key-value pairs
        into mapnik features. Return this from
        PythonDatasource.features() passing it a sequence of keys
        to appear in the output and an iterator yielding features.

        For example. One might have a features() method in a
        derived class like the following:

        def features(self, query):
            # ... create WKT features feat1 and feat2

            return mapnik.PythonDatasource.wkt_features(
                keys = ( 'name', 'author' ),
                features = [
                    (feat1, { 'name': 'feat1', 'author': 'alice' }),
                    (feat2, { 'name': 'feat2', 'author': 'bob' }),
                ]
            )

        """
        ctx = Context()
        [ctx.push(x) for x in keys]

        def make_it(feat, idx):
            f = Feature(ctx, idx)
            geom, attrs = feat
            f.add_geometries_from_wkt(geom)
            for k, v in attrs.iteritems():
                f[k] = v
            return f

        return itertools.imap(make_it, features, itertools.count(1))
```

These are two convenience functions (or methods). Take a look at the section *Integrating with the app* in *Chapter 4, Improving the App Search Capabilities*, if you don't remember what a convenience method is. We created one there.

Those methods are an easy shortcut to creating an iterable of Mapnik features from a list of lists (or tuples) containing the geometries and the attributes in a dictionary, one from WKT geometries and one from WKB geometries (again, if you need, take a look at the section *Knowing well-known text* in *Chapter 4, Improving the App Search Capabilities*).

One caveat is that these are not instance methods; they are class methods. Note the `@classmethod` before the method name; this is a decorator that changes the method's behavior.

I won't go into details about class methods and decorators (it would require an entire chapter). All we need to know is that we call this method from the class and not from the instance, using `PythonDatasource.wkt_features()` or `PythonDatasource.wkb_features()`.

Putting this into practice, what we need to do is create a class that inherits from `PythonDatasource` and reimplements its feature method. Let's start from the class skeleton and then later we will go back to the classes that we built in *Chapter 2, The Geocaching App*, *Chapter 3, Combining Multiple Data Sources*, and *Chapter 4, Improving the App Search Capabilities*, and use them as a source for the features:

1. Edit `my_datasource.py`; remove the previous code and add the new class:

    ```
    # coding=utf-8

    import mapnik

    class MapDatasource(mapnik.PythonDatasource):
        """Implementation of Mapinik's PythonDatasource."""

        def features(self, query=None):
            raise NotImplementedError
    ```

The first thing we did was to make the query an optional argument; we won't remove it because there is a risk of breaking compatibility. Then the function only raises an exception to the effect that it's not implemented yet.

Exporting geo objects

Before we continue, as part of the workaround for windows users we will need to export our geo objects as files.

Making Maps

We will use the GeoJSON file format. It's a good choice of format for exporting geographic data because:

- It's human-readable
- It's an open standard
- It's easy to make code that exports GeoJSON
- Mapnik can import it
- The properties/attributes can have multiple levels

Here you can see the same example of a GeoJSON file that we saw in *Chapter 3, Combining Multiple Data Sources – How Geographic Data is Represented*. You don't need to type it, we are just going to use it as a reference to write our export code:

```
{"type": "FeatureCollection",
 "features": [
   {"type": "Feature",
     "geometry": {
       "type": "Point",
       "coordinates": [102.0, 0.5]},
     "properties": {"prop0": "value0"}
   },
   {"type": "Feature",
     "geometry": {
       "type": "LineString",
       "coordinates": [[102.0, 0.0], [103.0, 1.0], [104.0, 0.0]]
     },
     "properties": {
       "prop0": "value0", "prop1": 0.0
     }
   },
   {"type": "Feature",
     "geometry": {
       "type": "Polygon",
       "coordinates": [
         [ [100.0, 0.0], [101.0, 0.0], [101.0, 1.0],
           [100.0, 1.0], [100.0, 0.0] ]
       ]
     },
     "properties": {"prop0": "value0",
       "prop1": {"this": "that"}
     }
   }
 ]
}
```

[146]

Looking at the file, we can see that the geo objects that we created have characteristics that conveniently make it very easy to export them to this file format. If we think of a `BaseGeoObject` being a GeoJSON `"Feature"` and a `BaseGeoCollection` being a `"FeatureCollection"`, it's easy to get started:

1. Open your `models.py` file and go to the `BaseGeoObject` class. Add the `export_geojson_feature` method:

   ```
   #...
       def export_geojson_feature(self):
           """Exports this object as dictionary formatted as a
            GeoJSON feature.
           """
           feature = {
               "type": "Feature",
               "geometry": mapping(self.geom),
               "properties": self.attributes}
           return feature
   ```

   The mapping function calls a *magic method* that every shapely geometry has; it returns the geometry as a GeoJSON representation.

2. Now, edit the `BaseGeoCollection` class. Add the `export_geojson` method:

   ```
   #...
       def export_geojson(self, file):
           """Exports the collection to a GeoJSON file."""
           features = [i.export_geojson_feature() for i in self.data]
           geojson = {"type": "FeatureCollection",
                      "features": features}
           with open(file, 'w') as out_file:
               json.dump(geojson, out_file, indent=2)
           print("File exported: {}".format(file))
   ```

   Here we used a *list comprehension* (`[i.export_geojson_feature() for i in self.data]`) to generate a list of features, then used the `json` module to serialize the dictionary into a JSON.

3. Import the mapping function from `shapely` and add the `json` module to your imports at the beginning of the file:

   ```
   # coding=utf-8

   from __future__ import print_function

   import json
   from shapely.geometry import Point, mapping
   ```

[147]

Making Maps

```
from shapely import wkb, wkt
import gdal
from utils.geo_functions import open_vector_file
from utils.geo_functions import transform_geometry
from utils.geo_functions import convert_length_unit
```

4. Finally, let's test it. Edit your `if __name__ == '__main__':` block:

```
if __name__ == '__main__':
    gdal.PushErrorHandler('CPLQuietErrorHandler')
    points = PointCollection("../data/geocaching.gpx")
    points.export_geojson("output/data.json")
```

5. Run the code and open the `output/data.json` file to check the results:

```
{
  "type": "FeatureCollection",
  "features": [
    {
      "geometry": {
        "type": "Point",
        "coordinates": [
          -78.90175,
          42.89648
        ]
      },
      "type": "Feature",
      "properties": {
        "status": "Available",
        "logs": {
          "log": [
            {
              "@id": "1",
              "time": "05/09/2015T11:04:05",
              "geocacher": "SYSTEM",
              "text": "Attributes: Quick Cache | Kid Friendly |\n
            },
...
```

Everything was neatly exported, including all the properties and logs. PyCharm can also inspect JSON files, so you can use the Structure panel (*Alt + 7*) to explore the file structure as you did with the GPX file.

Creating the Map Maker app

Now we will prepare an environment that is capable of using this data source. We are going to adapt the previous experiments into building blocks for the application and put them inside an application class, just as we did with the Geocaching app.

First let's organize the folder and files.

1. Create a new package called `map_maker` inside your `Chapter5` folder. To do this, right-click on the folder and chose **New | Python Package**.
2. Move the `my_datasource.py` file to the `map_make` folder (drag and drop it).
3. Copy the `map_style.xml` and `map_functions.py` files that are inside the `mapnik_experiments` folder to the `map_maker` folder.
4. Rename `map_style.xml` to `styles.xml`.
5. In the `Chapter5` root, create a file named `map_maker_app.py`. The complete tree structure should look like this:

    ```
    Chapter5
    |    geocaching_app.py
    |    map_maker_app.py
    |    models.py
    |
    ├──mapnik_experiments
    |
    ├──map_maker
    |    __init__.py
    |    my_datasource.py
    |    styles.xml
    |    map_functions.py
    |
    ├──utils
    ```

    Now we create the class that represents the application.

6. In the `map_maker_app.py` file, create this new class and its `__init__` method:

    ```
    # coding=utf-8

    import cv2
    import mapnik

    class MapMakerApp(object):
        def __init__(self, output_image=None):
            """Application class."""
            self.output_image = output_image
    ```

Making Maps

output_image will be the image that the app will write to the maps. It's not private because we may want to change it during the application execution.

7. Copy the `display_map` function from the `map_functions.py` file, and adapt it to work as a method of our new class:

```
class MapMakerApp(object):
    def __init__(self, output_image=None):
        """Application class."""
        self.output_image = output_image

    def display_map(self):
        """Opens and displays a map image file.

        :param image_file: Path to the image.
        """
        image = cv2.imread(self.output_image)
        cv2.imshow('image', image)
        cv2.waitKey(0)
        cv2.destroyAllWindows()
```

This function now uses the `output_image` property to display the map and takes no arguments apart from the class instance (`self`) when called.

Next, let's work on the `create_map` function.

8. Copy the `create_map` function from the `map_functions.py` file and make the following changes to the class:

```
# coding=utf-8

import cv2
import mapnik

class MapMakerApp(object):
    def __init__(self, output_image="map.png",
                 style_file="map_maker/styles.xml",
                 map_size=(800, 600)):
        """Application class.


        :param output_image: Path to the image output of the map.
        :param style_file: Mapnik XML file containing only the style
        for the map.
        :param map_size: Size of the map in pixels.
        """
```

[150]

```
            self.output_image = output_image
            self.style_file = style_file
            self.map_size = map_size

    def display_map(self):
        """Opens and displays a map image file."""
        image = cv2.imread(self.output_image)
        cv2.imshow('image', image)
        cv2.waitKey(0)
        cv2.destroyAllWindows()

    def create_map(self):
        """Creates a map and writes it to a file."""
        map = mapnik.Map(*self.map_size)
        mapnik.load_map(map, self.style_file)
        layers = map.layers

        map.zoom_all()
        mapnik.render_to_file(map, self.output_image)
```

As we did with `display_map`, now the `create_map` function takes no arguments (except for `self`) and all parameters come from the instance attributes, the ones that were added to the `__init__` method. We also improved the default values for those arguments.

All the layer and data source definitions were removed from `create_map` because in the next steps we will plug in the `PythonDatasource` that we created earlier.

Using PythonDatasource

To use this type of data source and implement the ability to display any number of data sources on the map, we will make our app class take control of the organization of the layers and the data that they use, always following the premise that the application should have a high level of abstraction:

1. Include this import at the beginning of the file:

   ```
   from map_maker.my_datasource import MapDatasource
   ```

2. Modify the class `__init__` method and create an `add_layer` method, as follows:

   ```
   class MapMakerApp(object):
       def __init__(self, output_image="map.png",
                    style_file="map_maker/styles.xml",
                    map_size=(800, 600)):
   ```

Making Maps

```
        """Application class.

        :param output_image: Path to the image output of the map.
        :param style_file: Mapnik XML file containing only the
style
        for the map.
        :param map_size: Size of the map in pixels.
        """
        self.output_image = output_image
        self.style_file = style_file
        self.map_size = map_size
        self._layers = {}

    def display_map(self):...
    def create_map(self):...

    def add_layer(self, geo_data, name, style='style1'):
        """Add data to the map to be displayed in a layer
        with a given style.

        :param geo_data: a BaseGeoCollection subclass instance.
        """
        data_source = mapnik.Python(factory='MapDatasource',
                                    data=geo_data)
        layer = {"data source": data_source,
                 "data": geo_data,
                 "style": style}
        self._layers[name] = layer
```

What we did here is use a private attribute (`_layers`) to keep track of the layers that we will use by their names. The `add_layer` method is responsible for instantiating the `MapDatasource` class and passing to it the data.

The data that we will use here is a subclass of `BaseGeoCollection` that we used in the previous chapters. With this, we will manipulate the map using only high-level objects, and also get all their functionality for free.

As we said before, *Python Datasource does not work on Windows*, so we need to create a workaround to make things work despite the operating system. What we are going to do is save the data to a temporary file and then use Mapnik's GeoJSON plugin to create a data source.

3. Add these imports to the beginning of the file:

```
# coding=utf-8

import platform
import tempfile
from models import BoundaryCollection, PointCollection
import cv2
import mapnik
```

4. Now let's create a folder to hold our temporary files. Create a new folder named `temp` inside your `Chapter5` folder.

5. Modify the `add_layer` method to include the workaround:

```
#...
    def add_layer(self, geo_data, name, style='style1'):
        """Add data to the map to be displayed in a layer
        with a given style.

        :param geo_data: a BaseGeoCollection subclass instance.
        """
        if platform.system() == "Windows":
            print("Windows system")
            temp_file, filename = tempfile.mkstemp(dir="temp")
            print temp_file, filename
            geo_data.export_geojson(filename)
            data_source = mapnik.GeoJSON(file=filename)
        else:
            data_source = mapnik.Python(factory='MapDatasource',
                                        data=geo_data)
        layer = {"data source": data_source,
                 "data": geo_data,
                 "style": style}
        self._layers[name] = layer
```

Here, we used `platform.system()` to detect whether the operating system is Windows. If so, instead of creating a Python DataSource, it creates a temporary file and exports `geo_data` to it. Then we use the GeoJSON plugin to open that file, creating a DataSource.

Now that the workaround is complete, we need to go back to the `MapDatasource` definition and make it accept the data that we are passing to it.

Making Maps

6. In the `my_datasource.py` file, include the following `__init__` method in the `MapDatasource` class:

   ```
   class MapDatasource(mapnik.PythonDatasource):
       """Implementation of Mapinik's PythonDatasource."""
       def __init__(self, data):
           super(MapDatasource, self).__init__(envelope, geometry_type,
               data_type)

           self.data = data

       def features(self, query=None):
           raise NotImplementedError
   ```

   Our subclass of `PythonDatasource` now takes one obligatory `data` argument. Since we are increasing the level of abstraction, we will make the `MapDatasource` class define all the other arguments automatically by inspecting the data it receives; with this change, we won't need to worry about the geometry type or data type.

7. Make another change to the `__init__` method:

   ```
   class MapDatasource(mapnik.PythonDatasource):
       """Implementation of Mapinik's PythonDatasource."""
       def __init__(self, data):
           data_type = mapnik.DataType.vector
           if isinstance(data, PointCollection):
               geometry_type = mapnik.GeometryType.Point
           elif isinstance(data, BoundaryCollection):
               geometry_type = mapnik.GeometryType.Polygon
           else:
               raise TypeError

           super(MapDatasource, self).__init__(
               envelope=None, geometry_type=geometry_type,
               data_type=data_type)

           self.data = data

       def features(self, query=None):
           raise NotImplementedError
   ```

   Here, `isinstance()` checks which type is `data`, and for each of the possible types it defines the corresponding `geometry_type` to be passed to the parent `__init__` method.

For now, we only have one data type: the vector. Anyway, we will make this definition explicit (`data_type = mapnik.DataType.vector`) because in the next chapter, the raster type will be introduced.

Before we go any further, let's test the app as it is.

8. Now edit the `if __name__ == '__main__':` block at the end of the file:

    ```
    if __name__ == '__main__':
        world_borders = BoundaryCollection(
            "../data/world_borders_simple.shp")
        map_app = MapMakerApp()
        map_app.add_layer(world_borders, 'world')
        map_app.create_map()
        map_app.display_map()
    ```

    > Note how Mapnik is completely abstracted; we now only deal with the high-level functionality provided by our models and the app.

9. Run the code; you should see an empty map and an output like this in the console:

    ```
    File imported: ../data/world_borders_simple.shp
    Windows system
    File exported: \geopy\Chapter5\temp\tmpfqv9ch
    ```

    The map is empty because two points are still missing: the `features` method, which is the glue between our geo data and the Mapnik data source, and making the `create_map` function use the layers that we have defined.

10. Let's start with the `create_map` method. Change its code so it can iterate over our layers and add them to the map:

    ```
    #...
        def create_map(self):
            """Creates a map and writes it to a file."""
            map = mapnik.Map(*self.map_size)
            mapnik.load_map(map, self.style_file)
            layers = map.layers
            for name, layer in self._layers.iteritems():
                new_layer = mapnik.Layer(name)
                new_layer.datasource = layer["data source"]
                new_layer.stylers.append(layer['style'])
                layers.append(new_layer)
            map.zoom_all()
            mapnik.render_to_file(map, self.output_image)
    ```

Making Maps

11. Now edit `styles.xml` in order to remove the extent restriction from it:

    ```xml
    <Map background-color="white">
      <Style name="style1">
        <Rule>
          <PolygonSymbolizer fill="#f2eff9" />
          <LineSymbolizer stroke="red" stroke-width="1.0" smooth="0.5" />
          <TextSymbolizer face-name="DejaVu Sans Book" size="10"
                          fill="black" halo-fill= "white"
                          halo-radius="1" placement="interior"
                          allow-overlap="false">[NAME]
          </TextSymbolizer>
        </Rule>
      </Style>
      <Style name="style2">
        <Rule>
          <PointSymbolizer file="marker.svg" transform="scale(0.3)"/>
        </Rule>
      </Style>
    </Map>
    ```

12. Now run the code again and look at the output. If you are using Windows, you should see a rendered map. If you are using Linux you should get an exception:

    ```
    Traceback (most recent call last):

      File ... in <module>
        raise NotImplementedError
    NotImplementedError

    Process finished with exit code 1
    ```

    If you got this exception (in Linux), it is because everything went fine and Mapnik called our unimplemented features method.

    So now let's implement this method.

13. Go to the `my_datasource.py` file and edit our class:

    ```python
    class MapDatasource(mapnik.PythonDatasource):
        """Implementation of Mapinik's PythonDatasource."""
        def __init__(self, data):
            data_type = mapnik.DataType.Vector
            if isinstance(data, PointCollection):
                geometry_type = mapnik.GeometryType.Point
            elif isinstance(data, BoundaryCollection):
    ```

[156]

```
            geometry_type = mapnik.GeometryType.Polygon
        else:
            raise TypeError

        super(MapDatasource, self).__init__(
            envelope=None, geometry_type=geometry_type,
            data_type=data_type)

        self.data = data

    def features(self, query=None):
        keys = ['name',]
        features = []
        for item in self.data.data:
            features.append([item.geom.wkb, {'name': item.name}])
        return mapnik.PythonDatasource.wkb_features(keys,
features)
```

14. Run the code again; now you should see the rendered map in the output:

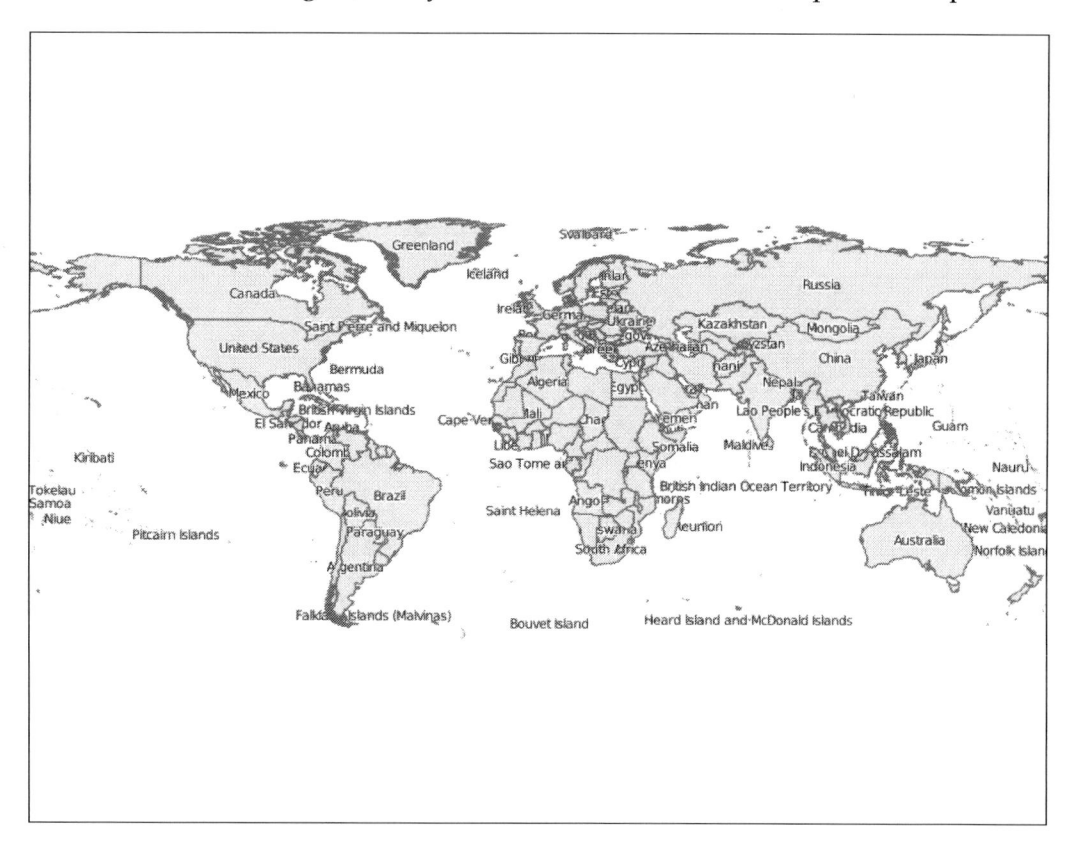

Making Maps

Using the app with filtering

Since the `BaseGeoCollection` class has filtering capabilities that were implemented before, it's possible to filter the data before passing it to the map.

Let's try some examples:

1. In the `map_maker_app.py` file, edit the `if __name__ == '__main__':` block:

   ```
   if __name__ == '__main__':
       world_borders = BoundaryCollection(
           "../data/world_borders_simple.shp")
       my_country = world_borders.filter('name', 'Brazil')
       map_app = MapMakerApp()
       map_app.add_layer(my_country, 'countries')
       map_app.create_map()
       map_app.display_map()
   ```

   Here, we are using the `filter` function of the `BaseGeoCollection` class to filter the countries by name; feel free to try to filter by your country.

2. Run the code and you should see a map containing only one country (zoom should be active), as in the following screenshot:

Chapter 5

3. Now try combining filters to show more than one country:

```
if __name__ == '__main__':
    world_borders = BoundaryCollection(
        "../data/world_borders_simple.shp")
    countries = world_borders.filter('name', 'China') +\
                world_borders.filter('name', 'India') +\
                world_borders.filter('name', 'Japan')
    map_app = MapMakerApp()
    map_app.add_layer(countries, 'countries')
    map_app.create_map()
    map_app.display_map()
```

4. Run the code again and see the results.

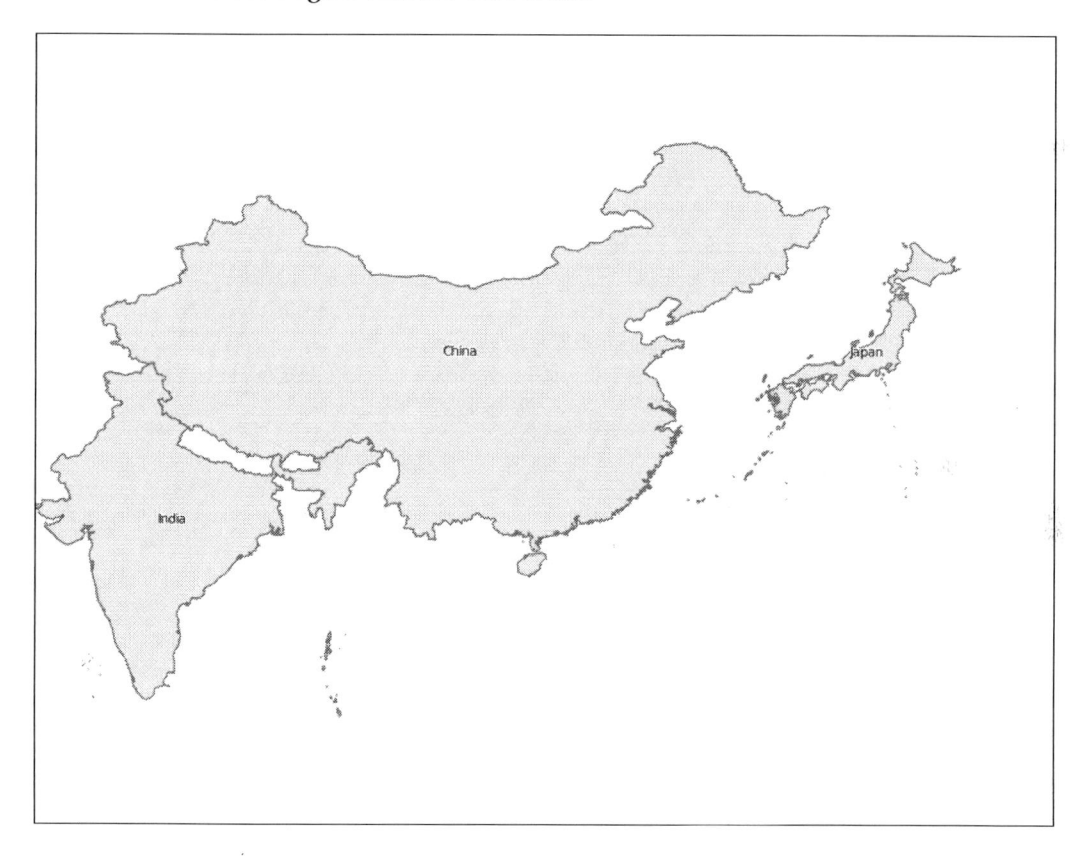

Summary

In this chapter we saw how Mapnik works and how maps are defined and styled using both Python and XML. Using Mapnik's Python API, it was possible to define the map in XML and then alter it in Python, showing great flexibility for all kinds of needs.

As the app was structured, Mapnik was hidden behind high-level functionalities that enabled us to use the geographic data objects that we created before, allowing the application to filter the data to be displayed in the map.

In the next chapter, we will meet raster data for the first time; we will see how it works and display it in our maps.

6
Working with Remote Sensing Images

In this chapter, we will start working with images—images that may come from a variety of sensors carried by satellites, drones, airplanes, and so on. These types of images, the ones collected from remote sensing devices, are images that contain pixels representing a spectral response from a given geographic region.

Besides just adding images to a map, it is important to prepare the images to be presented on the map. You may need to combine, cut, change the resolution, change values, and perform many other transformations in order to produce a visually appealing map or valuable information.

To perform these transformations on the images, we will go through a process of deduction that will result in a versatile and powerful software structure.

The topics covered here are:

- Understanding how the images are represented
- The relation of the images with the real world
- Combining, cropping, and adjusting the values of the images
- Creating shaded relief maps from the elevation data
- How to execute a sequence of processing steps

Working with Remote Sensing Images

Understanding how images are represented

In order to understand what images are in terms of computer representation and the data they contain, we are going to start with some examples. The first thing to do is to organize your project to follow this chapter's code as follows:

1. As before, inside your `geopy` project, make a copy of your `Chapter5` folder and rename it to `Chapter6`.
2. Inside `Chapter6`, navigate to the `experiments` folder and create a new file inside it named `image_experiments.py`. Open it for editing.

We will start by inspecting a small sample image that has a structure similar to a large satellite image.

Nothing fancy, you will see four squares of different colors. But if we take a step further and add a grid to it, we can see a little bit more information.

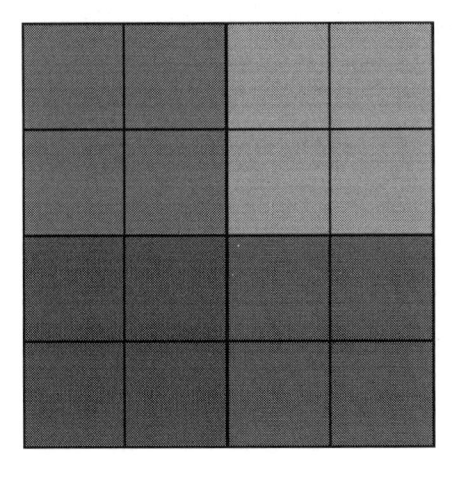

The image was divided into 16 squares of equal size. Each one of these squares is a so-called **pixel**. A pixel is the smallest portion of information that an image (that is, raster data) contains. While talking about geoprocessing, the image as a whole comprehends a space in the real world and each pixel is a fraction of that space.

When we added the sample image to the map in the beginning of the chapter, we manually defined the extent of this image (that is, its bounding box). This information told Mapnik how the coordinates in the image relates to the real world coordinates.

So far, we have seen that our sample image has 16 pixels with a shape of 4 x 4. But how this image or any other raster data relates to a real world space depends on the information that may or may not be stored in the data itself.

The first information that states the relation is where the image is in the world. Images and raster data normally have their point of origin in the top left corner. If we assign a coordinate to the point of origin, we will be able to place the image on the world.

Secondly, we need information on the area that this image covers. And there are three ways this information can appear:

- The size of the pixels of the image
- The size of the image
- The coordinates of the bounding box of the image

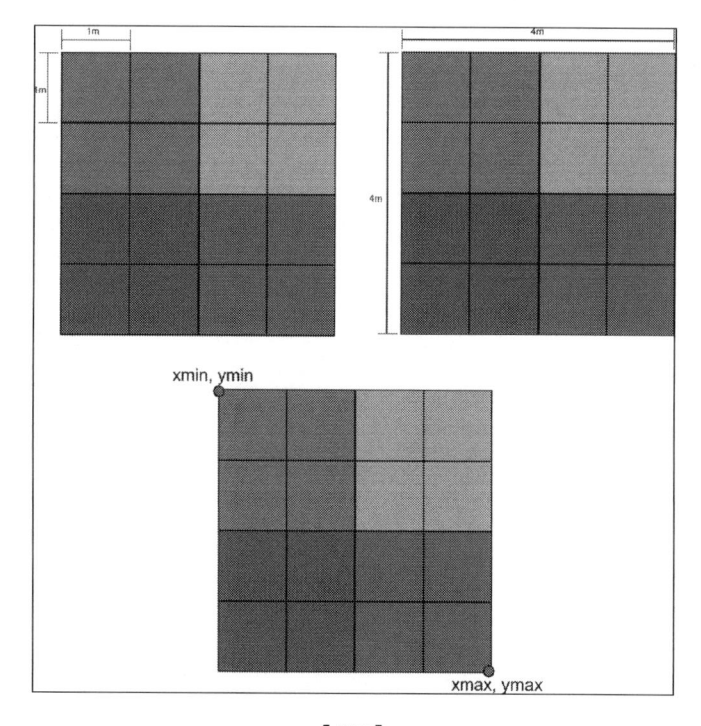

Working with Remote Sensing Images

This information is related by the following equations:

```
x_pixel_size = width / columns
y_pixel_size = height / lines
width = xmax - xmin
height = ymax - ymin
```

Opening images with OpenCV

For a better understanding, we will open the sample image with OpenCV and inspect its contents as follows:

1. In your `image_expriments.py` file, type the following code:

    ```
    def open_raster_file(image):
        """Opens a raster file.

        :param image: Path of the raster file or np array.
        """
        image = cv2.imread(image)
        return image


    if __name__ == '__main__':
        image = open_raster_file('../../data/sample_image.tiff')
        print(image)
        print(type(image))
        print(image.shape)
    ```

2. Run the code. Since it's the first time you have run this file, press *Alt + Shift + F10* and choose `image_experiments` from the list. You should see the following output:

    ```
    [[[  0   0 255]
      [  0   0 255]
      [  0 255   0]
      [  0 255   0]]

     [[  0   0 255]
      [  0   0 255]
      [  0 255   0]
      [  0 255   0]]

     [[255   0   0]
      [255   0   0]
      [100 100 100]
    ```

```
      [100 100 100]]

     [[255   0    0]
      [255   0    0]
      [100 100 100]
      [100 100 100]]]
    <type 'numpy.ndarray'>
    (4, 4, 3)

    Process finished with exit code 0
```

The expression `print(type(image))` prints the type of the object that is stored in the `image` variable. As you can see, it's a NumPy array with a shape of 4 x 4 x 3. OpenCV opens the image and put its data inside an array, although for now, it is a little bit hard to visualize how the data is organized. The array contains the color information for each pixel on the image.

For better visualization, I'm going to reorganize the print output for you:

```
    [[[  0   0 255] [  0   0 255] [  0   0 255] [  0   0 255]]
     [[  0   0 255] [  0   0 255] [  0   0 255] [  0   0 255]]
     [[255   0   0] [255   0   0] [100 100 100] [100 100 100]]
     [[255   0   0] [255   0   0] [100 100 100] [100 100 100]]]
```

Now the shape of the array makes more sense. Notice that we have four *lines* and each line has four *columns* exactly as it is seen in the image. By its turn, each item has a set of three numbers that represents the values for the blue, green, and red channels.

> Remember that when you import a colored image with OpenCV, the order of the channels will be BGR (blue, green, and red).

For example, take the first pixel in the top left corner. It's all red as we see in the image:

```
    Blue Green Red
    [  0    0   255]
```

So, the first and the most important implication of the images being imported as NumPy arrays is that they behave like arrays and have all the functions and methods that any NumPy array has, opening the possibility of using the full power of NumPy while working with raster data.

Knowing numerical types

Each pixel in the previous topic has three channels: blue, green, and red. Each one has a value ranging from 0 to 255 (256 possible values). The combination of these channels result in a visible color. This range of values is not random; 256 is the number of combinations that is possible to achieve with a single **byte**.

A byte is the smallest portion of data that a computer can store and retrieve from the memory. It's composed of 8 bits of zeros or ones.

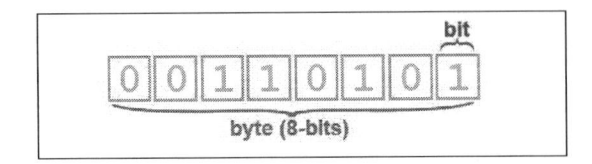

This is important to us because the computer uses its memory to store the image and it will reserve a given space to store the value for each channel for each pixel. We must be sure that the space reserved is adequate for the data we want to store.

Let's make an abstraction. Think that you have 1 liter (1,000 ml) of water and you want to store it. If you choose a 250 ml cup to store this water, the excess will spill out. If you choose a water truck with 10,000 liter capacity, you can store the water, but it will be a huge waste of space. So, you may choose a 3 liter bucket that would be sufficient to store the water. It's not big as a truck and you will have some extra space if you want to store a little bit more water.

In computing, things work similarly. You need to choose the size of the container before you put things in it. In the previous example, OpenCV made this choice for us. You will see a number of instances in the future where the programs we use will help us in these choices. But a clear understanding on how this works is very important because if the water spills out (that is, overflows), you will end up with unexpected behavior in your program. Or, if you choose a too large recipient, you may run out of computer memory.

The needs for value storage may vary in the aspects of:

- Only positive or positive and negative numbers
- Integers or fractions
- Small or large numbers
- Complex numbers

Chapter 6

The available options and their sizes may vary with the computer architecture and software. For a common 64-bit desktop, NumPy will give you these possible numerical types:

- `bool`: Boolean (True or False) stored as a byte
- `int8`: Byte (-128 to 127)
- `int16`: Integer (-32768 to 32767)
- `int32`: Integer (-2147483648 to 2147483647)
- `int64`: Integer (-9223372036854775808 to 9223372036854775807)
- `uint8`: Unsigned integer (0 to 255)
- `uint16`: Unsigned integer (0 to 65535)
- `uint32`: Unsigned integer (0 to 4294967295)
- `uint64`: Unsigned integer (0 to 18446744073709551615)
- `float16`: Half precision float: sign bit, 5 bits exponent, 10 bits mantissa
- `float32`: Single precision float: sign bit, 8 bits exponent, 23 bits mantissa
- `float64`: Double precision float: sign bit, 11 bits exponent, 52 bits mantissa
- `complex64`: Complex number represented by two 32-bit floats (real and imaginary components)
- `complex128`: Complex number represented by two 64-bit floats (real and imaginary components)

So, we may expect that our sample image has the type `uint8`. Let's check whether it's true:

1. Edit the `if __name__ == '__main__':` block:
   ```
   if __name__ == '__main__':
       image = open_raster_file('../../data/sample_image.tiff')
       print(type(image))
       print(image.dtype)
   ```

2. Run the code again. You should see an output matching our expectations:
   ```
   <type 'numpy.ndarray'>
   uint8
   
   Process finished with exit code 0
   ```

Processing remote sensing images and data

Satellite images come in a different format and serve different purposes. These images can be used to visualize features on Earth using real colors or they may be used to identify a variety of characteristics using parts of the spectrum invisible to the human eye.

As we saw, our sample image had three channels (blue, green, and red) that were combined in a single file to compose a real color image. Different from the sample image, most satellite data comes with each channel separated into a file for each one of them. These channels are called **bands** and comprise of a range of the electromagnetic spectrum visible or not to the human eye.

In the following examples, we are going to use the **digital elevation models (DEM)** generated with the data obtained by the **Advanced Spaceborne Thermal Emission and Reflection Radiometer (ASTER)**.

These DEM have a resolution of approximately 90 m and the values are stored in the 16 bits signed integers representing the elevation in meters.

The dataset we are going to use is included in the `data` folder and is from a Brazilian city called *Poços de Caldas*. This city is inside a giant extinct volcano crater, a feature we hope to see during data processing. For didactic reasons and in order to cover a big region, four images will be used:

> You can obtain more digital elevation models at `http://earthexplorer.usgs.gov/`.

1. If want to download and use your own DEM, you need to extract the downloaded ZIP file. Notice that each ZIP archive has two images. The one ending with `_dem` is the actual elevation data. The one ending with `_num` contains the quality assessment information. Take a look at the included `README.pdf` file for more information.
2. Move or copy all the images to the `data` folder of your `Chapter 6` code.

Each image represents a tile of 1 degree. The information on which tile the image covers is encoded in the name of the file, as seen in the following image:

```
          48°W              47°W
   22°S ┌──────────────┬──────────────┐
        │              │              │
        │              │              │
        │ ASTGTM2_S22W048_dem.tif │ ASTGTM2_S22W047_dem.tif │
        │              │              │
        │              │              │
   23°S ├──────────────┼──────────────┤
        │              │              │
        │              │              │
        │ ASTGTM2_S23W048_dem.tif │ ASTGTM2_S23W047_dem.tif │
        │              │              │
        │              │              │
        └──────────────┴──────────────┘
```

Mosaicking images

Mapnik has the ability to read tiled data from the disk using the raster data source. But we are not going to use it, because the process of patching images together is very important and is worth learning.

The next code will open the images, combine them, and save a single combined image in the disk. This process (with varying levels of complexity) is called **mosaicking**:

1. Still in the `image_experiments.py` file, add a new function after the `open_raster_file` function:

   ```
   def combine_images(input_images):
       """Combine images in a mosaic.

       :param input_images: Path to the input images.
       """
       images = []
       for item in input_images:
           images.append(open_raster_file(item))
       print images
   ```

Working with Remote Sensing Images

2. Now, edit the `if __name__ == '__main__':` block so we can test the code:

   ```
   if __name__ == '__main__':
       elevation_data = [
           '../../data/ASTGTM2_S22W048_dem.tif',
           '../../data/ASTGTM2_S22W047_dem.tif',
           '../../data/ASTGTM2_S23W048_dem.tif',
           '../../data/ASTGTM2_S23W047_dem.tif']
       combine_images(elevation_data)
   ```

3. Run the code and look at the output:

   ```
   [array([[[1, 1, 1],
            [1, 1, 1],
            [2, 2, 2],
            ...,
            [4, 4, 4],
            [4, 4, 4],
            [4, 4, 4]],
   ...

   Process finished with exit code 0
   ```

You should see a list of four arrays. PyCharm will hide some values so it can fit in the console.

The first thing we should notice is that the order of the images in the input images argument is the same as the order of the arrays in the output list. This will be very important later.

Secondly, although the elevation data is a 16-bit signed integer (`int16`), the arrays representing the images still have three bands of an 8-bit unsigned integer. This is an error. OpenCV is converting the grayscale image to a color image. We are going to fix it as follows:

1. Change the `open_raster_file` function to accept a new argument. It will allow us to open the images without changing them:

   ```
   def open_raster_file(image, unchanged=True):
       """Opens a raster file.

       :param image: Path of the raster file or np array.
       :param unchanged: Set to true to keep the original format.
       """
       flags = cv2.CV_LOAD_IMAGE_UNCHANGED if unchanged else -1
       image = cv2.imread(image, flags=flags)
       return image
   ```

The `flags` argument in `cv2.imread` allows us to tune how the images are opened and converted into arrays. If the flags are set to `cv2.CV_LOAD_IMAGE_UNCHANGED`, the image will open as it is without any conversion.

2. Since we set the default of `unchanged` to `true`, we will just run the code again and see the results:

```
[array([[ 508,  511,  514, ..., 1144, 1148, 1152],
        [ 507,  510,  510, ..., 1141, 1144, 1150],
        [ 510,  508,  506, ..., 1141, 1145, 1154],
        ...,
        [ 805,  805,  803, ...,  599,  596,  593],
        [ 802,  797,  803, ...,  598,  594,  590],
        [ 797,  797,  800, ...,  603,  596,  593]], dtype=uint16)
...

Process finished with exit code 0
```

The values now are correct and they are the measured elevation in meters for each pixel.

So far, we have a list of arrays in the order that the input files are listed. To figure out the next step, we can imagine this list as if the images were mosaicked as a strip:

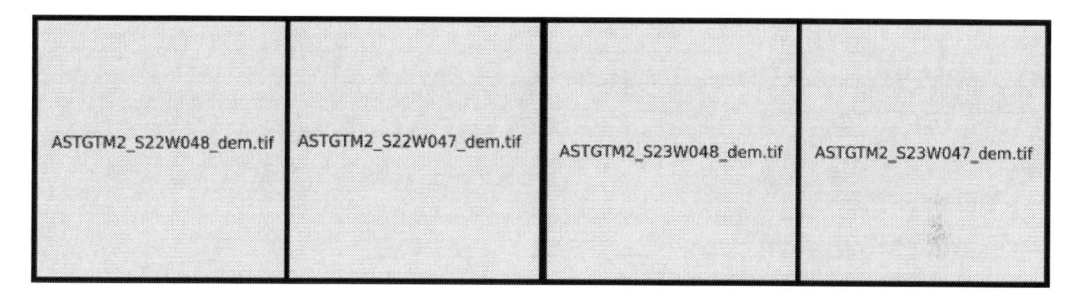

ASTGTM2_S22W048_dem.tif	ASTGTM2_S22W047_dem.tif	ASTGTM2_S23W048_dem.tif	ASTGTM2_S23W047_dem.tif

Now, we must reorganize this, so the images are placed in their correct position. Remember that NumPy arrays have a `shape` property. In a 2D array, it's a tuple containing the shape in columns and rows. NumPy arrays also have the `reshape()` method that performs a shape transformation.

> Take a look at the NumPy documentation on the reshape method and function. Changing the shape of an array is a very powerful tool at http://docs.scipy.org/doc/numpy/reference/generated/numpy.reshape.html.

Working with Remote Sensing Images

The reshape works by filling a row with the input values in order. When the row is full, the method jumps to the next row and continues until the end. So, if we pass the expected shape of the mosaic to the `combine_images` function, we can use this information to combine the images with respect to the proper positions.

But we need something else. We need to know the shape of the output image through the number of pixels, and this will be the product of the shape of each image by the shape of the mosaic. Let's try a few changes in the code as follows:

1. Edit the combine images function:

    ```
    def combine_images(input_images, shape, output_image):
        """Combine images in a mosaic.

        :param input_images: Path to the input images.
        :param shape: Shape of the mosaic in columns and rows.
        :param output_image: Path to the output image mosaic.
        """
        if len(input_images) != shape[0] * shape[1]:
            raise ValueError(
                "Number of images doesn't match the mosaic shape.")
        images = []
        for item in input_images:
            images.append(open_raster_file(item))
        rows = []
        for row in range(shape[0]):
            start = (row * shape[1])
            end = start + shape[1]
            rows.append(np.concatenate(images[start:end], axis=1))
        mosaic = np.concatenate(rows, axis=0)
        print(mosaic)
        print(mosaic.shape)
    ```

    Now the function accepts two more arguments, the shape of the mosaic (the number of images in the row and columns and not the number of pixels) and the path of the output image for later use.

    With this code, the list of images is separated into rows. Then, the rows are combined to form the complete mosaic.

2. Before you run the code, don't forget to import NumPy at the beginning of the file:

    ```
    # coding=utf-8

    import cv2
    ```

```
import numpy as np
```

And edit the if __name__ == '__main__': block:

```
if __name__ == '__main__':
    elevation_data = [
        '../../data/ASTGTM2_S22W048_dem.tif',
        '../../data/ASTGTM2_S22W047_dem.tif',
        '../../data/ASTGTM2_S23W048_dem.tif',
        '../../data/ASTGTM2_S23W047_dem.tif']
    combine_images(elevation_data, shape=(2, 2))
```

3. Now run the code and see the results:

```
[[508 511 514 ..., 761 761 761]
 [507 510 510 ..., 761 761 761]
 [510 508 506 ..., 761 761 761]
 ...,
 [514 520 517 ..., 751 745 739]
 [517 524 517 ..., 758 756 753]
 [509 509 510 ..., 757 759 760]]
(7202, 7202)

Process finished with exit code 0
```

It's now a single array with 7202 x 7202 pixels. The remaining task is to save this array to the disk as an image.

4. Just add two lines to the function and edit the if __name__ == '__main__': block:

```
def combine_images(input_images, shape, output_image):
    """Combine images in a mosaic.

    :param input_images: Path to the input images.
    :param shape: Shape of the mosaic in columns and rows.
    :param output_image: Path to the output image mosaic.
    """
    if len(input_images) != shape[0] * shape[1]:
        raise ValueError(
            "Number of images doesn't match the mosaic shape.")
    images = []
    for item in input_images:
        images.append(open_raster_file(item))
    rows = []
    for row in range(shape[0]):
```

[173]

Working with Remote Sensing Images

```
            start = (row * shape[1])
            end = start + shape[1]
            rows.append(np.concatenate(images[start:end], axis=1))
    mosaic = np.concatenate(rows, axis=0)
    print(mosaic)
    print(mosaic.shape)
    cv2.imwrite(output_image, mosaic)

if __name__ == '__main__':
    elevation_data = [
        '../../data/ASTGTM2_S22W048_dem.tif',
        '../../data/ASTGTM2_S22W047_dem.tif',
        '../../data/ASTGTM2_S23W048_dem.tif',
        '../../data/ASTGTM2_S23W047_dem.tif']
    combine_images(elevation_data, shape=(2, 2),
                   output_image="../output/mosaic.png")
```

Adjusting the values of the images

If you run the previous code, you will see a black image as an output. This happens because the value range that represents the actual data of this region is so narrow in comparison to the possible range of the 16-bit integer image that we can't distinguish the shades of gray. For better understanding, let's make a simple test as follows:

1. Still in the image_experiments.py file, comment the if __name__ == '__main__': block and add this new one:

   ```
   if __name__ == '__main__':
       image = open_raster_file("../output/mosaic.png")
       print(image.min(), image.max())
   ```

2. Run the code and look at the console output.

   ```
   (423, 2026)

   Process finished with exit code 0
   ```

   Precisely, the image ranges from -32768 to 32767 and the elevation of the region in it ranges from 423 to 2026. So what we need to do to make the image visible is to scale the altitude range to the range of the data type.

   Since we are making a data representation intended for human visualization, we don't need to use a big range of gray values. The researches vary, but some say that we can detect only 30 shades, so an 8-bit unsigned integer with 256 possible values should be more than enough for data visualization.

3. Add this new function:

```
def adjust_values(input_image, output_image, img_range=None):
    """Create a visualization of the data in the input_image by
    projecting a range of values into a grayscale image.

    :param input_image: Array containing the data
     or path to an image.
    :param output_image: The image path to write the output.
    :param img_range: specified range of values or None to use the
     range of the image (minimum and maximum).
    """
    image = open_raster_file(input_image)
    if img_range:
        min = img_range[0]
        max = img_range[1]
    else:
        min = image.min()
        max = image.max()
    interval = max - min
    factor = 256.0 / interval
    output = image * factor
    cv2.imwrite(output_image, output)
```

This function accepts either an array or the path to an image file. With this feature, we can later use this function as a sub-step in other processing procedures. The range of values that you want to use is also optional. It can be set manually or can be extracted from the images minimum and maximum value.

4. To test the code, edit the `if __name__ == '__main__':` block:

```
if __name__ == '__main__':
    # Adjust.
    adjust_values('../output/mosaic.png',
                  '../output/mosaic_grey.png')
```

Note that the output image is now a `png` file. Since we are preparing the image for visualization, we can afford to lose information in data compression in exchange for a smaller file.

5. Run the code and open the `mosaic_grey.png` file to see the results. You should see the following beautiful grayscale image now:

Cropping an image

We made a big mosaic of images in order to cover the region of interest, and in the process, we ended up with an image much bigger than the one we needed. Now, it's time to crop the image, so we end up with a smaller one comprising only of what we want to see, thus saving disk space and processing time.

In our example, we are interested in the volcano crater. It's the round object located on the right-hand side of the image. In order to obtain only that region of interest, we will write a function that can crop the image using a bounding box set of coordinates, as follows:

1. Add the new function to the `image_experiments.py` file:

```
def crop_image(input_image, image_extent, bbox, output_image):
    """Crops an image by a bounding box.
    bbox and image_extent format: (xmin, ymin, xmax, ymax).

    :param input_image: Array containing the data
```

```
    or path to an image.
:param image_extent: The geographic extent of the image.
:param output_image: The image path to write the output.
:param bbox: The bounding box of the region of interest.
"""
input_image = open_raster_file(input_image)
img_shape = input_image.shape
img_geo_width = abs(image_extent[2] - image_extent[0])
img_geo_height = abs(image_extent[3] - image_extent[1])

# How much pixels are contained in one geographic unit.
pixel_width = img_shape[1] / img_geo_width
pixel_height = img_shape[0] / img_geo_height

# Index of the pixel to cut.
x_min = abs(bbox[0] - image_extent[0]) * pixel_width
x_max = abs(bbox[2] - image_extent[0]) * pixel_width
y_min = abs(bbox[1] - image_extent[1]) * pixel_height
y_max = abs(bbox[3] - image_extent[1]) * pixel_height

output = input_image[y_min:y_max, x_min:x_max]
cv2.imwrite(output_image, output)
```

Since we are dealing with NumPy arrays, the cropping itself is a simple array slicing. The slicing of arrays is very similar to the Python lists' slicing, but with additional dimensions. The statement input_image[y_min:y_max, x_min:x_max] tells that we want only the portion of the array contained within the specified cells (that is, pixels). So, all the math involved is to convert geographic units into array indices.

2. Edit the if __name__ == '__main__': block to test the code:

```
if __name__ == '__main__':
    # Crop.
    roi = (-46.8, -21.7, -46.3, -22.1)   # Region of interest.
    crop_image('../output/mosaic_grey.png',
               (-48, -21, -46, -23), roi, "../output/cropped.png")
```

Working with Remote Sensing Images

3. Run the code and open the output image to see the results.

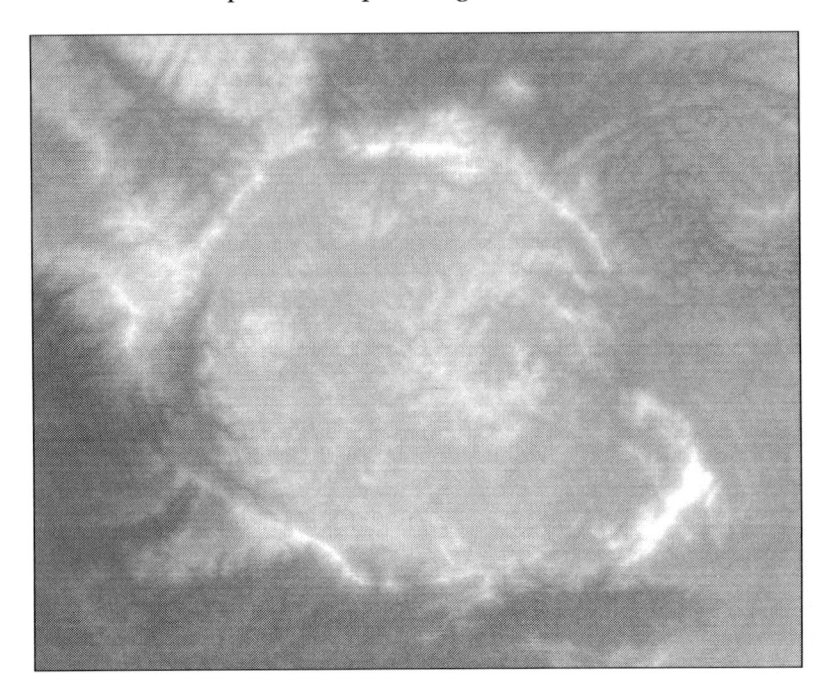

4. If you have missed any of the steps, you can run the whole process all at once. Just edit the `if __name__ == '__main__'` block:

```
if __name__ == '__main__':
    # Combine.
    elevation_data = [
        '../../data/ASTGTM2_S22W048_dem.tif',
        '../../data/ASTGTM2_S22W047_dem.tif',
        '../../data/ASTGTM2_S23W048_dem.tif',
        '../../data/ASTGTM2_S23W047_dem.tif']
    combine_images(elevation_data, shape=(2, 2),
                   output_image="../output/mosaic.png")

    # Adjust.
    adjust_values('../output/mosaic.png',
                  '../output/mosaic_grey.png')

    # Crop.
    roi = (-46.8, -21.7, -46.3, -22.1)  # Region of interest.
    crop_image('../output/mosaic_grey.png',
               (-48, -21, -46, -23), roi, "../output/cropped.png")
```

[178]

Creating a shaded relief image

Our digital elevation model image has improved a lot after we processed it, but it is still not suitable for a map. Untrained eyes may find it difficult to understand the relief only by looking at the different shades of gray.

Fortunately, there is a technique, called **hill shading** or **relief shading**, that transforms the elevation data into a simulated sun shading over the terrain. Look at the beautiful map in the following picture and note how much easier it is to understand the relief when it is presented as a shaded relief:

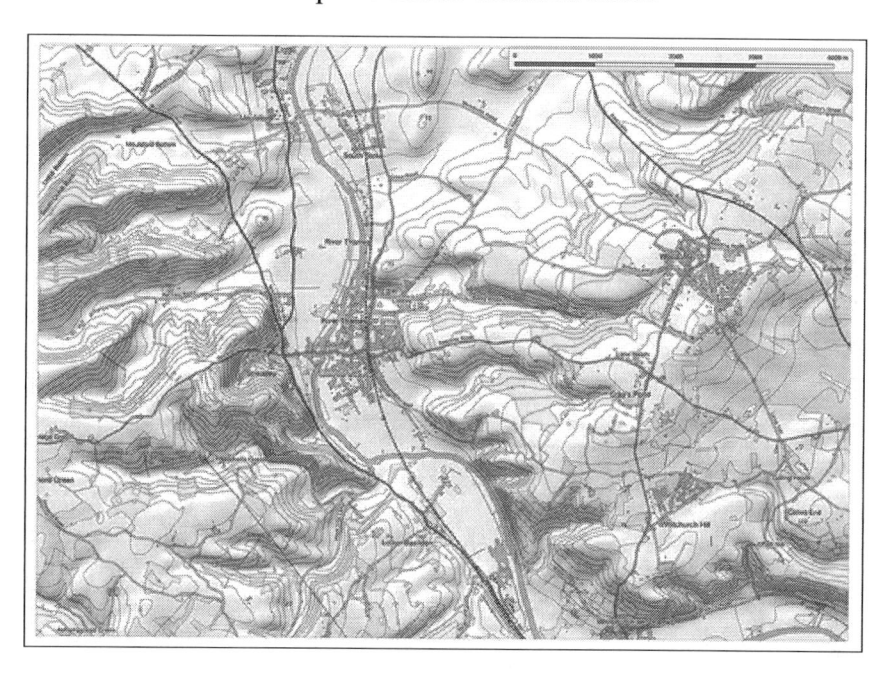

The process is simple and involves passing our image through a well-known algorithm as follows:

1. Add the `create_hillshade` function to your `image_experiments.py` file:

   ```
   def create_hillshade(input_image, output_image,
                       azimuth=90, angle_altitude=60):
       """Creates a shaded relief image from a digital elevation
       model.

       :param input_image: Array containing the data
        or path to an image.
       :param azimuth: Simulated sun azimuth.
       :param angle_altitude: Sun altitude angle.
   ```

```
    """
    input_image = open_raster_file(input_image)
    x, y = np.gradient(input_image)
    slope = np.pi / 2 - np.arctan(np.sqrt(x * x + y * y))
    aspect = np.arctan2(-x, y)
    az_rad = azimuth * np.pi / 180
    alt_rad = angle_altitude * np.pi / 180
    a = np.sin(alt_rad) * np.sin(slope)
    b = np.cos(alt_rad) * np.cos(slope) * np.cos(az_rad - aspect)
    output = 255 * (a + b + 1) / 2
    cv2.imwrite(output_image, output)
```

2. Now, alter the `if __name__ == '__main__':` block to test the code:

```
if __name__ == '__main__':
    create_hillshade("../output/cropped.png",
                    "../output/hillshade.png")
```

3. Run the code and open the output image to see the results. If everything goes fine, you should see a shaded relief representation of your data.

Building an image processing pipeline

Image processing, be it for geographic applications or not, generally requires the execution of a sequence of transformations (that is, steps) in order to obtain the desired final result. In these sequences, the output of one step is the input of the next one. In computing, this is called **processing pipeline**.

This type of data manipulation is very versatile, because you have a range of functions or steps than can be arranged into numerous combinations to produce a wide range of results.

What we did so far, in this chapter's examples, was we opened an image from the disk, performed a given operation, and saved the results to another image on the disk. Then, in the next step, we opened the result from the previous one and so on.

Despite the steps are not yet connected, we can imagine the following image processing pipeline:

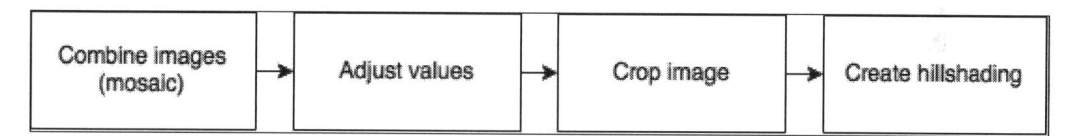

Combine images (mosaic) → Adjust values → Crop image → Create hillshading

Saving intermediary steps to the disk is useful when we want to use the images from them, or in other situations, when the pipeline uses parallel processing or other more complex methods.

For some cases, it would be more interesting just to pass data along the pipeline without touching the hard drive, only using the computer memory. With this, one should expect a noticeable gain in speed and a lesser production of residual files.

In order to conciliate these two situations, we can use type checks for our functions' arguments, making them accept either arrays or file paths. Navigate to your `open_raster_file` function and alter its code:

```
def open_raster_file(file_path, unchanged=True):
    """Opens a raster file.

    :param file_path: Path of the raster file or np array.
    :param unchanged: Set to true to keep the original format.
    """
    if isinstance(file_path, np.ndarray):
        return file_path
    flags = cv2.CV_LOAD_IMAGE_UNCHANGED if unchanged else -1
    image = cv2.imread(file_path, flags=flags)
    return image
```

Working with Remote Sensing Images

This function will now check the type of `file_path`. If it is already a NumPy array, it will be returned. This changes the behavior of all of our functions because they can now receive arrays as input.

If we add a `return` statement to all the functions and make them return the output arrays, we would be able to combine the function as follows:

```
create_hillshade(
    crop_image(
        adjust_values('mosaic.png'),
        (-48, -21, -46, -23), roi), 'shaded.png')
```

You don't need to type this code. This notation is hard to understand. The order in which the functions are called is unintuitive and it's difficult to figure out of which function is each argument.

It would be much nicer if we could execute the pipeline by chaining the functions, like we did in the *Chaining filters* section in *Chapter 4, Improving the App Search Capabilities*. Actually, it would be great to use something with a notation as follows:

```
adjust_values().crop_image().create_hillshade()
```

As in *Chapter 4, Improving the App Search Capabilities*, the only thing we need is to have a class and the methods that return the same type of class. With these two things, there are no limits on how the steps can be combined. So, let's do it.

Creating a RasterData class

Our `RasterData` class will follow the pattern used before with our vectors. When instantiated, the class will receive a file path or an array. As said before, in order to use method chaining to perform a processing pipeline, each processing method must return another instance of the `RasterData` class.

We will start with class declaration and then fill it with the methods. To make it easier to cut and paste the work we have already done, we will do the following steps inside the `image_experiments.py` file:

1. At the top of the `image_experiments.py` file, after the imports, create the class:

    ```
    # coding=utf-8


    import cv2
    ```

```
import numpy as np


class RasterData(object):
    def __init__(self, input_data, unchanged=True, shape=None):
        """Represents a raster data in the form of an array.

        :param input_data: Raster files or Numpy array.
        :param unchanged: True to keep the original format.
        :param shape: When using multiple input data, this param
         determines the shape of the composition.
        """
        self.data = None
        if isinstance(input_data, list) \
                or isinstance(input_data, tuple):
            self.combine_images(input_data, shape)
        else:
            self.import_data(input_data, unchanged)
```

The array will be stored in the `data` property, so we will initially set it to `None`.

There are a few other changes to make this class consistent with the others and avoid redundancy in the names. The first one is to use an `import_data` method like before.

2. Cut and paste the `open_raster_file` function into the class, rename it to `import_data`, and change it to behave like a method:

```
class RasterData(object):
    def __init__(self, input_data, unchanged=True, shape=None):
        ...

    def import_data(self, image, unchanged=True):
        """Opens a raster file.

        :param image: Path of the raster file or np array.
        :param unchanged: True to keep the original format.
        """
        if isinstance(image, np.ndarray):
            self.data = image
            return image
        flags = cv2.CV_LOAD_IMAGE_UNCHANGED if unchanged else -1
        self.data = cv2.imread(image, flags=flags)
```

Instead of returning an array, it will now put the array in the `data` property.

Next, since we will be removing the obligation of writing the image to the disk from the steps, we will need a method to perform this action.

Working with Remote Sensing Images

3. Add the `write_image` method:

   ```
   class RasterData(object):
       def __init__(self, input_data, unchanged=True, shape=None):
           ...

       def import_data(self, input_image, unchanged=True):
           ...

       def write_image(self, output_image):
           """Write the data to the disk as an image.

           :param output_image: Path and name of the output image.
           """
           cv2.imwrite(output_image, self.data)
           return self
   ```

4. Following the examples' order, cut and paste the `combine_images` function as a method to the class:

   ```
   class RasterData(object):
       def __init__(self, input_data, unchanged=True, shape=None):
           ...

       def import_data(self, input_image, unchanged=True):
           ...

       def write_image(self, output_image):
           ...

       def combine_images(self, input_images, shape):
           """Combine images in a mosaic.

           :param input_images: Path to the input images.
           :param shape: Shape of the mosaic in columns and rows.
           """
           if len(input_images) != shape[0] * shape[1]:
               raise ValueError("Number of images doesn't match the"
                                " mosaic shape.")
           images = []
           for item in input_images:
               if isinstance(item, RasterData):
                   images.append(item.data)
               else:
                   images.append(RasterData(item).data)
           rows = []
   ```

[184]

```
        for row in range(shape[0]):
            start = (row * shape[1])
            end = start + shape[1]
            rows.append(np.concatenate(images[start:end], axis=1))
        mosaic = np.concatenate(rows, axis=0)
        self.data = mosaic
        return self
```

Now, it's possible to create an empty RasterData instance and then populate it with a mosaic using this method. Or, you can create the instance with a list containing any combination of image paths, arrays, or even other RasterData instances as an argument. It will automatically combine them, put the result in the data property, and return itself.

Now that you got the hang of it, let's do the same transformation with the last three functions.

5. Cut and paste the `adjust_values`, `crop_image` and `create_hillshade` functions as methods into the class. Your complete class should be as follows:

```
class RasterData(object):
    def __init__(self, input_data, unchanged=True, shape=None):
        """Represents a raster data in the form of an array.

        :param input_data: Raster files or Numpy array.
        :param unchanged: True to keep the original format.
        :param shape: When using multiple input data, this param
          determines the shape of the composition.
        """
        self.data = None
        if isinstance(input_data, list) \
                or isinstance(input_data, tuple):
            self.combine_images(input_data, shape)
        else:
            self.import_data(input_data, unchanged)

    def import_data(self, image, unchanged=True):
        """Opens a raster file.

        :param image: Path of the raster file or np array.
        :param unchanged: True to keep the original format.
        """
        if isinstance(image, np.ndarray):
            self.data = image
            return image
        flags = cv2.CV_LOAD_IMAGE_UNCHANGED if unchanged else -1
```

```python
            self.data = cv2.imread(image, flags=flags)

        def write_image(self, output_image):
            """Write the data to the disk as an image.

            :param output_image: Path and name of the output image.
            """
            cv2.imwrite(output_image, self.data)
            return self

        def combine_images(self, input_images, shape):
            """Combine images in a mosaic.

            :param input_images: Path to the input images.
            :param shape: Shape of the mosaic in columns and rows.
            """
            if len(input_images) != shape[0] * shape[1]:
                raise ValueError("Number of images doesn't match the"
                                 " mosaic shape.")
            images = []
            for item in input_images:
                if isinstance(item, RasterData):
                    images.append(item.data)
                else:
                    images.append(RasterData(item).data)
            rows = []
            for row in range(shape[0]):
                start = (row * shape[1])
                end = start + shape[1]
                rows.append(np.concatenate(images[start:end], axis=1))
            mosaic = np.concatenate(rows, axis=0)
            self.data = mosaic
            return self

        def adjust_values(self, img_range=None):
            """Create a visualization of the data in the input_image by
            projecting a range of values into a grayscale image.

            :param img_range: specified range of values
            or None to use the range of the image
            (minimum and maximum).
            """
            image = self.data
```

```python
            if img_range:
                min = img_range[0]
                max = img_range[1]
            else:
                min = image.min()
                max = image.max()
            interval = max - min
            factor = 256.0 / interval
            output = image * factor
            self.data = output
            return self

    def crop_image(self, image_extent, bbox):
        """Crops an image by a bounding box.
        bbox and image_extent format: (xmin, ymin, xmax, ymax).

        :param input_image: Array containing the data
          or path to an image.
        :param image_extent: The geographic extent of the image.
        :param output_image: The image path to write the output.
        :param bbox: The bounding box of the region of interest.
        """
        input_image = self.data
        img_shape = input_image.shape
        img_geo_width = abs(image_extent[2] - image_extent[0])
        img_geo_height = abs(image_extent[3] - image_extent[1])
        # How much pixels are contained in one geographic unit.
        pixel_width = img_shape[1] / img_geo_width
        pixel_height = img_shape[0] / img_geo_height
        # Index of the pixel to cut.
        x_min = abs(bbox[0] - image_extent[0]) * pixel_width
        x_max = abs(bbox[2] - image_extent[0]) * pixel_width
        y_min = abs(bbox[1] - image_extent[1]) * pixel_height
        y_max = abs(bbox[3] - image_extent[1]) * pixel_height
        output = input_image[y_min:y_max, x_min:x_max]
        self.data = output
        return self

    def create_hillshade(self, azimuth=90, angle_altitude=60):
        """Creates a shaded relief image from a digital elevation
        model.

        :param input_image: Array containing the data
          or path to an image.
```

Working with Remote Sensing Images

```
        :param azimuth: Simulated sun azimuth.
        :param angle_altitude: Sun altitude angle.
        """
        input_image = self.data
        x, y = np.gradient(input_image)
        slope = np.pi / 2 - np.arctan(np.sqrt(x * x + y * y))
        aspect = np.arctan2(-x, y)
        az_rad = azimuth * np.pi / 180
        alt_rad = angle_altitude * np.pi / 180
        a = np.sin(alt_rad) * np.sin(slope)
        b = np.cos(alt_rad) * np.cos(slope) \
            * np.cos(az_rad - aspect)
        output = 255 * (a + b + 1) / 2
        self.data = output
        return self
```

The class is complete and we can make a pipeline to test it.

6. Edit and organize the `if __name__ == '__main__':` block to test the image processing pipeline:

```
if __name__ == '__main__':
    elevation_data = [
            '../../data/ASTGTM2_S22W048_dem.tif',
            '../../data/ASTGTM2_S22W047_dem.tif',
            '../../data/ASTGTM2_S23W048_dem.tif',
            '../../data/ASTGTM2_S23W047_dem.tif']
    roi = (-46.8, -21.7, -46.3, -22.1)  # Region of interest.
    iex = (-48, -21, -46, -23)  # Image extent.

    RasterData(elevation_data, shape=(2, 2)).adjust_values().\
        crop_image(iex, roi).create_hillshade().\
        write_image('../output/pipeline_output.png')
```

Due to the width limitation of the book, the pipeline is broken into three lines, but you can type it in a single line in PyCharm if you wish.

7. Run the code and admire the result.

At this point, you have a fantastic accomplishment. I'm not talking about the shaded relief image, I'm talking about the ability to consistently develop processing steps and combine them into a processing pipeline in order to achieve the final result. The structure that we developed here can be used to do almost anything in terms of geoprocessing.

Also, note that the image generated by the pipeline is of a much superior quality than the one created before. This happened because the data was in the memory the whole time. This avoided data loss due to compression when the data was saved to a file multiple times.

A few remarks about the functionality of the structure as we implemented it are as follows:

- All the processing methods do two things in the end: they change the instance data and return the instance itself. The implication of this is that the class instance will mutate along the pipeline and the old data will be replaced by new ones as the process goes on. With this, Python's garbage collector will eliminate old results from the memory and save space.
- If, at any step, you want to save the current state of processing, just insert a call to the `write_image` method (it will also return self and it can be piped). This is a powerful tool for debugging and also can save time when you only want to repeat the steps later in a long pipeline.

- You can fork the pipeline. You can create a bifurcation where more than one result can be produced by following different paths. To do this, you can use the `copy()` function or you can write the result to the disk before the bifurcation. Later in the book we will see that, sometimes, while performing parallel processing, we will need these techniques too.

Summary

In this chapter, we understood how remote sensing images are represented inside the computer as arrays and how we can use this characteristic to process them. We saw that, in order to use images on a map, it is common that we need to transform them to achieve better results. Then, we wrote processing functions to process the digital elevation model images, ending with a beautiful shaded relief map. Finally, we created a `RasterData` class and transformed our functions into the methods of this class. With a few additional changes, we made it possible to chain these methods into a processing pipeline.

In the next chapter, we will explore the data in the images and obtain valuable information.

7
Extract Information from Raster Data

More than just a resource for visual information, raster data are samples of a given spatial attribute, whose values can be analyzed in order to produce valuable information.

Is this chapter, we will extract information from raster data with special emphasis on statistical information. Following the previous examples, we will use the digital elevation model to obtain values such as the maximum and minimum altitude of a given region, separate altitude ranges into classes, and produce histograms and other statistical information. Going beyond simple numerical values, we will display all the information on beautifully colored maps.

The topics covered by this chapter are:

- How to obtain statistics from raster data
- The use of programming techniques, such as lazy evaluation and memorization, to avoid unnecessary calculation
- How to format tabular data output
- How to colorize maps and choose suitable colors for them
- How to blend color maps in order to produce colorized and shaded maps

Getting the basic statistics

As we have previously seen, images or raster data are arrays containing numerical values representing a given real world space. So, they are by consequence statistical samples and they can be used in statistical analysis.

Extract Information from Raster Data

When we import the data, it is converted into NumPy arrays. These arrays are packed with methods for basic statistical calculations. In this topic, we are going to obtain the results from these calculations and save them in a file.

At the end of the previous chapter, we made an image processing pipeline by combining steps that can be saved on the disk. Here, we will follow the same pattern. The statistical computation will be added as another step. Maintaining the same kind of organization allows the user to generate statistics at any point on the processing pipeline. It will be possible to save statistics from all the substeps if needed.

Let's start by organizing our code:

1. As we do at the beginning of every chapter, we will copy the code from the previous chapter. In your `geopy` project folder, copy the `Chapter 6` folder (*Ctrl* + *C*) and paste it (*Ctrl* + *V*). Name the copied folder as `Chapter7`.

    In the last chapter, we finished the `RasterData` class inside the `image_experiments.py` file. Since our experiments are over, let's move this class to a permanent and meaningful location.

2. Copy the file `Chapter7/experiments/image_experiments.py` (*Ctrl* + *C*).
3. Select the `Chapter7` folder and paste the file there (*Ctrl* + *V*).
4. Rename the file to `raster_data.py`. To do this, right-click on the file and select **Refactor | Rename...** or select the file and press *Ctrl* + *F6*. The refactor dialog will appear. Change the name in the dialog and click on the **Refactor** button. There are two checkboxes in the dialog asking whether you want to search for this file's references. If they are checked (on), PyCharm will search and automatically change these references, so the code will continue to work.
5. Remove the `image_experiments.py` file, as it won't be of use anymore.

Now that our code is organized, we are going to analyze a few aspects and review some points in order to plan our next step.

Let's take an instance of your `RasterData` class that has a base working pattern, as it is now:

- At the instancing moment, you can pass the data or you can import the data later. After this, the data will be stored as a NumPy array in the `data` property.
- When you run any method in the class, the operation is performed and the data is transformed if it's the case and the instance itself is returned along with the new data.
- No information is stored in the class, other than the data. And by consequence, some methods need to take manually defined parameters.
- The `data` property is a NumPy array, so it has all the NumPy array methods.

Preparing the data

The sample data that we will be using is composed of four images containing elevation data. The processing pipeline combines these images, adjusts the values to display on a map, cuts the image, and then generates the shaded relief image.

This pipeline is good for visualization, but data is lost in the moment we adjust the values. For this work, we don't want that to happen. We want the original values in meters. So, the first thing we need to do is build a pipeline adequate for our needs, and in the end, save the results, so we don't need to repeat all the steps in the following tests:

1. Open the `raster_data.py` file for editing, and at the end of it, add the `if __name__ == '__main__':` block with the following code:

   ```
   if __name__ == '__main__':
       elevation_data = [
           '../data/ASTGTM2_S22W048_dem.tif',
           '../data/ASTGTM2_S22W047_dem.tif',
           '../data/ASTGTM2_S23W048_dem.tif',
           '../data/ASTGTM2_S23W047_dem.tif']
       roi = (-46.8, -21.7, -46.3, -22.1)  # Region of interest.
       iex = (-48, -21, -46, -23)  # Image extent.

       data = RasterData(elevation_data, shape=(2, 2))
       data.crop_image(iex, roi).write_image(
           'output/dem.tif')
   ```

   This is very similar to what we did before, but the pipeline was simplified to combining the images and cropping and writing the results in the `dem.tif` file. It was chosen as a TIFF file, so the information isn't lost due to data compression.

2. Run the code. Remember that because it's a new file, you need to click on **Run** or press *Alt* + *Shift* + *F10* and choose `raster_data`. You should see an output telling you that everything went fine:

   ```
   Process finished with exit code 0
   ```

From now on, we can use the prepared image in `output/dem.tif` for our tests. This is simply a matter of speeding up the process. What we are going to do could be done in any `RasterData` instance.

If, by any reason, you couldn't generate `dem.tif`, copy the one provided with the sample data to your `output` folder.

Extract Information from Raster Data

Printing simple information

The first step for us to get some statistical output is to explore what NumPy has to offer. As we know, the `data` property of a `RasterData` instance is a NumPy array, so let's see what we can get from it:

1. First, check whether everything is working so far. Clean the `if __name__ == '__main__':` block and add this new code:

   ```
   if __name__ == '__main__':
       raster_data = RasterData('output/dem.tif')
       print raster_data.data
   ```

2. Run the code with *Shift + F10*. You should see this output:

   ```
   [[ 933  935  942 ...,  1077 1076 1078]
    [ 936  939  945 ...,  1075 1079 1076]
    [ 935  939  946 ...,  1064 1072 1075]
    ...,
    [ 780  781  781 ...,  1195 1193 1193]
    [ 781  784  782 ...,  1191 1189 1188]
    [ 781  784  785 ...,  1187 1185 1184]]

   Process finished with exit code 0
   ```

   This is the array containing the data in meters. NumPy automatically suppressed some rows and columns to make the output smaller. You see this output because a NumPy array has a `__repr__` method that tells what is to be shown when the print function is called.

   As we did before with the vector data, we will customize the `__repr__` method of our class, so it outputs some information from the data in it.

3. Edit the `RasterData` class and insert the `__repr__` method right after the `__init__` method:

   ```
   class RasterData(object):
       def __init__(self, input_data, unchanged=True, shape=None):
           ...

       def __repr__(self):
           return "Hi, I'm a raster data!"
   ```

4. Now, edit the `if __name__ == '__main__':` block and make it print the `RasterData` instance directly:

   ```
   if __name__ == '__main__':
       raster_data = RasterData('output/dem.tif')
       print raster_data
   ```

5. Run the code and see whether you get this output:

   ```
   Hi, I'm a raster data!

   Process finished with exit code 0
   ```

OK, nothing fancy here. It's just to remember that __repr__ takes no arguments except the instance (self) and should return only a string. Also, the method's position in the class makes no difference. We are placing it after the __init__ method for organization. All the *magic* methods go together at the beginning of the class.

Now that we have everything set, let's explore the NumPy array in the data property.

In order to avoid repetition, I'll suppress the class' declaration and the __init__ method in the code and replace it by #....

1. Edit the __repr__ method to look as follows:

   ```
   # ...
       def __repr__(self):
           if self.data is None:
               return "No data to display!"

           data = self.data
           min = "Min: {}".format(data.min())
           mean = "Mean: {}".format(data.mean())
           max = "Max: {}".format(data.max())

           return "Hi, I'm a raster data!\n {} {} {}".format(
               min, mean, max)
   ```

   The first thing is to avoid an exception if the data is empty (None). In this case, the method prints a nice message telling that the instance has no data. If the instance has data, then it prepares three strings with the minimum, mean, and maximum values by calling the respective methods. In the end, a string is formatted to contain all the information.

2. Run the code with *Shift + F10*. You should see this output:

   ```
   Hi, I'm a raster data!
   Min: 671 Mean: 1139.06559874 Max: 1798

   Process finished with exit code 0
   ```

That's great! Now, we have some statistical information on our data.

[195]

Extract Information from Raster Data

But this code is clumsy and if we want to add or remove information returned from `__repr__`, we need to do a lot of editing. So, before we proceed on to obtaining more statistics, we will make a few changes and automate the process of formatting the information that we want to display.

Formatting the output information

At this point, we are displaying three parameters in a simple string output. We want to improve this code, so we can easily add or remove parameters from the output.

Before we modify the code, let's think ahead and foresee that we may also need to output these statistics in other formats, for example:

- To a file on the disk in a human-friendly format
- To a file on the disk in a computer-friendly format, such as CSV or JSON
- As parameters to be passed to the other function or method

So, a good way we can prepare the code to fulfill these requirements is to separate the statistic generation from the output as follows:

1. First, separate the data verification from the `__repr__` method. Create a new method to handle this task:

    ```
    # ...
        def _check_data(self):
            """Check if has data and if it's a Numpy array."""
            if self.data is None:
                raise ValueError("No data defined.")
            elif not isinstance(self.data, np.ndarray):
                raise TypeError("Wrong type of data.")
    ```

    The verification is more rigorous and it raises different types of exceptions for each possible failure. This makes the code mode useful and safe, because it allows error-handling to be done in the other functions and because it stops the program's execution if the exception is not properly caught.

2. Now, create a new method to calculate and collect the statistics that we have so far:

    ```
    # ...
        def _calculate_stats(self):
            """Calculate and return basic statistical information from
            the data.
            """
            self._check_data()
            data = self.data
    ```

Chapter 7

```
        stats = {
            "Minimum": data.min(),
            "Mean": data.mean(),
            "Maximum": data.max()}
        return stats
```

Here, the statistics are stored in a dictionary for two reasons: it allows the items to have readable names (including accents and spaces if you wish) and it avoids name collisions.

Finally, it lets us prepare a human-readable output with the statistics calculated. For this, we will use the `tabulate` module.

3. Insert this import at the beginning of the file:

```
# coding=utf-8


import cv2
import numpy as np
from tabulate import tabulate
```

4. Add this new method:

```
# ...
    def _format_stats(self, stats, out_format='human'):
        """Format the statistical data in a given output format.

        :param out_format: 'human' or 'csv'
        """
        table = []
        for key, value in stats.iteritems():
            table.append([key, value])
        return tabulate(table)
```

The `tabulate` function takes a list of lists representing a table. It then prepares a string containing a well-formatted table with this data.

5. Finally, edit the `__repr__` method:

```
# ...
    def __repr__(self):
        stats = self._calculate_stats()
        stats = self._format_stats(stats)
        return "Raster data - basic statistics.\n {}".format(stats)
```

[197]

Extract Information from Raster Data

6. Now, run the code again with *Shift + F10*. You should see this output:

   ```
   Raster data - basic statistics.
   -------   -------
   Minimum   671
   Maximum   1798
   Mean      1139.07
   -------   -------

   Process finished with exit code 0
   ```

The presentation is much better now. If we want to add or remove elements, we just need to edit the dictionary in the `_calculate_stats` method.

Calculating quartiles, histograms, and other statistics

We have the minimum, maximum, and mean values for our data. In our case, it is the minimum, maximum, and mean elevation of the given region. In the next few steps, we will obtain more information from our data:

1. Edit the `_calculate_stats` method, adding more items to the dictionary:

   ```
   # ...
       def _calculate_stats(self):
           """Calculate and return basic statistical information from
           the data.
           """
           self._check_data()
           data = self.data
           stats = {
               "Minimum": data.min(),
               "Mean": data.mean(),
               "Maximum": data.max(),
               "Q1": np.percentile(data, 25),
               "Median": np.median(data),
               "Q3": np.percentile(data, 75),
               "Variance": data.var(),
               "Histogram": np.histogram(data)
           }
           return stats
   ```

   You can add any value to the dictionary. Maybe, you can obtain it from a NumPy function or method or from a function developed by you.

[198]

> You can find more information on NumPy statistics in http://docs.scipy.org/doc/numpy/reference/routines.statistics.html and http://docs.scipy.org/doc/numpy/reference/arrays.ndarray.html#array-methods.

2. Run the code with *Shift* + *F10*. You should get more values as the output:

```
Raster data - basic statistics.
---------
Q1          992.0
Q3          1303.0
Minimum     671
Variance    37075.0925323
Histogram   (array([ 83917, 254729,   ..., 44225, 8279, 2068]),
             array([ 671. ,    783.7, ..., 1685.3, 1798.]))
Median      1140.0
Maximum     1798
Mean        1139.06559874
---------   ---------------

Process finished with exit code 0
```

Note in the output that the histogram is composed of two arrays: one containing the number of occurrences and the other containing the top limit for each bin. Since we are dealing with geographic data, it would be better if this information came translated into the amount of area for each interval.

To do this, we just need to multiply the number of currencies (the number of pixels within a given range) by the area represented by each pixel. We will get to this after we prepare a few things in the next topics.

Making statistics a lazy property

Our statistics is working fine and we will make an improvement now. Instead of calculating the statistics that we need all the time, we will calculate it only once and only when it's needed for the first time.

We will use two very useful programming techniques: **lazy evaluation** and **memoization**. Lazy evaluation is when a process or calculation is delayed and only performed when needed. Memoization is when the results of an expensive process are stored for later use to avoid them being recalculated every time we may need them.

Extract Information from Raster Data

Let's see how it works:

1. Add a new `_stats` property to the `__init__` method:
   ```
   class RasterData(object):
       def __init__(self, input_data, unchanged=True, shape=None):
           """Represents a raster data in the form of an array.

           :param input_data: Raster files or Numpy array.
           :param unchanged: True to keep the original format.
           :param shape: When using multiple input data, this param
            determines the shape of the composition.
           """
           self.data = None
           self._stats = None
           if isinstance(input_data, list) \
                   or isinstance(input_data, tuple):
               self.combine_images(input_data, shape)
           else:
               self.import_data(input_data, unchanged)
   ```

   The property name starts with an underscore. Remember that this notation shows that the property should only be accessed from the instance itself. This property will work as a cache to store the statistics.

2. Now add a `property` method that will return the statistics:
   ```
   #...
       @property
       def stats(self):
           if self._stats is None:
               self._stats = self._calculate_stats()
           return self._stats
   ```

   When this property is accessed, it verifies that `if _stats is None`. If so, it calculates the statistics and stores the results into `_stats`. The next time we need it, it only returns what's stored.

   Making a property lazy and adding memoization to it is important when the process to obtain this information is costly. The processing power and time is used only once when the given property is needed.

3. Now, change the `__repr__` method to use this new functionality:
   ```
   # ...
       def __repr__(self):
           stats = self._format_stats(self.stats)
           return "Raster data basic statistics.\n {}".format(stats)
   ```

Creating color classified images

If we want to display image information on a map, we must prepare a visual output of what we got. A common and efficient form of visual representation is to separate values into classes and give each class a different color. In our case, we can split the data into altitude classes. NumPy makes it easy for us. Let's write a method that can be called in the pipeline to get started:

1. Add a new method to the `RasterData` class:

    ```
    #...
        def colorize(self, style):
            """Produces an BGR image based on a style containing
               limits and colors.

            :param style: A list of limits and colors.
            """
            shape = self.data.shape
            limits = []
            colors = []
            # Separate the limits and colors.
            for item in style:
                limits.append(item[0])
                colors.append(self._convert_color(item[1]))
            colors = np.array(colors)
            # Put each color in its limits.
            flat_array = self.data.flatten()
            di_array = np.digitize(flat_array, limits)
            di_array = di_array.reshape((shape[0], shape[1], 1))
            results = np.choose(di_array, colors)
            # Convert from  RGB to BGR.
            results = np.asarray(results, dtype=np.uint8)
            results = cv2.cvtColor(results, cv2.COLOR_RGB2BGR)
            self.data = results
            return self
    ```

    In order to achieve what we want, two important things happen here. First, the data is indexed into classes by NumPy's `digitize` function. Then, each class receives an RGB value with the defined color. This is done using the `choose` function.

    This method takes a `style` as an argument. This style is a list of limits and colors, like a map legend. For example, the `style` can be defined as:

    ```
    style = [[700, "#f6eff7"],
             [900, "#bdc9e1"],
             [1100, "#67a9cf"],
             [1300, "#1c9099"],
             [1800, "#016c59"]]
    ```

Extract Information from Raster Data

This means that all the values below 700 will have the color `"#f6eff7"` and so on. The colors are expressed in hex notations. This notation is popular with web applications and is chosen here because it's short and easy to type or copy.

At this point, note that inside this method, we called the `_convert_color` method that will perform the conversion of the color notation. Let's add this method to the class:

1. Add the `_convert_color` method to the class:

    ```
    #...
        def _convert_color(self, color_code):
            """Converts the color notation.

            :param color_code: A string containing the color in hex
            or JavaScript notation.
            """
            if color_code[0] == "#":
                result = (int(color_code[1:3], 16),
                          int(color_code[3:5], 16),
                          int(color_code[5:7], 16))
            elif color_code[:3] == "rgb":
                result = map(int, color_code[4:-1].split(','))
            else:
                raise ValueError("Invalid color code.")
            return result
    ```

2. Finally, edit the `if __name__ == '__main__':` block to test our code:

    ```
    if __name__ == '__main__':
        raster_data = RasterData('output/dem.tif')
        style = [[700, "#f6eff7"],
                 [900, "#bdc9e1"],
                 [1100, "#67a9cf"],
                 [1300, "#1c9099"],
                 [1800, "#016c59"]]
        raster_data.colorize(style).write_image(
            'output/classified.png')
    ```

3. Run the code and then open the output image to see the results:

Choosing the right colors for a map

The choice of what colors to use in a map is one determining factor as to whether the map would be capable of correctly passing the desired information. In order to choose a good set of colors, some factors should be considered:

- The ability of the human eye to distinguish hues — the classes need to be visually distinguishable, otherwise the map may contain colors that may look the same to some people
- The media that the map will be presented on (for example, paper or screen) — depending on the media, the colors may suffer small changes that may compromise the readability of the map
- Colorblind safety — this is an inclusion measure and it allows the information to be interpreted by a wider audience
- The type of data (for example, sequential or qualitative) — use colors that match what you want to show

Extract Information from Raster Data

There are a number of studies on this subject and the ones made by Cynthia Brewer are very practical and popular among modern map makers. She produced an extensive set of colors to be used in maps and made this information available for use under the name of ColorBrewer.

Let's change the colors of our map with the help of ColorBrewer:

1. Access the http://colorbrewer2.org/ website. You should see this interface:

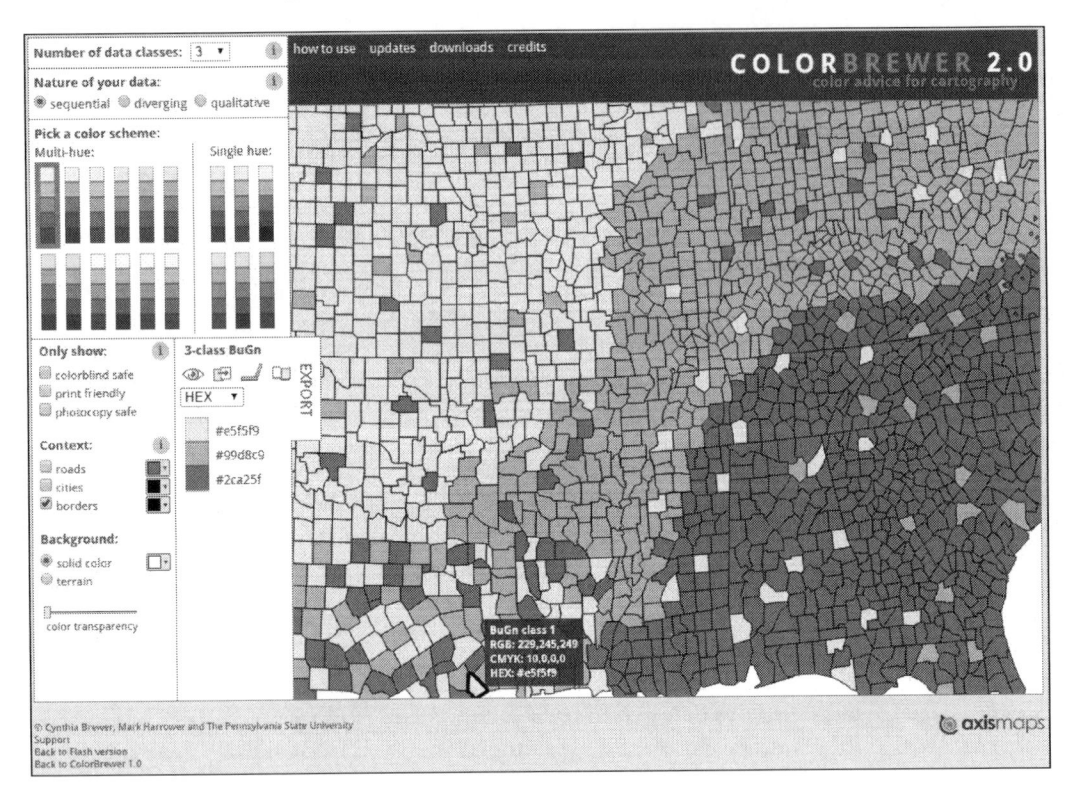

2. The left-hand side panel allows you to set the parameters to choose the color. At the top, change **Number of data classes** to **5** as in our data.

3. About the nature of our data, two options would go well, sequential or diverging. I will choose diverging for this example.

4. Before choosing a color scheme, if you wish, you can filter the schemes by **colorblind safe**, **print friendly** and **photocopy safe**.

5. Now, pick a color scheme that pleases you and note that the bottom right section of the panel and the map will change to show the colors of this scheme.

6. Let's export this scheme in a practical way to it use in our code. Click on the **EXPORT** tab just to the right of the colors. A new panel will open as follows:

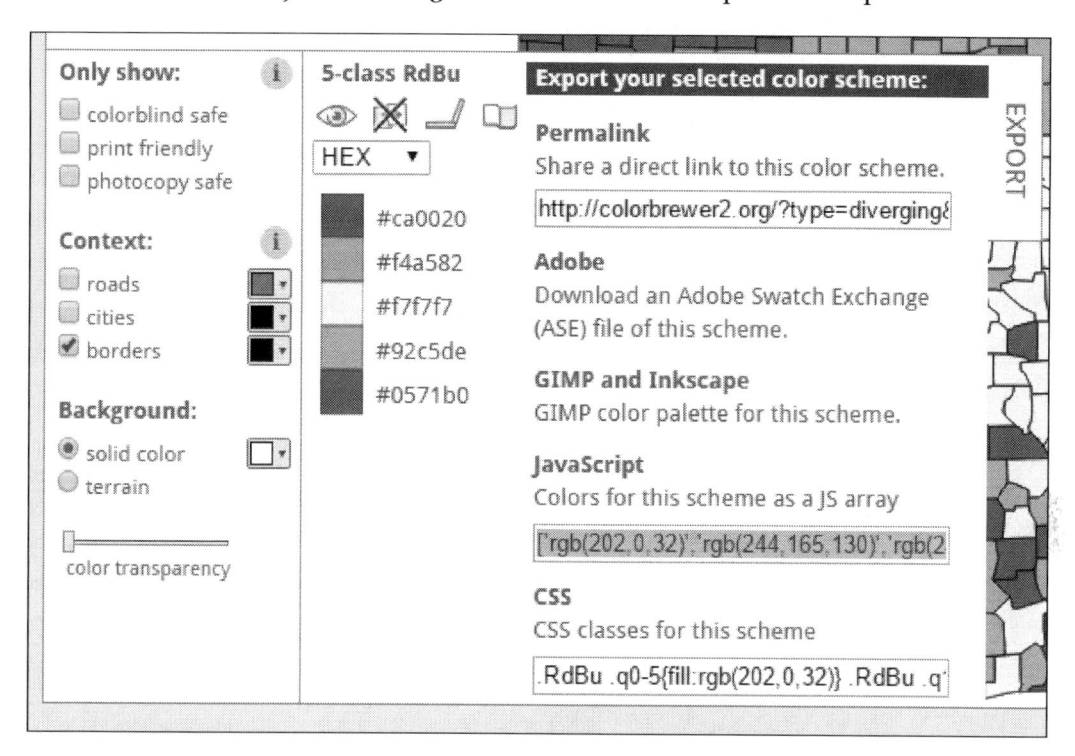

7. Note that the **JavaScript** box contains a list of RGB values. We can easily parse this information in our code. So, we will select its contents and copy it.

8. Go back to our code and paste the colors to a variable named `colorbrewer` in the `if __name__ == '__main__':` block:

```
if __name__ == '__main__':
    colorbrewer = ['rgb(202,0,32)','rgb(244,165,130)',
                   'rgb(247,247,247)','rgb(146,197,222)',
                   'rgb(5,113,176)']
    raster_data = RasterData('data/dem.tif')
    style = [[700, "#f6eff7"],
             [900, "#bdc9e1"],
             [1100, "#67a9cf"],
             [1300, "#1c9099"],
             [1800, "#016c59"]]
    raster_data.colorize(style).write_image(
        'output/classified.png')
```

Extract Information from Raster Data

At this point, the style is not yet complete. There are two problems: the colors are in a format different from what we need and we don't have the limits associated with them. Since we want the process to be as practical as possible, we will write the code to solve these two issues instead of manually converting the colors and associating them with the limits.

First, let's implement the capability of our program to accept colors and limits separately.

9. Put the limits that were in the style definition into a different list:

```
if __name__ == '__main__':
    colorbrewer = ['rgb(202,0,32)','rgb(244,165,130)',
                   'rgb(247,247,247)','rgb(146,197,222)',
                   'rgb(5,113,176)']
    limits = [700, 900, 1100, 1300, 1800]
    raster_data = RasterData('data/dem.tif')
    raster_data.colorize(style).write_image('output/classified.png')
```

10. Now edit the `colorize` method:

```
#..
    def colorize(self, limits, raw_colors):
        """Produces an BGR image based on a style containing
            limits and colors.

        :param limits: A list of limits.
        :param raw_colors: A list of color codes.
        """
        shape = self.data.shape
        colors = []
        for item in raw_colors:
            colors.append(self._convert_color(item))
        colors = np.array(colors)
        # Put each color in its limits.
        flat_array = self.data.flatten()
        di_array = np.digitize(flat_array, limits, right=True)
        di_array = di_array.reshape((shape[0], shape[1], 1))
        results = np.choose(di_array, colors)
        # Convert from RGB to BGR.
        results = np.asarray(results, dtype=np.uint8)
        results = cv2.cvtColor(results, cv2.COLOR_RGB2BGR)
        self.data = results
        return self
```

This method now takes two arguments instead of just the style. The only task that remains is to convert this new color format.

Chapter 7

11. Edit the `_convert_color` method:

    ```
    #...
        def _convert_color(self, color_code):
            """Converts the color notation.

            :param color_code: A string containing the color in hex
            or JavaScript notation.
            """
            if color_code[0] == "#":
                result = (int(color_code[1:3], 16),
                          int(color_code[3:5], 16),
                          int(color_code[5:7], 16))
            elif color_code[:3] == "rgb":
                result = map(int, color_code[4:-1].split(','))
            else:
                raise ValueError("Invalid color code.")
            return result
    ```

    This method is now able to detect and convert the two color codes that we use. It can also raise an exception in case the color code is not recognized.

12. To test the code, edit the `if __name__ == '__main__':` block to be compliant with the new format:

    ```
    if __name__ == '__main__':
        raster_data = RasterData('output/dem.tif')
        colors = ['rgb(202,0,32)', 'rgb(244,165,130)',
                  'rgb(247,247,247)', 'rgb(146,197,222)',
                  'rgb(5,113,176)']
        limits = [700, 900, 1100, 1300, 1800]
        raster_data.colorize(limits, colors).write_image(
            'output/classified.png')
    ```

[207]

13. Finally, run the code with *Shift + F10* and check the output. The schema I chose produced the following result:

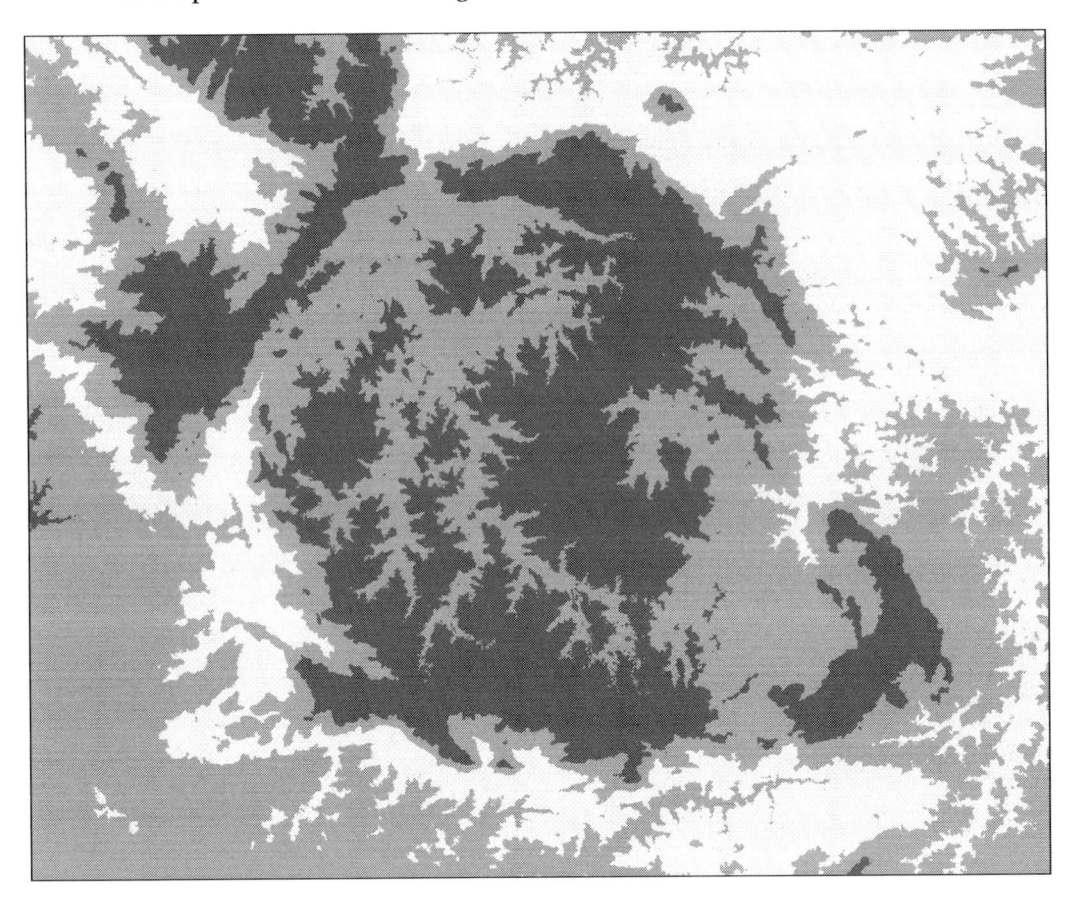

Despite the fact that this is a beautiful image, there is a mistake in the choice of colors. The warm colors are representing lower altitudes. This could lead to confusions, since on most maps, the rule is warmer the color, higher is the value.

It's only a mater of inverting the colors. Let's add an option to our `colorize` method to do this.

14. Edit the `colorize` method:

```
#...
    def colorize(self, limits, raw_colors, invert_colors=False):
        """Produces an BGR image based on a style containing
           limits and colors.

        :param limits: A list of limits.
        :param raw_colors: A list of color codes.
        :param invert_colors: Invert the order of the colors.
        """
        shape = self.data.shape
        colors = []
        if invert_colors:
            raw_colors = list(reversed(raw_colors))
        # Convert the colors.
        for item in raw_colors:
            colors.append(self._convert_color(item))
        colors = np.array(colors)
        # Put each color in its limits.
        flat_array = self.data.flatten()
        di_array = np.digitize(flat_array, limits, right=True)
        di_array = di_array.reshape((shape[0], shape[1], 1))
        results = np.choose(di_array, colors)
        # Convert from  RGB to BGR.
        results = np.asarray(results, dtype=np.uint8)
        results = cv2.cvtColor(results, cv2.COLOR_RGB2BGR)
        self.data = results
        return self
```

15. Now, edit the `if __name__ == '__main__':` block again:

```
if __name__ == '__main__':
    raster_data = RasterData('output/dem.tif')
    colors = ['rgb(202,0,32)', 'rgb(244,165,130)',
              'rgb(247,247,247)', 'rgb(146,197,222)',
              'rgb(5,113,176)']
    limits = [700, 900, 1100, 1300, 1800]
    raster_data.colorize(limits, colors, True).write_image(
        'output/classified.png')
```

Extract Information from Raster Data

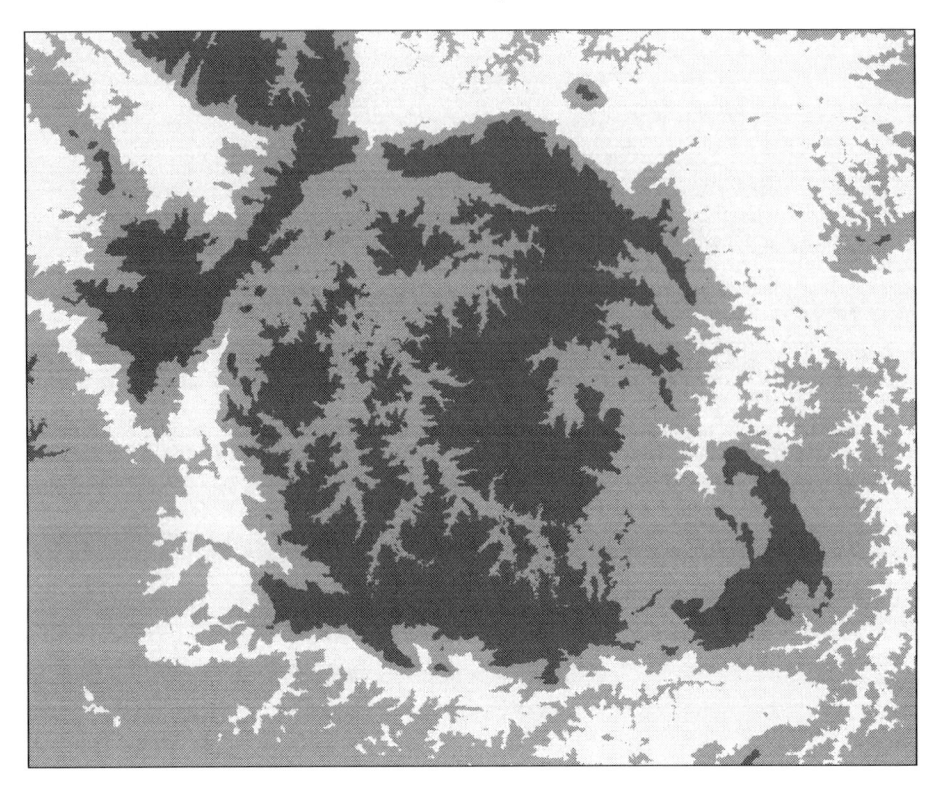

16. Run the code and look at the new output:

Blending images

We can make our results even more visually appealing and informative if we can combine the colorized image with the shaded relief image. Again, since we are dealing with arrays, we may deduce that this kind of composition can be achieved by performing an arithmetic operation between the two arrays.

In image processing, this is called **alpha blending**. Basically, a *transparency* is applied to both of the images and then they are blended into a new one. In the next steps, we are going to create a function that performs this operation:

1. First, to avoid generating the shaded relief multiple times, let's save it on the disk and edit the `if __name__ == '__main__':` block of the `raster_data.py` file:

   ```
   if __name__ == '__main__':
       raster_data = RasterData('output/dem.tif')
       raster_data.adjust_values().create_hillshade(
           10, 60).write_image('output/shaded.png')
   ```

2. Run the code and check whether the image was correctly written on the disk.
3. Now, add the `alpha_blend` method to the `RasterData` class:

   ```
   #...
       def alpha_blend(self, raster_data, alpha=0.5):
           """Blend this raster data with another one.

           :param raster_data: RasterData instance.
           :param alpha: Amount of transparency to apply.
           """
           shade = cv2.cvtColor(raster_data.data, cv2.COLOR_GRAY2BGR)
           result = (1-alpha) * self.data + alpha * shade
           self.data = result
           return self
   ```

4. Finally, edit the `if __name__ == '__main__':` block again to test the code:

   ```
   if __name__ == '__main__':
       shaded = RasterData('output/shaded.png')
       classified = RasterData('output/classified.png')
       classified.alpha_blend(shaded).write_image(
           'output/color_shade.png')
   ```

5. Run the code and check the image in the output folder:

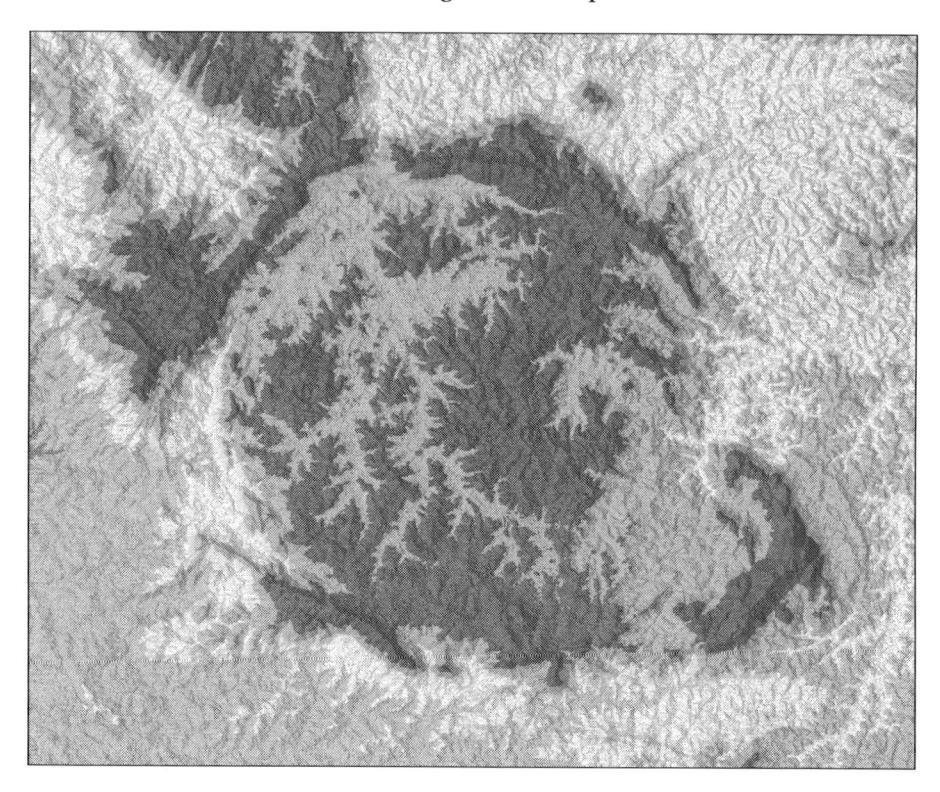

Extract Information from Raster Data

You should see this beautiful output. Note how the combination of the shaded relief with the colorized image produces a map that transmits a lot of information even for untrained eyes.

Showing statistics with colors

How the map is colorized is only a matter of defining the limits and colors in the style. So, if we want to translate statistical information into colors, we just need to associate the values that we want with a sequence of colors.

First, let's try it with the quartiles:

1. Since everything is prepared in our class, we just need to change the code in the `if __name__ == '__main__':` block:

```
if __name__ == '__main__':
    dem = RasterData('output/dem.tif')
    shaded = RasterData('output/shaded.png')
    limits = [dem.stats['Q1'],
              dem.stats['Q3'],
              dem.stats['Maximum']]
    colors = ["#fc8d59", "#ffffbf", "#91cf60"]
    dem.colorize(limits, colors).write_image('output/stats.png')
    dem.alpha_blend(shaded).write_image('output/shaded_stats.png')
```

The following image illustrates the colored output for the analyzed parameters:

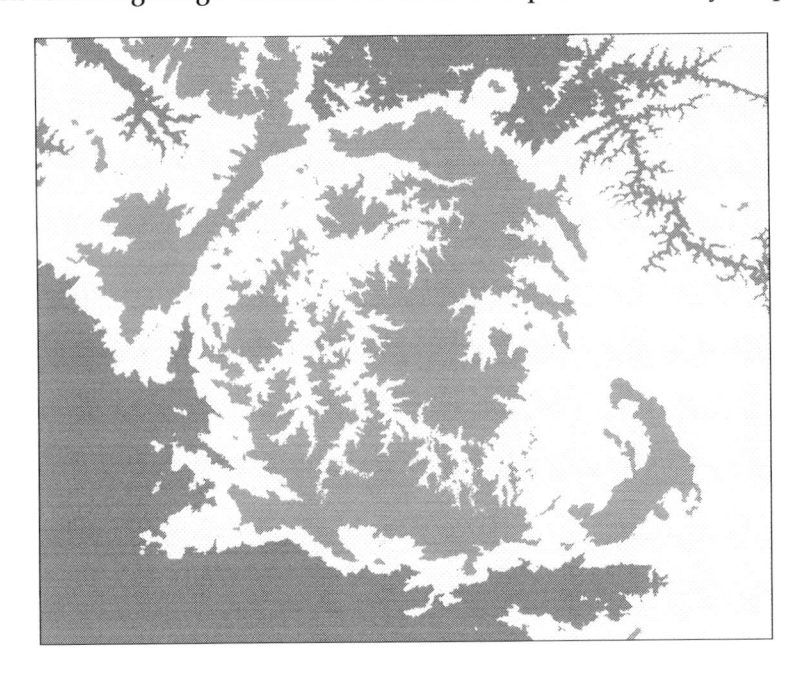

For this image you can start the lead-in this way:

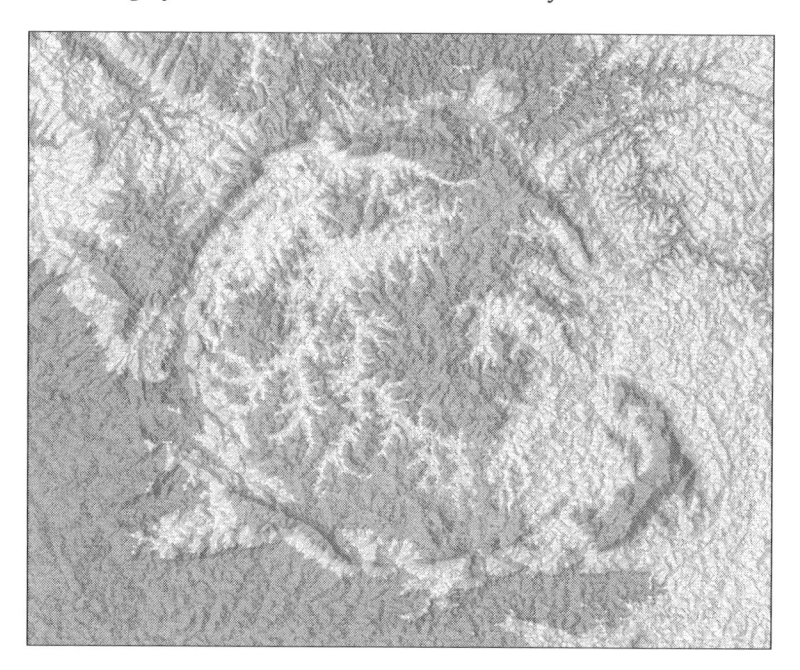

Using the histogram to colorize the image

We can also use the histogram to colorize the maps. The histogram generated by NumPy is composed of two one-dimensional arrays. The first contains the number of occurrences in a given interval (that is, the number of pixels). The second one contains the *bins* or the limits. By default, the histogram is produced with 11 bins, so we also need 11 different colors to produce a map. Let's change our tests to see how this works:

1. Edit the `if __name__ == '__main__':` block:

```
if __name__ == '__main__':
    dem = RasterData('data/dem.tif')
    shaded = RasterData('output/shaded.png')
    colors = ['rgb(103,0,31)','rgb(178,24,43)','rgb(214,96,77)',
              'rgb(244,165,130)','rgb(253,219,199)',
              'rgb(247,247,247)','rgb(209,229,240)',
              'rgb(146,197,222)','rgb(67,147,195)',
              'rgb(33,102,172)','rgb(5,48,97)']

    limits = dem.stats['Histogram'][1]
    dem.colorize(limits, colors, True).write_image('output/hist.png')
    dem.alpha_blend(shaded).write_image('output/shaded_hist.png')
```

Extract Information from Raster Data

The colors here are also obtained from ColorBrewer. They are of a diverging nature from red to blue. The limits were taken from the histogram by simply using the `stats` property and the second array, which contains the bins.

2. Run the code and look at the output.

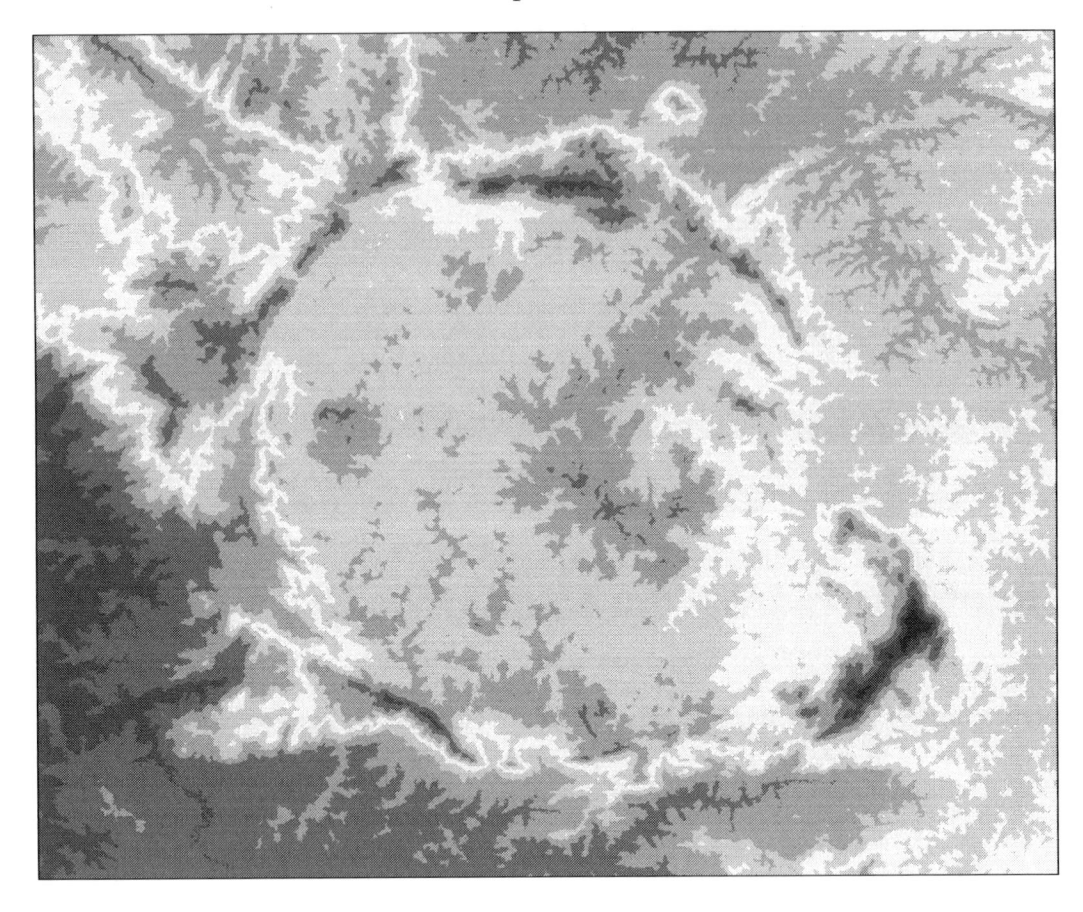

And the shaded result should look as the following image:

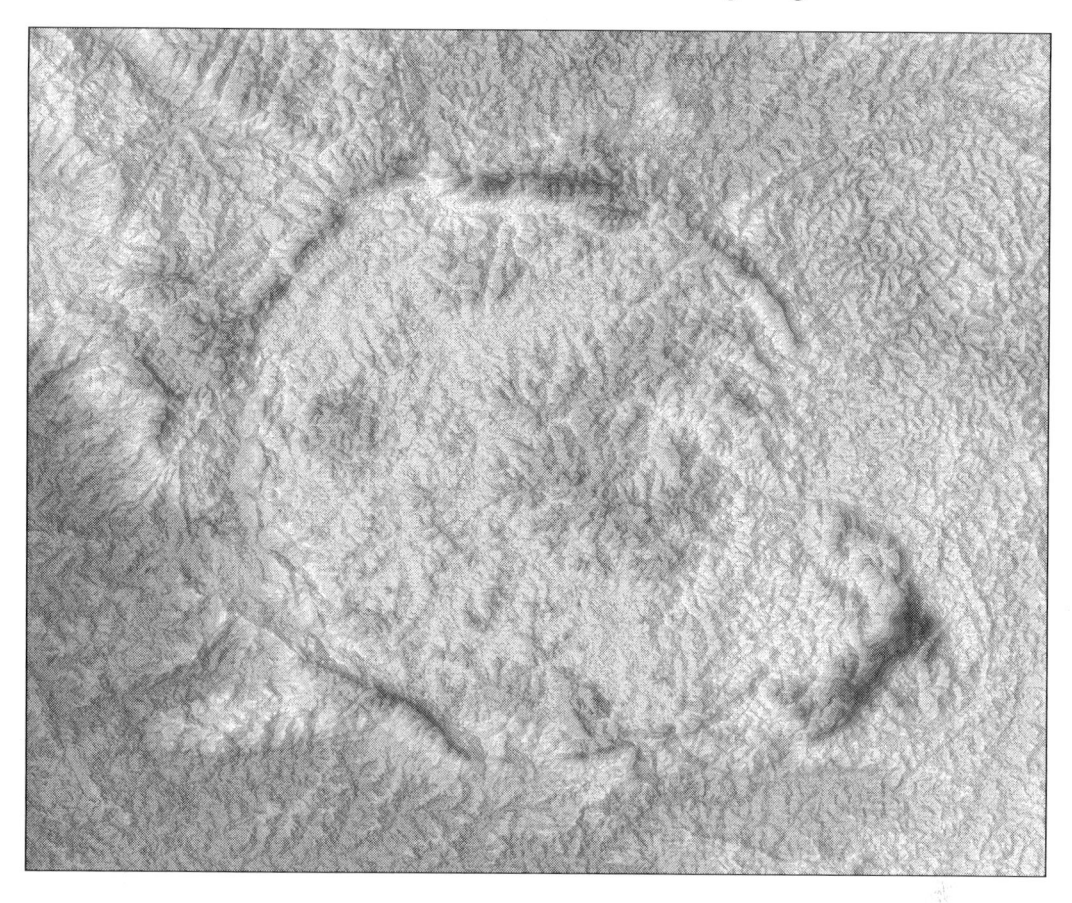

Using more classes resulted in a better representation of the altitude variation and it allowed us to clearly see the peaks with high altitudes.

Summary

In this chapter, we took raw raster data, and with a series of techniques, we were able to extract statistical information from it and display it on high quality maps. These procedures took us to a high level of communication in terms of geospatial information because the material produced is easy to interpret, even for untrained eyes.

In the next chapter, we will enter a new field and start taking care of the efficiency of our code in order to process massive geospatial datasets in a timely manner.

8
Data Miner App

New challenges appear, to the extent that data size increases. Large sets of data bring problems related to excessive processing time and great memory consumption. These problems may turn data analysis into a painful process or may even make it completely impossible.

In this chapter, we will create an application capable of processing huge datasets in an efficient way. We will review our code, implementing new tools and techniques that will make our analysis not only run faster, but also make better use of computer hardware, allowing virtually any amount of data to be processed.

In order to achieve those goals, we will learn how to use databases and how to stream the data into them, making the use of computing power constant and stable regardless of the amount of data.

These tools will also enable us to perform more advanced searches, calculations, and cross information from different sources, allowing you to mine the data for precious information.

This chapter will cover the following topics:

- What code efficiency is and how to measure it
- How to import data into a spatial database
- How to abstract database data into Python objects
- Making queries and getting information from a spatial database
- Understanding code efficiency

What constitutes efficient code depends on the points that are being analyzed. When we talk about computational efficiency, there are four points that may be taken into consideration:

- The time the code takes to execute
- How much memory it uses to run
- How much disk space it uses
- Whether the code uses all the available computing power

Good and efficient code is not only about computational efficiency; it's also about writing code that brings these favorable qualities to the development process (to cite just a few of them):

- Clean and organized code
- Readable code
- Easy to maintain and debug
- Generalized
- Shielded against misuse

It's obvious that some points are contradictory. Here are just a few examples. To speed up a process, you may need to use more memory. To use less memory, you may need more disk space. Alternatively, for faster code, you may need to give up on generalization and write very specific functions.

It is the developer who determines the balance between antagonistic characteristics, based on the software requirements and the gains obtained by investing in one point or another. For example, if much cleaner code can be written with very little penalty in terms of execution time, the developer may opt for clean and maintainable code that will be easier for him and his team to understand.

The second block of good characteristics is prone to human evaluation, whereas the items in the first block can be measured and compared by the computer.

Measuring execution time

In order to measure how fast a piece of code is executed, we need to measure its execution time. The time measured is relative and varies, depending on a number of factors: the operating system, whether there are other programs running, the hardware, and so on.

For our efficiency tests, we will measure the execution time, make changes in the code, and measure it again. In this way, we will see if the changes improve the code efficiency or not.

Let's start with a simple example and measure how long it takes to run.

1. As before, make a copy of the previous chapter folder in your geopy project and rename it as Chapter8. Your project structure should look like this:

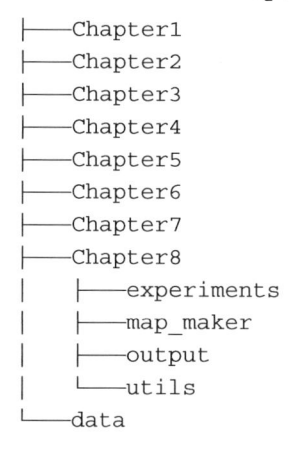

    ```
    ├───Chapter1
    ├───Chapter2
    ├───Chapter3
    ├───Chapter4
    ├───Chapter5
    ├───Chapter6
    ├───Chapter7
    ├───Chapter8
    │   ├───experiments
    │   ├───map_maker
    │   ├───output
    │   └───utils
    └───data
    ```

2. Click on your experiments folder and create a new Python file inside it. Name that file timing.py.

3. Now add the following code to that file:

    ```
    # coding=utf-8


    def make_list1(items_list):
        result = ""
        for item in items_list:
            template = "I like {}. \n"
            text = template.format(item)
            result = result + text
        return result


    if __name__ == '__main__':
        my_list = ['bacon', 'lasagna', 'salad', 'eggs', 'apples']
        print(make_list1(my_list))
    ```

4. Run the code. Press *Alt + Shift + F10* and select a timing from the list. You should get this output:

   ```
   I like bacon.
   I like lasagna.
   I like salad.
   I like eggs.
   I like apples.
   ```

   Nothing fancy, it's a simple inefficient function to format texts and produce a printable list of things.

5. Now we are going to measure how long it takes to execute. Modify your code:

   ```
   # coding=utf-8


   from timeit import timeit


   def make_list1(items_list):
       result = ""
       for item in items_list:
           template = "I like {}. \n"
           text = template.format(item)
           result = result + text
       return result


   if __name__ == '__main__':
       my_list = ['bacon', 'lasagna', 'salad', 'eggs', 'apples']
       number = 100
       execution_time = timeit('make_list1(my_list)',
           setup='from __main__ import make_list1, my_list',
           number=number)
       print("It took {}s to execute the code {} times".format(
           execution_time, number))
   ```

6. Run your code again with *Shift + F10* and look at the results:

   ```
   It took 0.000379365835017s to execute the code 100 times

   Process finished with exit code 0
   ```

Here we are using the `timeit` module to measure the execution time of our function. Since some pieces of code run vary fast, we need to repeat the execution many times to get a more precise measurement and a more meaningful number. The number of times that the statement is repeated is given by the number parameter.

7. Increase your number parameter to `1000000` and run the code again:

    ```
    It took 3.66938576408s to execute the code 1000000 times

    Process finished with exit code 0
    ```

    Now we have a more consistent number to work with. If your computer is much faster than mine you can increase the number. If it's slower, decrease it.

    Grab a piece of paper and take note of that result. We are going to change the function and see if we make the code more efficient.

8. Add another version of our function; name it `make_list2`:

    ```
    def make_list2(items_list):
        result = ""
        template = "I like {}. \n"
        for item in items_list:
            text = template.format(item)
            result = result + text
        return result
    ```

9. Also change your `if __name__ == '__main__':` block. We will make it clear which version of the function we are executing:

    ```
    if __name__ == '__main__':
        my_list = ['bacon', 'lasagna', 'salad', 'eggs', 'apples']
        number = 1000000
        function_version = 2
        statement = 'make_list{}(my_list)'.format(function_version)
        setup = 'from __main__ import make_list{}, my_list'.format(
            function_version)
        execution_time = timeit(statement, setup=setup, number=number)
        print("Version {}.".format(function_version))
        print("It took {}s to execute the code {} times".format(
            execution_time, number))
    ```

[221]

Data Miner App

10. Run the code again and see your results. On my computer, I got this:

    ```
    Version 2.
    It took 3.5384931206s to execute the code 1000000 times

    Process finished with exit code 0
    ```

    That was a slight improvement in execution time. The only change that was made in version 2 was that we moved the template out of the `for` loop.

11. Make a third version of the function:

    ```
    def make_list3(items_list):
        result = ""
        template = "I like "
        for item in items_list:
            text = template + item + ". \n"
            result = result + text
        return result
    ```

12. Change your `function_version` variable to 3 and run the code again:

    ```
    Version 3.
    It took 1.88675713574s to execute the code 1000000 times

    Process finished with exit code 0
    ```

Now we changed how the string `"I like "` is formed. Instead of using string formatting, we added parts of the string and got code that ran almost twice as fast as the previous version.

You can find out which small changes will reduce the execution time by trial and error, by consulting articles on the Internet, or by experience. But there is a more assertive and powerful way to find out where your code spends more time; this is called **profiling**.

Code profiling

By trial, we found that the most expensive part of our code was the string formatting. When your code gets more complex, finding bottlenecks by this method gets harder and at some point becomes impractical.

The solution is to break and analyze small pieces of code. To see how long they take to execute, make a profile of the code.

Python comes with a good profiling tool that automates this process to a certain level. Let's use it on our code to see what it tells us:

1. Add this import at the beginning of the file:
   ```
   from timeit import timeit
   import cProfile
   ```

2. Edit your `if __name__ == '__main__':` block to use the profiler:
   ```
   if __name__ == '__main__':
       my_list = ['bacon', 'lasagna', 'salad', 'eggs', 'apples']
       number = 1000000
       profile = cProfile.Profile()
       profile.enable()
       for i in range(number):
           make_list1(my_list)
       profile.disable()
       profile.print_stats(sort='cumulative')
   ```

3. Run the code. You should see the profiler statistics on the console. (I suppressed some information for reasons of space):
   ```
           6000002 function calls in 4.755 seconds

      Ordered by: cumulative time

      ncalls  tottime  percall  cumtime  percall
      1000000   2.718    0.000    4.738    0.000 timing.py
      5000000   2.019    0.000    2.019    0.000 {'format' ...}
            1   0.017    0.017    0.017    0.017 {range}
            1   0.000    0.000    0.000    0.000 {'disable' ...}
   ```

There are many ways to execute the profiler. In our case, we instantiated the `Profile` class and used the `enable` and `disable` methods to tell the profiler where to start and stop collecting data. Again, the call to `make_list1` was repeated `1000000` times to generate bigger numbers.

In the output, we can see that `make_list1` was called `1000000` times and the `format` method was called five million times, taking `2.019` seconds. Note that the profiler only gave information regarding methods and functions.

Storing information on a database

In the previous chapters, the basic workflow was to import all the data into memory as Python objects every time we ran the code. That's perfectly fine and efficient when we work with small pieces of data.

At some point, you may have noticed that the performance of our code was debilitated, especially when we started importing country boundaries along with all the attributes. This happened because importing attributes is slow.

Secondly, although our filtering mechanisms worked pretty well, we may have problems when dealing with huge datasets.

The formula to solve these problems is very simple and consists of only two basic ingredients:

- Get only what you need
- Use indexed searches

The first point is about getting only the records you need, as well as getting only the attributes that are desired for a given analysis.

The second point is about how things are found. In our method, a loop tests every record for a condition until the desired one is found (that is, the test returns `True`). Alternatively, if the computer somehow had an idea of where the item was, the search would be much faster; this is indexing.

Instead of trying to implement these features by ourselves, we can use a database to handle these mechanisms for us; they are state-of-the-art for this kind of job.

Here we have two options:

- Use a **SQLite** database with the **Spatialite** extension, which is an open source, simple, and very efficient SQL database. It doesn't require a server or installation, and Python comes bundled with a connector to it.
- Use a **PostgreSQL** database with the **Postgis** extension. Also open source and powerful, this is a full-featured database server.

The choice is up to you and will have no influence on the code except for a small change in the settings.

> PostgreSQL can be download from: http://www.postgresql.org/. In order to enable Postgis, you just need to select it in the stack builder during the installation.
>
> If you are using Ubuntu, you can find more details at: https://wiki.ubuntu.com/UbuntuGIS.

Creating an Object Relational Mapping

Object Relational Mapping (ORM) is a method that we will use to convert the data stored in a database into Python objects. This no different from what we did before in our `models.py` file, where we made code that transformed data stored in geographic files (for example, a GPX shapefile) into Python objects.

This time, we will close the circle by importing the data into the database, and then later retrieve data or information from it in the same elegant and intuitive manner as before.

SQL databases, such as SQLite, store the data in tables with row and columns. The following table illustrates how the geocaching data that we previously used would be represented in this format:

ID	Geom	Name	Status	Owner	Hints
1	(wkb)	LaSalle Park	Available	John	Under sign
2	(wkb)	Parking	Available	Nina	Big tree

We can guess that this is incompatible with the premise of being able to import any type of data, because the type of column is fixed. If we have data with different attributes or more attributes, we need different tables or to add more columns to match every possibility.

To overcome the limitation of this schema, we will use the relational capabilities of SQL databases. We will store items and attributes in different tables and relate them:

Points	
ID	Geom
1	42.89 - 78.90
2	43.00 - 78.0

Attributes			
ID	Key	Value	point_id
1	name	LaSalle Park	1
2	status	Available	1
3	owner	John	1
4	hints	under sign	1
5	name	Parking	2
6	status	Available	2

Data Miner App

Attributes			
ID	Key	Value	point_id
7	owner	Nina	2
8	hints	big tree	2

This key/value data model allows each point (or other objects) to have arbitrary numbers and types of attributes. Each attribute is attached to its owner by an ID.

You may have heard of Django, *batteries-included* Python web framework. It happens that Django has a fantastic ORM included in it, and it has very developed support for geospatial databases and geospatial operations (this part of Django is called **GeoDjango** and is included by default). You will also notice that the transition from our models to Django will be smooth and they will remain easy to use, as before.

Preparing the environment

In order to use Django's ORM we need to setup a Django project. To do that we will prepare the minimum required structure, which consists of a few files and settings.

First, let's set up our application to use Django.

1. Inside your `Chapter8` folder, create a new Python file named `settings.py`. If you are using PostgreSQL/Postgis, add the following code to the file:

   ```python
   DATABASES = {
       'default': {
           'ENGINE': 'django.contrib.gis.db.backends.postgis',
           'NAME': 'postgres',
           'USER': 'postgres',
           'PASSWORD': 'mypassword',
           'PORT': 5432
       }}
   ```

   The first item (DATABASES) is the database settings. If you have a default PostgreSQL/Postgis installation, this will work. Just change your password for the one you set during the installation.

2. If you are using SQLite/Spatialite, use this configuration:

   ```python
   DATABASES = {
       'default': {
           'ENGINE': 'django.contrib.gis.db.backends.spatialite',
           'NAME': 'mydatabase.db'
       }}
   ```

3. After the database configuration, add these items:

   ```
   INSTALLED_APPS = ('django.contrib.gis', 'geodata')
   SECRET_KEY = 'abc'
   ```

   The `INSTALLED_APPS` item tells Django where to look for models. `SECRET_KEY` is used for Django's user management. Although we won't use it, this needs to be set (you can use any value as the secret key).

4. Now create a Python package that will be our Django app. Right-click the `Chapter8` folder and select **New | Python Package**. Name it `geodata`.

5. Create a new Python file inside `Chapter8` and name it `geodata_app.py`.

Changing our models

We have the basic structure ready, now we need to adapt our models so they can use the database instead of storing all the information in memory. Django's model definition is very similar to ours.

Using the new capabilities provided by Django, we will make one change in the choice of design: instead of one class for each type of object (geocaching, roads, boundaries, and so on) we will have only one class that can store data for all of them and any others that we can think of.

1. Create a file `models.py` inside the `geodata` folder and add this code:

   ```
   # coding=utf-8


   from django.contrib.gis.db import models


   class GeoObject(models.Model):
       geom = models.GeometryField()
       atype = models.CharField(max_length=20)
       objects = models.GeoManager()
   ```

   The `GeoObject` class represents a single object (a single row in a table). It can accept any kind of geometry (a point, polygon, and so on) in the `geom` field. The `atype` property represents the high-level type of the object. This property will tell us if it's a geocaching point or something else (we are using `atype` and not `type` to avoid conflicts with the internal `type()` function).

   Finally, the `objects` property represents the collection of `GeoObject` (the table in the database). In Django this is called a **manager**; don't worry, we will see more about this later.

Data Miner App

2. Now we need the tags for our `GeoObject`; the tags will contain every attribute. Add another class after the `GeoObject` class.

```
class Tag(models.Model):
    key = models.CharField(max_length=250)
    value = models.CharField(max_length=250)
    geo_object = models.ForeignKey(GeoObject, related_name='tags')
```

Again, this class represents a single object, a single tag with a key and a value that is connected with a GeoObject by a foreign key. The result is that a `Tag` class has a GeoObject and a GeoObject has many tags.

Customizing a manager

As said before, a manager can be considered as something that represents a table in a database. It contains methods to retrieve records, add, delete, and many other operations.

Django comes with the `GeoManager` class that is used for tables that contain spatial objects. If we want to add more functionalities to our GeoData manager, we just need to inherit from `GeoManager` and then add a class property with an instance of it in the `GeoObject` class. Actually, we will just replace the instance in the objects property.

Let's adapt our `BaseGeoCollection` class to be a manager for the `GeoObject` class:

1. Navigate to your `Chapter8/models.py` file (the one that we wrote in previous chapters) and rename it to `Chapter8/old_models.py`. With this, we avoid confusion about which model we are talking about.

2. Create a file named `managers.py` inside the `geodata` folder. Add this code to the file:

```
# coding=utf-8


from django.contrib.gis.db.models import GeoManager
from utils.geo_functions import open_vector_file


class GeoCollection(GeoManager):
    """This class represents a collection of spatial data."""
    Pass
```

[228]

This is the first step in migrating our `BaseGeoCollection` class. Note that we named it `GeoCollection` because it won't be a base class anymore. We will simplify our code so this class will manage all types of geo objects. To do that, we will add the `import_data` method from the `BaseGeoCollection` class and combine it with the `_parse_data` method from the `PointCollection` class. Before we continue, let's take a look at these methods as they are (you don't need to type this code):

```
#...
    def import_data(self, file_path):
        """Opens an vector file compatible with OGR and parses
            the data.

        :param str file_path: The full path to the file.
        """
        features, metadata = open_vector_file(file_path)
        self._parse_data(features)
        self.epsg = metadata['epsg']
        print("File imported: {}".format(file_path))
#...
    def _parse_data(self, features):
        """Transforms the data into Geocache objects.

        :param features: A list of features.
        """
        for feature in features:
            coords = feature['geometry']['coordinates']
            point = Point(float(coords[1]), float(coords[0]))
            attributes = feature['properties']
            cache_point = Geocache(point, attributes=attributes)
            self.data.append(cache_point)
```

Note that `import_data` opens the vector file and then sends the features to `_parse_data`, which iterates over the data, creating points and putting the `feature` properties into a dictionary. If we manage to import any kind of geometry and pass the `feature` properties to the `tag` model, we end with a piece of code that will serve any kind of geospatial object.

3. Edit the code in `geodata/managers.py` again. Whether you want to copy and edit the mentioned methods or type the new `import_data` method from scratch is up to you. The resulting code should be the following:

```
# coding=utf-8

from django.contrib.gis.db.models import GeoManager
```

Data Miner App

```python
from django.db import IntegrityError, DataError
from utils.geo_functions import open_vector_file
from shapely.geometry import shape

class GeoCollection(GeoManager):
    """This class represents a collection of spatial data."""

    def import_data(self, file_path, atype):
        """Opens an vector file compatible with OGR and parses
        the data.

        :param str file_path: The full path to the file.
        """
        features = open_vector_file(file_path)
        for feature in features:
            geom = shape(feature['geometry'])
            geo_object = self.model(geom=geom.wkt, atype=atype)
            geo_object.save()
            for key, value in feature['properties'].iteritems():
                try:
                    geo_object.tags.create(key=key, value=value)
                except (IntegrityError, DataError):
                    pass
        print("File imported: {}".format(file_path))
```

We used Shapley's `shape` function to directly convert `feature['geometry']`, which is a GeoJSON geometry-like dictionary, into a shapely geometry of the correct type. Then we used that geometry to get a WKT representation of it.

The `atype` argument was included on the method, so we can use it to define the type of the `GeoObject`. Remember that `atype` is not a type of geometry; it represents the high-level type of the object (geocaching, boundary, road, river, waypoint, and so on).

In the statement `geo_object = self.model(geom=geom.wkt, atype=atype)`, we see a great feature of Django managers: the same manager can be used by many models, and `self.model` contains a reference to the class that this manager was called from. If we had decided on another design pattern and used one class for each object type, we would still be able to use the same manager for all of them.

In the sequence, the model is saved and then the `properties` dictionary is iterated and for every item a tag is created. We are catching exceptions here because we have two special conditions that may happen: if the value of a property is `None` it will raise an `IntegrityError`; if the length of the value is larger than 250, it will raise a `DataError`. If you are interested in long fields, such as the logs from the geocaching data, you can increase the field `max_length` or try a different field type.

Chapter 8

4. We are not using the metadata here, and reading it can cause an incompatibility error between libraries for Windows users. So we will remove it from the `open_vector_file` function. Edit your `utils/geo_functions.py` file to change this function. As a plus, let's print the number of features read:

```python
def open_vector_file(file_path):
    """Opens an vector file compatible with OGR or a GPX file.
    Returns a list of features and informations about the file.

    :param str file_path: The full path to the file.
    """
    datasource = ogr.Open(file_path)
    # Check if the file was opened.
    if not datasource:
        if not os.path.isfile(file_path):
            message = "Wrong path."
        else:
            message = "File format is invalid."
        raise IOError('Error opening the file {}\n{}'.format(
            file_path, message))
    file_name, file_extension = os.path.splitext(file_path)
    # Check if it's a GPX and read it if so.
    if file_extension in ['.gpx', '.GPX']:
        features = read_gpx_file(file_path)
    # If not, use OGR to get the features.
    else:
        features = read_ogr_features(datasource.
GetLayerByIndex(0))
    print("{} features.".format(len(features)))
    return features
```

5. Finally, edit `geodata/models.py` to import and use the new manager:

```python
# coding=utf-8


from django.contrib.gis.db import models
from managers import GeoCollection


class GeoObject(models.Model):
    geom = models.GeometryField()
    atype = models.CharField(max_length=20)
    objects = GeoCollection()
```

[231]

Data Miner App

```
class Tag(models.Model):
    key = models.CharField(max_length=250)
    value = models.CharField(max_length=250)
    geo_object = models.ForeignKey(GeoObject, related_name='tags')
```

We are almost ready to begin testing. At this point, your `Chapter 8` structure should be like this:

```
+---Chapter8
|       geocaching_app.py
|       geodata_app.py
|       map_maker_app.py
|       models_old.py
|       raster_data.py
|       settings.py
|       settings.pyc
|       __init__.py
|
+---experiments
|
+---geodata
|   |   managers.py
|   |   models.py
|   |   __init__.py
|
+---map_maker
|
+---output
|
\---utils
        check_plugins.py
        data_transfer.py
        geo_functions.py
```

Generating the tables and importing data

Now it's time to make Django generate the database tables for us. Since our models are defined, we just need to call a pair of commands and Django will perform its magic.

1. Go back to the `geodata_app.py` file and add some content to it:

    ```
    # coding=utf-8


    import os
    ```

```
import django

os.environ.setdefault("DJANGO_SETTINGS_MODULE", "settings")
django.setup()

from django.core.management import call_command
from geodata.models import *


def prepare_database():
    """Call this to setup the database or any time you change your
    models.
    """
    call_command('makemigrations', 'geodata')
    call_command('migrate', 'geodata')


if __name__ == '__main__':
    prepare_database()
```

After we import `os` and `django` we need to specify which settings file it should look for. After that, `django.setup()` initializes Django.

The `prepare_database` function calls two Django management commands responsible for database creation. We will need to call it every time we change our models. Internally, Django keeps a record of the changes made and automatically generates SQL queries that perform the modifications on the database.

2. Run your code now. If everything goes fine, you should see the database migration results in the output:

```
Migrations for 'geodata':
  0001_initial.py:
    - Create model GeoObject
    - Create model Tag
Operations to perform:
  Apply all migrations: geodata
Running migrations:
  Rendering model states... DONE
  Applying geodata.0001_initial... OK

Process finished with exit code 0
```

Data Miner App

3. Now, edit `geodata_app.py` again to add a convenience function to import some data. We will begin with the geocaching data as a test:

   ```
   # coding=utf-8


   import os
   import django

   os.environ.setdefault("DJANGO_SETTINGS_MODULE", "settings")
   django.setup()

   from django.core.management import call_command
   from geodata.models import *


   def prepare_database():
       """Call this to setup the database or any time you change your
       models.
       """
       call_command('makemigrations', 'geodata')
       call_command('migrate', 'geodata')


   def import_initial_data(input_file, atype):
       """Import new data into the database."""
       print("Importing {}...".format(atype))
       GeoObject.objects.import_data(input_file, atype)
       print("Done!")

   if __name__ == '__main__':
       # prepare_database()
       import_initial_data("../data/geocaching.gpx", 'geocaching')
   ```

   This new function is only a convenience function to reduce typing since we will import a lot of data very soon. We are commenting the `prepare_database()` statement because we will use it later.

4. Run your code (make sure you run it only once to avoid duplicated entries). In your output you should see this:

   ```
   Importing geocaching...
   112 features.
   Done!

   Process finished with exit code 0
   ```

Filtering the data

Now that we have some data in the database, it's time to test it and see if we can filter some points as we did before.

1. Edit your `if __name__ == '__main__':` block (remember to comment the previous commands):

   ```
   if __name__ == '__main__':
       # prepare_database()
       # import_initial_data("../data/geocaching.gpx", 'geocaching')
       points = GeoObject.objects.filter(atype='geocaching',
                                          tags__key='status',
                                          tags__value='Available')
       print(len(points))
       for tag in points[0].tags.all():
           print(tag.key, tag.value)
   ```

   Here we are using the `filter` method inherited by our manager to filter the records of geocaching type. Plus we are accessing the related tags to filter only the available geocaches. This is done by using a double underscore after the property name. In the end, we print all the tags for the first of the points returned.

2. Run your code and you should see a list of tags like this:

   ```
   224
   (u'type', u'Other')
   (u'hints', u'under sign')
   (u'time', u'2013-09-29T00:00:00Z')
   (u'state', u'New York')
   (u'country', u'United States')
   (u'url', u'http://www.opencaching.us/viewcache.php?cacheid=1728')
   (u'name', u'LaSalle Park No 1')
   (u'container', u'Virtual')
   (u'src', u'www.opencaching.us')
   (u'@xmlns', u'http://geocaching.com.au/geocache/1')
   (u'desc', u'LaSalle Park No 1 by Mr.Yuck, Unknown Cache (1/1)')
   (u'urlname', u'LaSalle Park No 1')
   (u'owner', u'Mr.Yuck')
   (u'difficulty', u'1')
   (u'sym', u'Geocache')
   (u'terrain', u'1')
   (u'status', u'Available')

   Process finished with exit code 0
   ```

Data Miner App

Importing massive amount of data

Now that our environment is ready, we can begin working with bigger datasets. Let's start by profiling the import process and then optimize it. We will start with our small geocaching dataset and after the code is optimized we will move to bigger sets.

1. In your `geodata_app.py` file, edit the `if __name__ == '__main__':` block to call the profiler.

   ```
   if __name__ == '__main__':
       profile = cProfile.Profile()
       profile.enable()
       import_initial_data("../data/geocaching.gpx", 'geocaching')
       profile.disable()
       profile.print_stats(sort='cumulative')
   ```

2. Run the code and see the results. Don't worry about duplicated entries in the database now, we will clean it later. (I removed some information from the following output for space reasons.)

   ```
   Importing geocaching...
   112 features.
   Done!
   1649407 function calls (1635888 primitive calls) in 5.858 seconds

   cumtime   percall  filename:lineno(function)
     5.863    5.863   geodata_app.py:24(import_initial_data)
     5.862    5.862   managers.py:11(import_data)
     4.899    0.002   related.py:749(create)
     4.888    0.002   manager.py:126(manager_method)
     3.621    0.001   base.py:654(save)
     3.582    0.001   base.py:737(save_base)
     3.491    0.001   query.py:341(create)
     1.924    0.001   base.py:799(_save_table)

   ncalls   tottime  percall  cumtime  percall  filename:lineno(function)
        1    0.001    0.001    5.863    5.863  (import_initial_data)
        1    0.029    0.029    5.862    5.862  (import_data)
     2497    0.018    0.000    4.899    0.002  related.py:749(create)
   ```

Take a look at `ncalls` and `cumtime` for each of the functions. The `create` function is called a lot of times and accumulates almost five seconds on my computer. This is the function (method) called when we add a tag to a GeoObject. The time spent on this function is relevant when we import geocaching data because every point has a lot of attributes. Maybe we can make this process more efficient.

Optimizing database inserts

As we saw in the profiler, the method we are using to insert the tags into the database creates a bottleneck when we import geocaching data with our current code. If we can change how it's done, we can make the code run faster.

1. Go to your manager and edit the `import_data` method of the `GeoCollection` **manager**:

    ```
    class GeoCollection(GeoManager):
        """This class represents a collection of spatial data."""

        def import_data(self, file_path, atype):
            """Opens an vector file compatible with OGR and parses
            the data.

            :param str file_path: The full path to the file.
            """
            from models import Tag
            features = open_vector_file(file_path)
            tags = []
            for feature in features:
                geom = shape(feature['geometry'])
                geo_object = self.model(geom=geom.wkt, atype=atype)
                geo_object.save()
                geoo_id = geo_object.id
                for key, value in feature['properties'].iteritems():
                    tags.append(Tag(key=key, value=value,
                                    geo_object_id=geoo_id))
            Tag.objects.bulk_create(tags)
    ```

    Instead of creating the tags one by one, now we add them to a list without hitting the database; only in the end do we call `bulk_create`, which inserts all entries in a single request. Note that the `import` statements for the `Tag` model are inside the function. This will avoid an error with circular imports, because `models` also import the managers.

2. Run your code and see what happens:

    ```
    django.db.utils.DataError: value too long for type character
    varying(250)



    Process finished with exit code 1
    ```

    Since `bulk_insert` sends everything together to the database, we can't catch exceptions for individual tags.

Data Miner App

The solution is to validate the tag before we insert it. At this point we are making a trade-off between generalization and performance because the validation may fail depending on the type of data, whereas the error catching could be triggered by a wide range of reasons.

3. Edit the code again:

```
class GeoCollection(GeoManager):
    """This class represents a collection of spatial data."""

    def import_data(self, file_path, atype):
        """Opens an vector file compatible with OGR and parses
        the data.

        :param str file_path: The full path to the file.
        """
        from models import Tag
        features = open_vector_file(file_path)
        tags = []
        for feature in features:
            geom = shape(feature['geometry'])
            geo_object = self.model(geom=geom.wkt, atype=atype)
            geo_object.save()
            geoo_id = geo_object.id
            for key, value in feature['properties'].iteritems():
                if value and (isinstance(value, unicode)
                        or isinstance(value, str)):
                    if len(value) <= 250:
                        tags.append(Tag(key=key, value=value,
                                    geo_object_id=geoo_id))
        Tag.objects.bulk_create(tags)
```

4. Now run `geodata_app.py` again and look at the profiler results:

```
506679 function calls (506308 primitive calls) in 1.144 seconds
Ordered by: cumulative time
ncalls  cumtime  percall  filename:lineno(function)
     1    1.144    1.144  geodata_app.py:24(import_initial_data)
     1    1.142    1.142  managers.py:12(import_data)
     1    0.556    0.556  geo_functions.py:91(open_vector_file)
     1    0.549    0.549  geo_functions.py:9(read_gpx_file)
     1    0.541    0.541  xmltodict.py:155(parse)
     1    0.541    0.541  {built-in method Parse}
  6186    0.387    0.000  pyexpat.c:566(StartElement)
  6186    0.380    0.000  xmltodict.py:89(startElement)
   112    0.317    0.003  base.py:654(save)
```

[238]

```
    112      0.316    0.003  base.py:737(save_base)
 14/113      0.290    0.003  manager.py:126(manager_method)
  12487     0.278    0.000  collections.py:38(__init__)
    113      0.235    0.002  query.py:910(_insert)
    113      0.228    0.002  compiler.py:969(execute_sql)
   6186     0.178    0.000  xmltodict.py:84(_attrs_to_dict)
      1      0.170    0.170  query.py:356(bulk_create)
```

The import now runs five times faster. Note how the profile changed. The database part of the process felt down on the list and now the most time-consuming part is the conversion from XML (the GPX file) to a dictionary.

Looking at the output, we also see that we have another.

At this point, we have much more efficient code and we won't change how the XML conversion is done. Instead, we will move on to testing and optimizing the process for other types of data.

Optimizing data parsing

Remember that we made a branch in our code to import GPX files, because OGR/GDAL was unable to import the nested data inside those files. So we should expect that when importing shapefiles or GML files, we will have a different profile for code execution time. Let's try it:

1. Now we will test the code with the world borders dataset. Change the `if __name__ == '__main__':` block of `geodata_app.py`:

   ```
   if __name__ == '__main__':
       profile = cProfile.Profile()
       profile.enable()
       import_initial_data("../data/world_borders_simple.shp",
                           'boundary')
       profile.disable()
       profile.print_stats(sort='cumulative')
   ```

2. Run the code:

   ```
   ValueError: A LinearRing must have at least 3 coordinate tuples

   Process finished with exit code 1
   ```

Well, it doesn't work. What is happening here is that Shapely is complaining about the geometry that is being passed to it. This is because this branch of the code is passing a WKT geometry instead of coordinates.

Data Miner App

Django can receive the geometry as a WKT and we are using Shapely for the conversion. This may be a time-consuming step and we are going to eliminate it. At this point, we are just using common sense to optimize the code: the fewer the steps, the faster the code.

1. Edit the `GeoCollection` manager:

   ```
   class GeoCollection(GeoManager):
       """This class represents a collection of spatial data."""

       def import_data(self, file_path, atype):
           """Opens an vector file compatible with OGR and parses
             the data.

           :param str file_path: The full path to the file.
           """
           from models import Tag
           features = open_vector_file(file_path)
           tags = []
           for feature in features:
               geo_object = self.model(geom=feature['geom'],
                                       atype=atype)
               geo_object.save()
               geoo_id = geo_object.id
               for key, value in feature['properties'].iteritems():
                   if value and (isinstance(value, unicode)
                                 or isinstance(value, str)):
                       if len(value) <= 250:
                           tags.append(Tag(key=key, value=value,
                                           geo_object_id=geoo_id))
           Tag.objects.bulk_create(tags)
   ```

   We eliminated the Shapely use (you can remove it from the imports too) and changed how the geometry is retrieved from the dictionary.

2. Now go to `geo_functions.py` and edit the `read_ogr_features` function:

   ```
   def read_ogr_features(layer):
       """Convert OGR features from a layer into dictionaries.

       :param layer: OGR layer.
       """
       features = []
       layer_defn = layer.GetLayerDefn()
       layer.ResetReading()
       type = ogr.GeometryTypeToName(layer.GetGeomType())
   ```

```
    for item in layer:
        attributes = {}
        for index in range(layer_defn.GetFieldCount()):
            field_defn = layer_defn.GetFieldDefn(index)
            key = field_defn.GetName()
            value = item.GetFieldAsString(index)
            attributes[key] = value
        feature = {
            "geom": item.GetGeometryRef().ExportToWkt(),
            "properties": attributes}
        features.append(feature)
    return features
```

As a trade-off between generalization and performance, we changed the `feature` dictionary from the universal GeoJSON format to contain only two keys: `geom` with a WKT geometry and `properties`.

3. Now edit the `read_gpx_file` function so it's compliant with the new format:

```
def read_gpx_file(file_path):
    """Reads a GPX file containing geocaching points.

    :param str file_path: The full path to the file.
    """
    with open(file_path) as gpx_file:
        gpx_dict = xmltodict.parse(gpx_file.read())
    output = []
    for wpt in gpx_dict['gpx']['wpt']:
        geometry = "POINT(" + wpt.pop('@lat') + " " + \
                   wpt.pop('@lon') + ")"
        # If geocache is not on the dict, skip this wpt.
        try:
            geocache = wpt.pop('geocache')
        except KeyError:
            continue
        attributes = {'status': geocache.pop('@status')}
        # Merge the dictionaries.
        attributes.update(wpt)
        attributes.update(geocache)
        # Construct a GeoJSON feature and append to the list.
        feature = {
            "geom": geometry,
            "properties": attributes}
        output.append(feature)
    return output
```

4. Run your code again (you can also test importing points again if you wish, you will get a few milliseconds of improvement). Look at the result:

```
Importing boundary...
245 features.
Done!
90746 function calls (90228 primitive calls) in 5.164 seconds
```

Importing OpenStreetMap points of interest

OpenStreetMap (**OSM**) is a collaborative mapping project where everyone can make an account and collaborate in the map making. It's something like Wikipedia, but instead of articles the community make maps.

The data is all available for download, and some regions have incredibly detailed maps. What we want here is to get **points of interest** (**POI**). These are points that represent the location of restaurants, supermarkets, banks, and so on.

Take a look at the following screenshot of Boulevard Saint-Laurent in Montreal. Each one of those small icons is a POI:

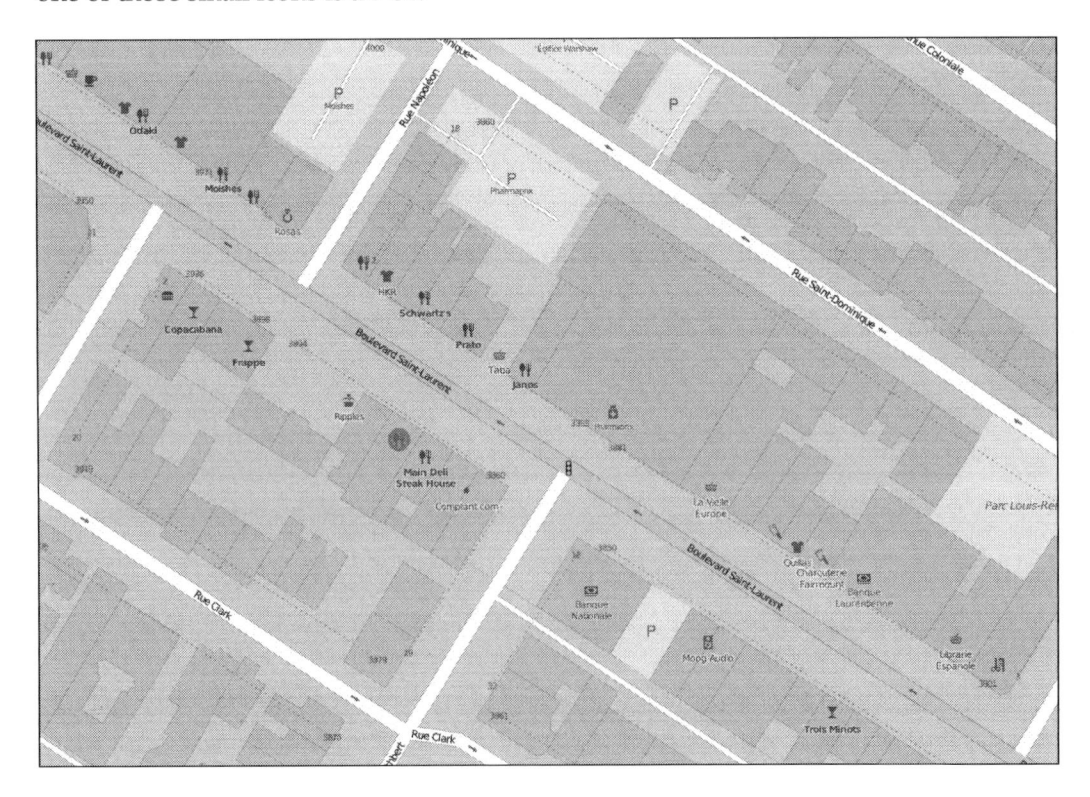

Chapter 8

OSM data can be easily obtained using its API, which is called **Overpass API**. It allows the user to make advanced queries and filter data of interest.

The obtained data is in XML format adapted for OSM needs. We are going to use `overpy`, a Python package that translates this data into Python objects.

At this point, I have to admit that through my career I have been deeply inspired by OSM and its data format. It's simple and yet flexible, to the point where everything in OSM is represented by the same schema.

OSM consists of nodes, a lot of nodes. Actually by this date it had 3,037,479,553 nodes. That's right, more than three billion nodes. Nodes can be points or can be related to other nodes as part of something represented by a line or polygon.

Every node can have an arbitrary number of tags made of key/value pairs, just like our data. Take a look at the information obtained from one of the POI:

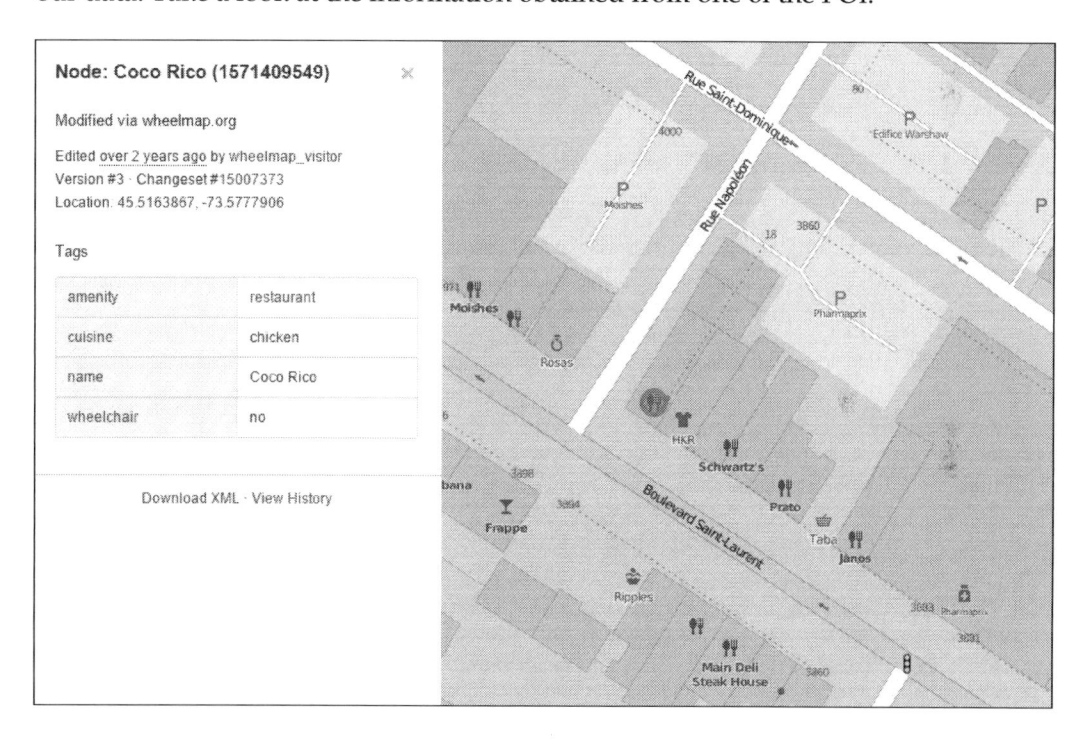

So, storing OpenStreetMap POIs in our database will be pretty straightforward. First, let's create a utility function to download points for a given region of interest.

1. Go to the `utils` folder and create a new Python file named `osm_data.py`.

Data Miner App

2. Add the following code to this file:

```python
# coding=utf-8


import overpy


def get_osm_poi(bbox):
    """Downloads points of interest from OpenStreetMap.

    :param bbox: The bounding box of the region to get the points.
    """
    api = overpy.Overpass()
    result = api.query("""
      <osm-script>
          <query type="node">
            <bbox-query s="{ymin}" n="{ymax}" w="{xmin}" e="{xmax}"/>
            <has-kv k="amenity"/>
          </query>
          <print/>
      </osm-script>
      """.format(**bbox))
    print("Found {} POIs".format(len(result.nodes)))
    return result


if __name__ == "__main__":
    bbox = {"xmin":-71.606, "ymin":46.714,
            "xmax":-71.140, "ymax":48.982}
    result = get_osm_poi(bbox)
    print(result.nodes[0].tags)
```

This is a simple wrapper for `overpy` that queries all points in a given region and has the `amenity` key. In the `if __name__ == '__main__':` block, we make a simple test, get some points, and print the tags of one of them.

> You can get more information on the Overpass API at this site: `http://wiki.openstreetmap.org/wiki/Overpass_API/Language_Guide`.

[244]

Chapter 8

3. Run the code on this file. Remember to press *Alt + Shift + F10* to choose a different file and select `osm_data` in the list. You should get an output like this:

    ```
    Found 3523 POIs
    {'operator': 'Desjardins', 'amenity': 'bank', 'atm': 'yes',
    'name': 'Caisse Populaire Desjardins'}

    Process finished with exit code 0
    ```
    If you don't have overpy installed, just click on it in your code, press Alt + F10 and select "Install Package"

    Now, let's import this data into our database. Open your `manage.py` file. We will create a new method to our `GeoCollection` manager, very similar to `import_data`, but specific to OSM data.

4. Edit your `manage.py` file and add this new method to the `GeoCollection` class:

    ```
    #...
        def import_osm_data(self, result):
            """Import OpenStreetMap points of interest.

            :param str file_path: The full path to the file.
            """
            from models import Tag
            tags = []
            for node in result.nodes:
                geometry = "POINT(" + str(node.lat) + " " + \
                           str(node.lon) + ")"
                geo_object = self.model(geom=geometry, atype="poi")
                geo_object.save()
                geoo_id = geo_object.id
                for key, value in node.tags.iteritems():
                    tags.append(Tag(key=key, value=value,
                                    geo_object_id=geoo_id))

            Tag.objects.bulk_create(tags)
    ```

    We could have reused the code that is common for both `import_data` and `import_osm_data`, but in this chapter we are emphasizing speed and, as was stated earlier, sometimes it's easier to achieve better execution times with specific functions. In this case, we were able to remove the verifications when creating the tags, making the loop run faster.

    Now let's test this new method:

Data Miner App

5. Open the `geodata_app.py` file and add this import at the beginning of the file:

   ```
   from utils.osm_data import get_osm_poi
   ```

6. Now edit the `if __name__ == '__main__':` block:

   ```
   if __name__ == '__main__':
       bbox = {"xmin":-71.206, "ymin":47.714,
               "xmax":-71.140, "ymax":48.982}
       result = get_osm_poi(bbox)
       GeoObject.objects.import_osm_data(result)
       points = GeoObject.objects.filter(atype='poi')
       print(len(points))
   ```

7. Finally, run the code and see if you get an output resembling the following (the number of points may be different for you):

   ```
   Found 14 POIs
   14

   Process finished with exit code 0
   ```

Removing the test data

Before we continue with real imports, let's clean the database of all the data we put into it for testing. Let's make a simple function for this job in our app:

1. In `geodata_app.py`, add this function:

   ```
   def clean_database():
       """Remove all records from the database."""
       from django.db import connection
       cursor = connection.cursor()
       cursor.execute('DELETE FROM geodata_tag;')
       cursor.execute('DELETE FROM geodata_geoobject;')
   ```

   Here we are calling SQL commands directly on the database in order to avoid all Django overheads and get a better performance.

2. Now call it from the `if __name__ == '__main__':` block:

   ```
   if __name__ == '__main__':
       clean_database()
   ```

3. Run the code; it may take a while to finish.

4. Keep it as a resource in case you want to make other tests or if you need to start over.

[246]

Populating the database with real data

Now it's time to put real data into our database. We will import all the data that we used so far, plus additional data:

- Geocaching points (extended version)
- World borders
- Canadian districts borders
- Points of interest in Canada

1. Go to your `geodata_app.py` file and edit the `if __name__ == '__main__':` block:

   ```
   if __name__ == '__main__':
       import_initial_data("../data/canada_div.gml", 'canada')
       import_initial_data("../data/world_borders_simple.shp", 'world')
       import_initial_data("../data/geocaching_big.gpx", 'geocaching')
   ```

This time we are setting more specific types for our data to make our queries easier.

1. Now, run the code to begin importing. In the end you should have this output:

   ```
   Importing canada...
   293 features.
   Done!
   Importing world...
   245 features.
   Done!
   Importing geocaching...
   1638 features.
   Done!

   Process finished with exit code 0
   ```

   Now it's time to fetch points of interest from OpenStreetMap and add them to our database.

2. Add this function to your `geodata_app.py`:

   ```
   def import_from_osm(district):
       # tags = Tag.objects.filter(value="Montreal")
       borders = GeoObject.objects.get(atype='canada',
                                       tags__key='CDNAME',
                                       tags__value=district)
   ```

[247]

```
        extent = borders.geom.extent
        print("Extent: {}".format(extent))
        bbox = {"xmin":extent[0], "ymin":extent[1],
                "xmax":extent[2], "ymax":extent[3]}
        osm_poi = get_osm_poi(bbox)
        GeoObject.objects.import_osm_data(osm_poi)
        print("Done!")
```

This function takes a district name. Get it from our database and use its extent to query the OSM API.

3. Change the `if __name__ == '__main__':` block:

```
if __name__ == '__main__':
    import_from_osm('Montréal')
```

4. Now, run the code. It may take some time to download the data from OSM. When it's done, your output should be something like the following (the number of features may be different):

```
Extent: (-73.9763757739999, 45.4021292300001, -73.476065978, 45.703747476)
Found 5430 POIs
Done!
```

--- Memory Error ----

At this point, you will probably have your first contact with another issue in code optimization: memory consumption. Unless you have a large amount of RAM, you'll be faced with Python's `MemoryError`. This means that your computer ran out of memory while parsing the huge amount of POIs acquired from OSM.

This happened because the whole XML from OSM was parsed into Python objects and later into Django objects, and they were all stored in the memory at the same time.

The solution here is to read one XML tag at a time. If it's a node, put it into the database, get its tags, and release the memory. To do that, we will use a XML file available on the sample data, so we don't need to download it again.

1. Open the `managers.py` file and add this import at the beginning of the file:

```
import xml.etree.cElementTree as ET
```

2. Go to your `GeoCollection` manager and edit the `import_osm_data` method:

```
#...
    #...
    def import_osm_data(self, input_file):
        """Import OpenStreetMap points of interest.
```

```
    :param str input_file: The full path to the file.
    """
    from models import Tag
    tags = []
    tags_counter = 0
    nodes_counter = 0
    xml_iter = ET.iterparse(input_file)
    for event, elem in xml_iter:
        if elem.tag == 'node':
            lat, lon = elem.get('lat'), elem.get('lon')
            geometry = "POINT(" + str(lat) + " " + str(lon) + ")"
            geo_object = self.model(geom=geometry, atype="poi")
            geo_object.save()
            geoo_id = geo_object.id
            nodes_counter += 1
            if nodes_counter % 10000 == 0:
                print("{} Nodes...".format(nodes_counter))
                print("Creating tags...")
                Tag.objects.bulk_create(tags)
                tags = []
            for child_tag in elem:
                key = child_tag.get('k')
                value = child_tag.get('v')
                if len(value) <= 250:
                    tags.append(Tag(key=key,
                                    value=value,
                                    geo_object_id=geoo_id))
                    tags_counter += 1
            elem.clear()
    print("Creating tags...")
    Tag.objects.bulk_create(tags)
    print("Imported {} nodes with {} tags.".format(
        nodes_counter, tags_counter))
    print("Done!")
```

ElementTree is a Python module designed for XML parsing; `cElementTree` has the same functionality but is implemented in C. The only restriction on using `cElementTree` is when C library loading is not available, which is not the case here.

Note that the solution to optimizing tag creation is to accumulate the tags in a list, bulk-create tags every 10,000 nodes, and then clear the list.

Data Miner App

3. Edit the `if __name__ == '__main__':` block of the `geodata_app.py` file to test the code:

   ```
   if __name__ == '__main__':
       GeoObject.objects.import_osm_data("../data/osm.xml")
   ```

4. Now run it. While you wait, you can open the Windows Task Manager, or the system monitor on Ubuntu, and see how your computer resources are being consumed and/or watch the progress in the console output:

   ```
   10000 Nodes...
   Creating tags...
   20000 Nodes...
   Creating tags...
   30000 Nodes...
   Creating tags...
   40000 Nodes...
   Creating tags...
   50000 Nodes...

   ...

   Imported 269300 nodes with 1272599 tags.
   Done!
   ```

If you were watching your computer resources, you should have seen that the memory consumption fluctuated around some value. As the memory didn't keep increasing as more and more nodes were imported, we would be able to import virtually any given number of points on files of any size because the code is stable and has no memory leaks.

On my computer, Python consumed something around 100 Mb of memory during the program execution. The processor cores stayed mostly at 5% of load (Python and PostgreSQL) and the hard drive was 100% occupied with database writing.

It would be possible to tweak the database for a better performance, but this is beyond the scope of this book.

Remember that, if you want to make more tests, you can always clean the database with the function that we created before. Just remember to import all the data again before we continue.

Searching for data and crossing information

Now that we have our database populated with some data, it's time to get some information from it; let's explore what kind of information all those POIs hold. We know that we downloaded points that contain at least one of the `amenity` or `store` keys.

Amenities are described by OSM as any type of community facilities. As an exercise, let's see a list of amenity types that we got from the points:

1. Edit your `geodata_app.py` file's `if __name__ == '__main__':` block:

    ```
    if __name__ == '__main__':
        amenity_values = Tag.objects.filter(
            key='amenity').distinct('value').values_list('value')
        for item in amenity_values:
            print(item[0])
    ```

    Here we take the `Tag` model, access its manager (objects), then filter the tags whose `key='amenity'`. Then we separate only distinct values (exclude repeated values from the query). The final part—`values_list('value')`—tells Django that we don't want it to create `Tag` models, we only want a list of values.

2. Run the code, and take a look at the huge list of amenity types:

    ```
    atm, fuel
    atm;telephone
    audiologist
    auditorium
    Auto Body Repair Shop
    auto_club
    automobile_club
    baby_hatch
    bail_bonds
    bakery
    ball_washer
    ballet
    bandshell
    bank
    bank_construction
    banquet_hall
    bar
    bar/food
    ```

```
barber
barbershop
bathroom
bbq
beauty
Beauty Services
bell_tower
bench
betting
bicycle_dirt jumping
bicycle_parking
bicycle_parking; bicycle_rental
bicycle_parking;bank
bicycle_rental

...
```

You can also spot some misuse of this OSM tag as people mistakenly put street names, business names, and so on instead of the amenity type.

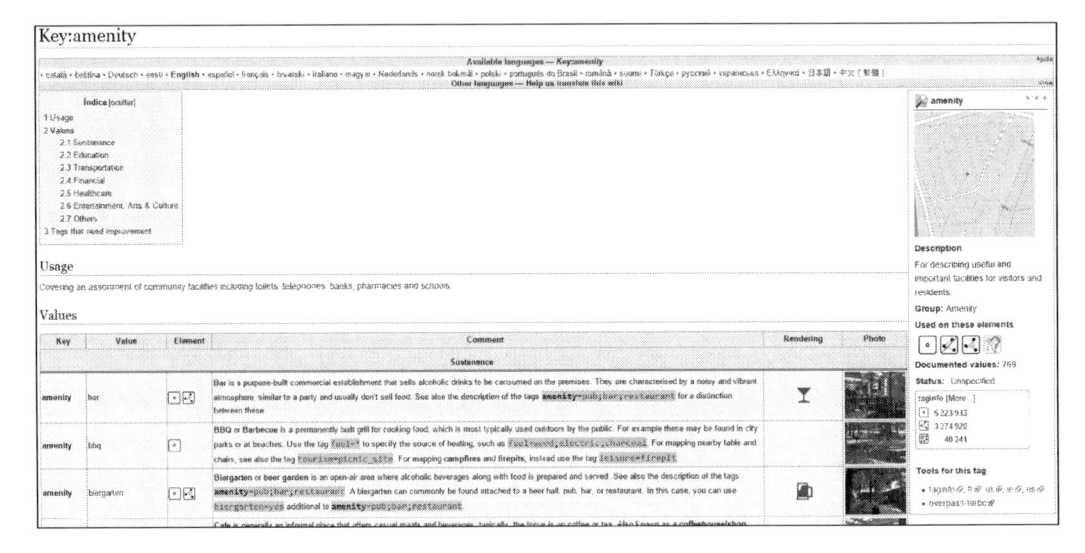

> For a list of common amenity types, you can check the OpenStreetMap wiki: `http://wiki.openstreetmap.org/wiki/Key:amenity`.

Filtering using boundaries

Now, let's try getting only the amenities that are at Montréal. The procedure is similar to what we did before. We will use one of the known predicates to filter objects by a geometry relationship, but this time the searches are powered by the database and spatial indexes, making them incredibly fast.

> Take a look at the *Geometry relationships* section in *Chapter 4*, *Improving the App Search Capabilities* for a list of predicates.

```
if __name__ == '__main__':
    # Get Montreal object.
    montreal = GeoObject.objects.get(atype='canada',
                                     tags__key='CDNAME',
                                     tags__value='Montréal')

    # Filter tags whose POI is within Montreal.
    amenities = Tag.objects.filter(
        key='amenity', geo_object__geom__within=montreal.geom)

    # Filter only the distinct values.
    amenities = amenities.distinct('value')

    # Get the list of 'values'
    amenity_values = amenities.values_list('value')

    for item in amenity_values:
        print(item[0])
```

Here I separated each part into a different statement to facilitate understanding.

It doesn't make any difference if you put everything together or keep it separated, Django query sets are lazy (somewhat like what we did in *Chapter 7*, *Extract Information from Raster Data*), and they are evaluated only when a value is needed. This means that Django will only hit the database once when we start iterating through the values (`for item in amenity_values`).

1. Run the code. You should get a more modest list of amenity types:

   ```
   arts_centre
   atm
   audiologist
   bakery
   bank
   bar
   ```

Data Miner App

```
bbq
bench
bicycle_parking
bicycle_rental
billboard
bureau_de_change
bus_station
cafe
car_rental
car_repair
car_sharing
car_wash
childcare
cinema
city_hall
clinic
clock
college
```

...

Now, let's find out how many cinemas (movie theatres) we can find in Montreal:

2. Edit the `if __name__ == '__main__':` block:

```
if __name__ == '__main__':
    montreal = GeoObject.objects.get(atype='canada',
                                     tags__key='CDNAME',
                                     tags__value='Montréal')

    cinemas = GeoObject.objects.filter(atype='poi',
                                       geom__within=montreal.geom,
                                       tags__key='amenity',
                                       tags__value='cinema')
    print("{} cinemas.".format(cinemas.count()))
```

> Note that we are using the `count` method instead of Python's `len` function. This makes the counting happen on the database and only the output value is returned. This is much faster than getting all the objects and then counting with Python.

3. Now run it and check the output:

   ```
   16 cinemas.

   Process finished with exit code 0
   ```

Summary

In this chapter, we explored introductory concepts about code efficiency and how to measure it. Equipped with the right tools, we optimized our code to make it run faster.

Instead of storing data into Python objects, we turned to SQL databases. We thereby enhanced our app with state-of-the-art filtering and got information in an efficient way.

Later, we came across a large amount of data that was impossible to import with ordinary computers. We optimized our code again, making it memory-efficient and stable, allowing us to import this data. Finally, we queried the data, testing the new feature capabilities.

In the next chapter, we will face similar speed and memory problems but with images (raster) data. This will require us to develop new and creative solutions.

9
Processing Big Images

Processing satellite images (or other remote sensing data) is a computational challenge for two reasons: normally, the images are big (many megabytes or gigabytes) and many images are needed in combination to produce the desired information.

Opening and processing many big images can consume a lot of computer memory. This condition sets a tight limit on what the user can do before running out of memory.

In this chapter, we will focus on how to perform sustainable image processing and how to open and make calculations with many big images while keeping the memory consumption low with efficient code.

The following topics will be covered:

- An introduction to satellite images and Landsat 8 data
- How to select and download Landsat 8 data
- What happens to the computer memory when we work with images?
- How to read images in chunks
- What are Python iterators and generators?
- How to iterate through an image
- How to create color compositions with the new techniques

Working with satellite images

Satellite images are a form of remote sensing data. They are composed of the information collected by satellites and are made available to users as image files. Just like the digital elevation model that we worked on before, these images are made of pixels, each one representing the value of a given attribute for a given geographic extent.

Processing Big Images

These images can be used to visualize features on Earth using real colors or they can be used to identify a variety of characteristics using parts of the light spectrum invisible to the human eyes.

In order to follow the examples, we will use images from the Landsat 8 satellite. They are available for free on the Internet. Let's take a look at some of the characteristics of this satellite.

Landsat 8 carries two instruments: the **Operational Land Imager (OLI)** and the **Thermal Infrared Sensor (TIRS)**.

These sensors can collect data in a total of 10 different bands processed in a resolution of 4096 possible levels (12-bit). The data is encoded into 16-bit TIFF images scaled to 55000 possible values.

Bands	Wavelength (micrometers)	Resolution (meters)	Common uses
Band 1 – Coastal aerosol	0.43 - 0.45	30	Shallow coastal water studies and estimation of the concentration of aerosols in the atmosphere
Band 2 – Blue	0.45 - 0.51	30	Visible blue channel, distinguish soil from vegetation

Bands	Wavelength (micrometers)	Resolution (meters)	Common uses
Band 3 — Green	0.53 - 0.59	30	Visible green channel
Band 4 — Red	0.64 - 0.67	30	Visible red channel
Band 5 — Near Infrared (NIR)	0.85 - 0.88	30	Biomass estimation
Band 6 — SWIR 1	1.57 - 1.65	30	Soil moisture
Band 7 — SWIR 2	2.11 - 2.29	30	Soil moisture
Band 8 — Panchromatic	0.50 - 0.68	15	Sharper resolution
Band 9 — Cirrus	1.36 - 1.38	30	Detection of cirrus cloud contamination
Band 10 — Thermal Infrared (TIRS) 1	10.60 - 11.19	30	Thermal mapping and estimating soil moisture
Band 11 — Thermal Infrared (TIRS) 2	11.50 - 12.51	30	Thermal mapping and estimating soil moisture

Getting Landsat 8 images

Landsat 8 images are available freely on the Internet and there are some nice tools to find and download these images. For the book, we will use **U.S Geological Survey (USGS)** EarthExplorer. It's a web app packed with resources to obtain geographic data.

In order to follow the book's examples, we will download data for the same Montreal (Quebec, Canada) area that we obtained the points of interest of the previous chapter. This data is included in the book's sample data and you can skip these steps if you wish.

Processing Big Images

First, we will open the website and select our region of interest as follows:

1. Go to the `http://earthexplorer.usgs.gov/` website. You will see a map, some options at the top, and a panel with search tools on the left-hand side:

2. At the top right, you will see a **Login/Register** button. If you don't have an account, click on **Register** and create a new one. Otherwise, log in to the system.

3. The next step is to search for the location of interest. You can search by entering `Montreal` in the box and clicking on **Show**. A list will appear with the search results. Click on **Montreal** on the list. A marker will appear and the coordinates will be set.

4. Click on the **Data Sets** button to show the available data for this coordinate.

Chapter 9

5. On the next screen, expand the **Landsat Archive** item, select **L8 OLI/TIRS**, and click on the **Additional Criteria** button.

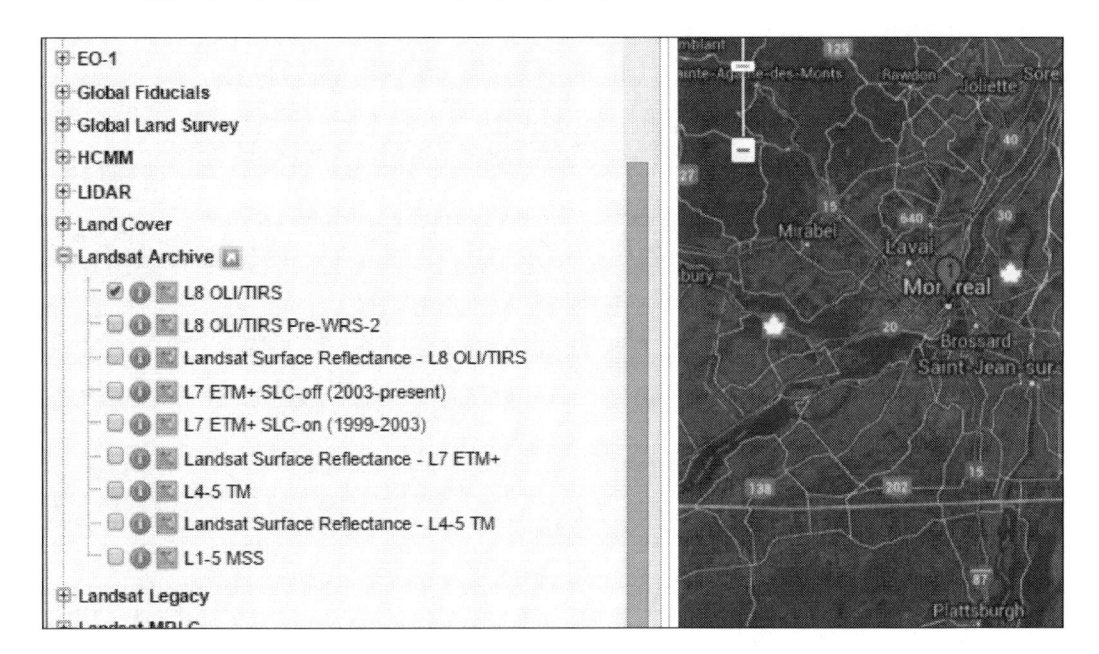

6. Now, let's make sure that we get images with little cloud cover. Use the scroll bar to find the **Cloud Cover** item and select **Less than 10%**. Now, click on **Results** to see what was found.

[261]

Processing Big Images

7. A new tab will open showing the results. Note that each item contains a small toolbar with a set of icons. Click on the feet icon of some of the images to see their extent on the map:

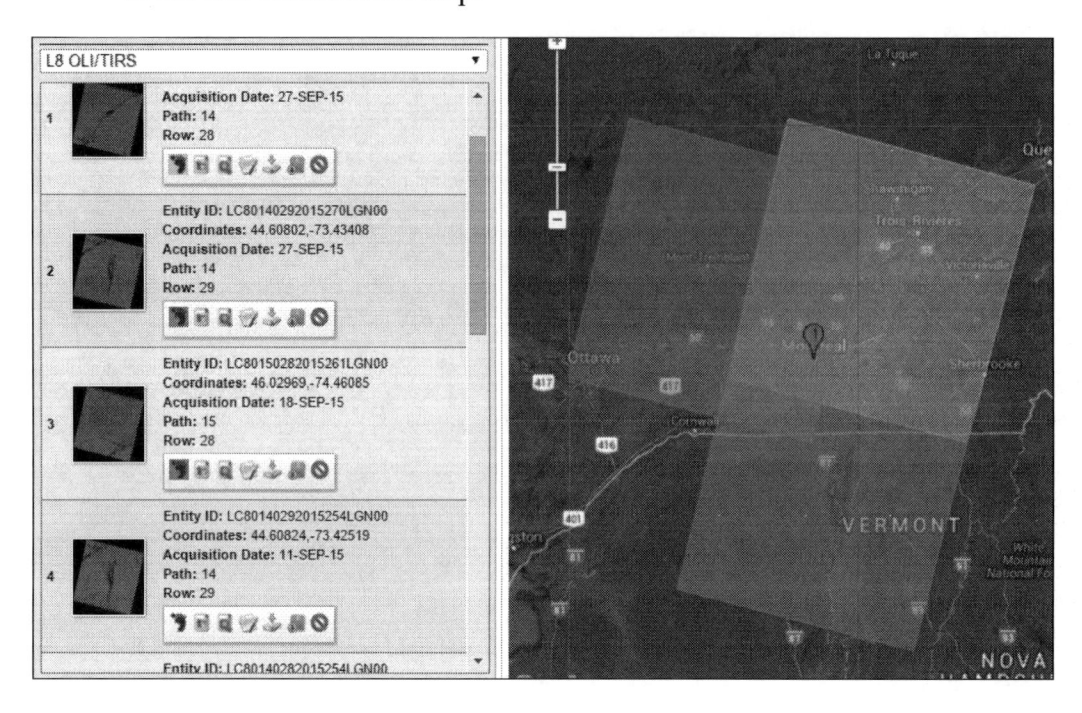

8. For our examples, we need just one data set: one for path 14, row 28. Find the data for this set of rows and columns (you can use an image from any date; it's up to you) and then click on the **Download Options** button on the mini toolbar (it's the icon with a green arrow pointing to a hard drive).

9. A window will pop up with the download options. Click on **Download Level 1 GeoTIFF Data Product**.

> USGS has an application that can manage and resume large downloads. Take a look at https://lta.cr.usgs.gov/BulkDownloadApplication for more information.

10. After the download is complete, create a new folder in your `data` folder and name it `landsat`. Unpack all the images in this folder.

Each package contains 12 `.tif` images and a text file containing the metadata. Each image name is composed of the row, column, date, and band of the image. Note that the band 8 image (B8) is much larger than the other images. This is because it has a better resolution. BQA is a quality assessment band. It contains information on the quality of each of the pixels in the image. We will see more about this band later.

LC80140282015270LGN00_B1.TIF	117,848 KB	TIF File
LC80140282015270LGN00_B2.TIF	117,848 KB	TIF File
LC80140282015270LGN00_B3.TIF	117,848 KB	TIF File
LC80140282015270LGN00_B4.TIF	117,848 KB	TIF File
LC80140282015270LGN00_B5.TIF	117,848 KB	TIF File
LC80140282015270LGN00_B6.TIF	117,848 KB	TIF File
LC80140282015270LGN00_B7.TIF	117,848 KB	TIF File
LC80140282015270LGN00_B8.TIF	471,207 KB	TIF File
LC80140282015270LGN00_B9.TIF	117,848 KB	TIF File
LC80140282015270LGN00_B10.TIF	117,848 KB	TIF File
LC80140282015270LGN00_B11.TIF	117,848 KB	TIF File
LC80140282015270LGN00_BQA.TIF	117,848 KB	TIF File
LC80140282015270LGN00_MTL.txt	8 KB	TXT File

Memory and images

First, we will check how opening images affects random access memory (RAM) usage. In our first example, we will try to open band 8 of the Landsat data using the same technique as before:

1. Prepare the working environment for Chapter 9 by making a copy of the `Chapter8` folder in your `geopy` project. Name the copied folder as `Chapter9`.
2. In `Chapter9` folder, open the `experiments` folder and delete all the files inside it.
3. In the `experiments` folder, create a new Python file and name it `images.py`. Open it for editing.
4. Now type the following code in this file:

    ```
    # coding=utf-8

    import cv2 as cv

    def open_image(img_path):
        image = cv.imread(img_path)
    ```

```
        print(type(image))
        raw_input("Press any key.")


if __name__ == '__main__':
    image_path = "../../data/landsat/LC80140282015270LGN00_B8.TIF"
    open_image(image_path)
```

5. Run the code. Press *Alt + Shift + F10* and select the images on the list.
6. Depending on your computer's memory and the OpenCV version, you may succeed. Otherwise, you will see this nice exception:

```
OpenCV Error: Insufficient memory (Failed to allocate 723585188
bytes) in cv::OutOfMemoryError, file ..\..\..\opencv-2.4.11\
modules\core\src\alloc.cpp, line 52
Traceback (most recent call last):
  File "Chapter9/experiments/images.py", line 14, in <module>
    open_image(image_path)
  File " experiments/images.py", line 6, in open_image
    image = cv.imread(img_path)
cv2.error: ..\..\..\opencv-2.4.11\modules\core\src\alloc.cpp:52:
error: (-4) Failed to allocate 723585188 bytes in function
cv::OutOfMemoryError


Process finished with exit code 1
```

This happens because we are using the 32-bit version of the Python interpreter (that is, x86) and the program fails to allocate enough memory to open the whole image at once.

7. Let's try with a band with a smaller file size. Change the filename to match band 1 of any of the images. It could be `LC80140282015270LGN00_B1.TIF`.
8. Run the code again. You should see a prompt asking you to press any key:

```
<type 'numpy.ndarray'>
Press any key.
```

This was done on purpose in order to halt the program execution while the image is still in the memory.

9. Now, if you are using Windows, press *Ctrl + Alt + Del* and open the task manager. If you are using Ubuntu Linux, open the system monitor.

10. Look for the Python process and see how much memory it's using. You should see something as follows:

Name	Status	CPU 1%	Memory 32%	Disk 0%	Network 0%
PyCharm Community Edition (32 bit)		0%	423,6 MB	0 MB/s	0 Mbps
python.exe (32 bit)		0%	182,3 MB	0 MB/s	0 Mbps

That's OK. The image has opened and isn't consuming much memory.

11. Press any key on the console to finish program execution.
12. Now, let's simulate opening more than one image and see what happens. Change your `open_image` function:

```
def open_image(img_path):
    image = cv.imread(img_path)
    image2 = cv.imread(img_path)
    image3 = cv.imread(img_path)
    image4 = cv.imread(img_path)
    image5 = cv.imread(img_path)
    raw_input("Press any key.")
```

13. Run the code again and check the memory used by Python. For me, it's 872 MB.
14. Press any key in the console to exit the program and release the memory.
15. For our last test, open the image one more time to see what happens:

```
def open_image(img_path):
    image = cv.imread(img_path)
    image2 = cv.imread(img_path)
    image3 = cv.imread(img_path)
    image4 = cv.imread(img_path)
    image5 = cv.imread(img_path)
    image6 = cv.imread(img_path)
    raw_input("Press any key.")
```

16. Run the code and see the result:

```
cv2.error: D:\Build\OpenCV\OpenCV-2.4.11\modules//python//src2//
cv2.cpp:201: error: (-2) The numpy array of typenum=2, ndims=3 can
not be created in function NumpyAllocator::allocate

Process finished with exit code 1
```

Again, the program failed to allocate enough memory to open the image.

Processing Big Images

The point of these experiments was to show that, while processing images, there is a good chance of facing memory problems. With band 8, it was even impossible to begin processing it because we couldn't open it.

With band 1, we simulated a common situation where we wanted to perform a calculation involving many images and this calculation had sub-steps. The memory consumption would escalate until the program crashes.

The maximum amount of memory that Python is allowed to use is limited by the operation system and the Python version (64 or 32 bits). Probably, if you are running the 64 bits version of Python, or using Linux, you won't face any error during the examples.

Independent of being able to run this program or not, these examples show a code whose success is tied to the image size. Even while running a 64-bit Python on a Linux machine with 32 GB of RAM, the program may run out of memory if the images are too big and the process is complex. Remember that some satellite images could be pretty large.

Processing images in chunks

We will change the code, so we can open images of any size. The principle is the same as the one we applied in the previous chapter: in order to read and import an arbitrary number of points, we made the program read, import, and release the memory after each small set of points.

Instead of reading points, we will read a small piece from the image, make some calculations, write the output on the disk, and release the memory before repeating the process with the next piece.

Using GDAL to open images

The process of reading selected regions of a given image is no easy task. Many factors are relevant, such as how the data is encoded in the image, the type of data, how to read the data, and so on. Fortunately, GDAL is equipped with great functions and methods that abstract most of the low-level process. Let's experiment with it:

1. In the `images.py` file, import GDAL at the beginning of the file:
   ```
   import gdal
   ```

2. Now, create a new function to open the Landsat band 8 using GDAL:
   ```
   def open_image_gdal(img_path):
       dataset = gdal.Open(img_path)
   ```

```
        cols = dataset.RasterXSize
        rows = dataset.RasterYSize
        print "Image dimensions: {} x {}px".format(cols, rows)
        raw_input("Press any key.")
```

3. Change the `if __name__ == '__main__':` block to use the new function:
    ```
    if __name__ == '__main__':
        image_path = "../../data/landsat/LC80140282015270LGN00_B8.TIF"
        open_image_gdal(image_path)
    ```

4. Run your code and check the output:
    ```
    Image dimensions: 15401 x 15661px
    Press any key.
    ```

We simply opened the image and printed its dimensions. You should have noticed that the code ran incredibly fast and with no errors. If you wish, you can check how much memory the Python process is using (using the Task Manager or the system monitor).

What happened this time is that the data wasn't read when the file was opened. GDAL only got the information about the image, but the actual data wasn't touched.

Let's try reading a few pixels from this image:

1. Press any key to exit the program.
2. Edit the function:
    ```
    def open_image_gdal(img_path):
        dataset = gdal.Open(img_path)
        cols = dataset.RasterXSize
        rows = dataset.RasterYSize
        print "Image dimensions: {} x {}px".format(cols, rows)
        middle_col = int(cols / 2)
        middle_row = int(rows / 2)
        array = dataset.ReadAsArray(xoff=middle_col - 50,
                                    yoff=middle_row - 50,
                                    xsize=100, ysize=100)
        print(array)
        print(array.shape)
    ```

3. Run the code again and check the output:
    ```
    Image dimensions: 15401 x 15661px
    [[8826 8821 8846 ..., 8001 7965 7806]
     [8842 8838 8853 ..., 7982 7931 7676]
     [8844 8860 8849 ..., 8050 7958 7693]
     ...,
    ```

Processing Big Images

```
        [7530 7451 7531 ..., 7471 7457 7494]
        [7605 7620 7555 ..., 7533 7519 7610]
        [7542 7542 7499 ..., 7620 7947 7728]]
(100, 100)

Process finished with exit code 0
```

We just read a chunk of 100 x 100 pixels from the centre of the image. Again, the code ran fast and little memory was consumed.

Now let's try something fancier. Read a region from the image and save it on the disk, so we can visualize it.

4. First, delete all the files from the `Chapter9/output` folder. We will save our image here.

5. Add the `adjust_values` function and edit the code of the `open_image_gdal` function:

```python
def adjust_values(array, img_range=None):
    """Projects a range of values into a grayscale image.

    :param array: A Numpy array containing the image data.
    :param img_range: specified range of values or None to use
    the range of the image (minimum and maximum).
    """
    if img_range:
        min = img_range[0]
        max = img_range[1]
    else:
        min = array.min()
        max = array.max()
    interval = max - min
    factor = 256.0 / interval
    output = array * factor
    return output


def open_image_gdal(img_path):
    dataset = gdal.Open(img_path)
    cols = dataset.RasterXSize
    rows = dataset.RasterYSize
    print "Image dimensions: {} x {}px".format(cols, rows)
    middle_col = int(cols / 2)
    middle_row = int(rows / 2)
    array = dataset.ReadAsArray(xoff=middle_col - 50,
                                yoff=middle_row - 50,
```

[268]

```
                              xsize=1000, ysize=1000)
print(array.shape)
greyscale_img = adjust_values(array)
cv.imwrite('../output/landsat_chunk.jpg', greyscale_img)
```

The `adjust_values` function is the same that we used before to adjust the gray values of the elevation data in order to visualize it.

We are using OpenCV to write the JPG image for two reasons: by default, GDAL can't write JPG on Windows, and OpenCV is easier to use in this simple case.

6. Run the code and open the image in the `output` folder. If you are using the same Landsat data as I am, you should see this beautiful image of Quebec's rural area:

Iterating through the whole image

We saw that we can read specific parts of an image. With this concept, we can process the whole image one piece at a time. By doing this, it's possible to make calculations that involve many bands. We just need to read the same region of each band, obtain the results, write them, release the memory, and move to the next piece.

The most obvious way to iterate through something in Python is to use a `for` loop. We can iterate through the elements on a list, characters on a string, keys on a dictionary, features on a vector layer, and so on.

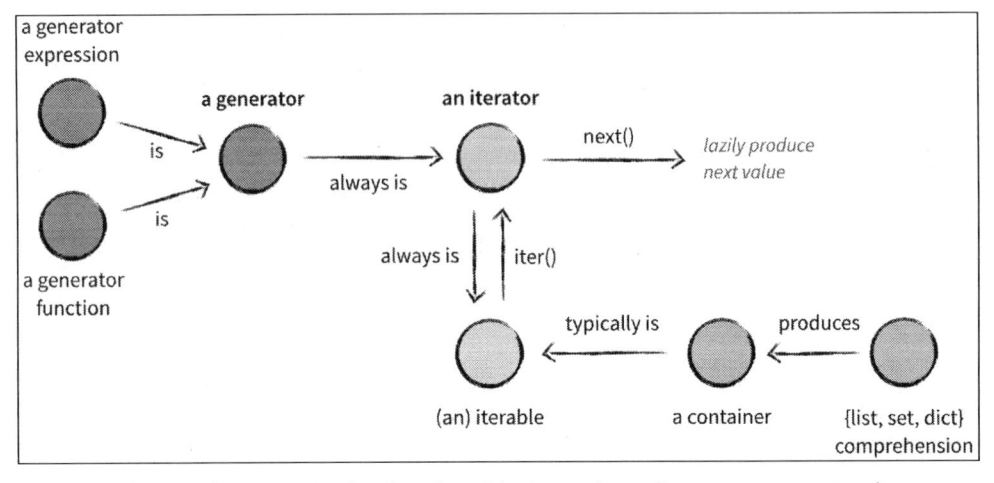

The preceding image is taken from http://nvie.com/posts/iterators-vs-generators/

You may have heard the concepts of iterables, iterators, and generators. **Iterables**, like a list, become iterators when they are used in a `for` loop. But we don't want to create a list of image chunks, because in order to do this, we would need to read the whole image upfront to produce the list. That's when a special feature of iterators comes into light: they are lazy.

An **iterator** is nothing more than a class with specific magic methods. At every loop, this class `next()` method is called and a new value is returned. Python has handy tools to create iterators and that's the point when we are going to see what are generators. Let's write some code:

1. In your `images.py` file, add a new function:

    ```
    def create_image_generator(dataset):
        cols = dataset.RasterXSize
        rows = dataset.RasterYSize
        for row_index in xrange(0, rows):
            yield dataset.ReadAsArray(xoff=0, yoff=row_index,
                                     xsize=cols, ysize=1)
    ```

2. Now edit the `if __name__ == '__main__':` block:

```
if __name__ == '__main__':
    base_path = "../../data/landsat"
    img_name = "LC80140282015270LGN00_B8.TIF"

    img_path = os.path.join(base_path, img_name)
    dataset = gdal.Open(img_path)
    img_generator = create_image_generator(dataset)

    print(img_generator)
    print(type(img_generator))
```

3. Run the code and check the output:

```
<generator object create_image_generator at 0x0791D968>
<type 'generator'>

Process finished with exit code 0
```

Our `create_image_generator` function has a special behavior because of the `yield` word in the `for` loop. When we iterate through the generator object created by this function, the `yield` statement halts the function execution and returns a value at each loop. In our case, the generator/iterator will return one image row at a time.

4. Just to check whether it works, try this in the `if __name__ == '__main__':` block:

```
if __name__ == '__main__':
    base_path = "../../data/landsat"
    img_name = "LC80140282015270LGN00_B8.TIF"

    img_path = os.path.join(base_path, img_name)
    dataset = gdal.Open(img_path)
    img_generator = create_image_generator(dataset)

    print(img_generator)
    print(type(img_generator))

    for row in img_generator:
        print(row)
```

5. Run the code and look at the output:

```
...
[[0 0 0 ..., 0 0 0]]
[[0 0 0 ..., 0 0 0]]
```

Processing Big Images

```
[[0 0 0 ..., 0 0 0]]
[[0 0 0 ..., 0 0 0]]
[[0 0 0 ..., 0 0 0]]
[[0 0 0 ..., 0 0 0]]

Process finished with exit code 0
```

What you see is Python printing a lot of arrays, each containing the data of one row. You see zeros because the borders of the image are black and all the other values are suppressed by NumPy to fit the console. Let's make a few tests to explore the characteristics of iterators:

1. Now, try this concept test just to check another characteristic of iterators:

    ```
    if __name__ == '__main__':
        base_path = "../../data/landsat"
        base_path = "C:/Users/Pablo/Desktop/landsat"
        img_name = "LC80140282015270LGN00_B8.TIF"

        img_path = os.path.join(base_path, img_name)
        dataset = gdal.Open(img_path)
        img_generator = create_image_generator(dataset)


        print(img_generator[4])
    ```

2. Run the code and an error will be raised:

    ```
    Traceback (most recent call last):
      File "Chapter9/experiments/images.py", line 98, in <module>
        print(img_generator[4])
    TypeError: 'generator' object has no attribute '__getitem__'
    ```

    Remember that iterators are lazy and do not behave like sequences (for example, lists). The elements are calculated one at a time and we can't get the 5th element directly.

3. Now, to check whether it really works, let's make a copy of the image one line at a time. Create this new function:

    ```
    def copy_image(src_image, dst_image):
        try:
            os.remove(dst_image)
        except OSError:
            pass

        src_dataset = gdal.Open(src_image)
        cols = src_dataset.RasterXSize
    ```

```
        rows = src_dataset.RasterYSize

        driver = gdal.GetDriverByName('GTiff')
        new_dataset = driver.Create(dst_image, cols, rows,
                                    eType=gdal.GDT_UInt16)
        gdal_array.CopyDatasetInfo(src_dataset, new_dataset)
        band = new_dataset.GetRasterBand(1)

        for index, img_row in enumerate(
                create_image_generator(src_dataset)):
            band.WriteArray(xoff=0, yoff=index, array=img_row)
```

In order to copy the image, we created a new dataset using GDAL's GTiff driver. The new dataset has the same number of rows, columns, and data types (an unsigned 16-bit integer).

To ensure that the copy has the same projection information as the source, we used the function `gdal_array.CopyDatasetInfo`, thus saving us a lot of code.

Finally, using our generator, we read one line at a time and wrote it to the output band.

4. Edit the `if __name__ == '__main__':` block and run the following code to test it:

```
if __name__ == '__main__':
    base_path = "../../data/landsat"
    img_name = "LC80140282015270LGN00_B8.TIF"
    img_path = os.path.join(base_path, img_name)

    img_copy = "../output/B8_copy.TIF"
    copy_image(img_path, img_copy)
```

Open both of the images (the original and the copy) just to check whether they look the same.

Creating image compositions

Now that we know the basics of iterating through the image, which allows us to process many bands together without running out of memory, let's produce some fancier results.

True color compositions

Since we have Landsat's red, green, and blue bands, we can create an image with *true colors*. This means an image with colors similar to what they would be if we were directly observing the scene (for example, the grass is green and the soil is brown). To do this, we will explore a little bit more of Python's iterators.

The Landsat 8 RGB bands are respectively bands 4, 3, and 2. Following the concept that we want to automate tasks and processes, we won't repeat the commands for each one of the bands. We will program Python to do this as follows:

1. Edit your imports at the beginning of the file to be as follows:

    ```
    import os
    import cv2 as cv
    import itertools
    from osgeo import gdal, gdal_array
    import numpy as np
    ```

2. Now add this new function. It will prepare the bands' paths for us:

    ```
    def compose_band_path(base_path, base_name, band_number):
        return os.path.join(
            base_path, base_name) + str(band_number) + ".TIF"
    ```

3. To check the purpose of this function and `itertools` we imported, edit the `if __name__ == '__main__':` block with this code:

    ```
    if __name__ == '__main__':
        base_path = "../../data/landsat"
        base_name = 'LC80140282015270LGN00_B'

        bands_numbers = [4, 3, 2]
        bands = itertools.imap(
            compose_band_path,
            itertools.repeat(base_path),
            itertools.repeat(base_name),
            bands_numbers)

        print(bands)
        for item in bands:
            print(item)
    ```

4. Now run the code and check the results:

    ```
    <itertools.imap object at 0x02DE9510>
    ../../data/landsat/LC80140282015270LGN00_B4.TIF
    ../../data/landsat/LC80140282015270LGN00_B3.TIF
    ```

```
../../data/landsat/LC80140282015270LGN00_B2.TIF
```

```
Process finished with exit code 0
```

The compose band path simply joins the base path, the name of the band, and the band number in order to output a band filename with its path.

Instead of calling the function in a `for` loop and appending the results to a list, we used the `itertools.imap` function. This function takes another function as the first argument and any iterables as the other arguments. It creates an iterator that will call the function with the arguments at each iteration. The `itertools.repeat` function is responsible for repeating a given value infinite times when iterated.

5. Now, we will write the function that will combine the bands into an RGB image. Add this function to your file:

```
def create_color_composition(bands, dst_image):
    try:
        os.remove(dst_image)
    except OSError:
        pass
    # Part1
    datasets = map(gdal.Open, bands)
    img_iterators = map(create_image_generator, datasets)
    cols = datasets[0].RasterXSize
    rows = datasets[0].RasterYSize

    # Part2
    driver = gdal.GetDriverByName('GTiff')
    new_dataset = driver.Create(dst_image, cols, rows,
                                eType=gdal.GDT_Byte,
                                bands=3,
                                options=["PHOTOMETRIC=RGB"])
    gdal_array.CopyDatasetInfo(datasets[0], new_dataset)

    # Part3
    rgb_bands = map(new_dataset.GetRasterBand, [1, 2, 3])
    for index, bands_rows in enumerate(
            itertools.izip(*img_iterators)):
        for band, row in zip(rgb_bands, bands_rows):
            row = adjust_values(row, [0, 30000])
            band.WriteArray(xoff=0, yoff=index, array=row)
```

Processing Big Images

In Part 1, Python's built-in map function works like `itertools.imap`, but instead of an iterator, it creates a list with the results. This means that all the items are calculated and available. First, we used it to create a list of GDAL datasets by calling `gdal.Open` on all the bands. Then, the map function is used to create a list of image iterators, one for each band.

In Part 2, we created the output database just like we did before. But this time, we told the driver to create a dataset with three bands, each with byte data type (256 possible values). We also tell that it's an RGB photo in the options.

In Part 3, we used the map function again to get the reference to the bands in the dataset. In the first for loop, at each iteration, we got an index, that is, the row number, and a tuple containing a row for every band.

In the nested for loop, each iteration gets one of the output image bands and one row of the input bands. The values of the row are then converted from 16-bit to 8-bit (byte) with our `adjust_values` function. To adjust the values, we passed a magic number in order to get a brighter image. Finally, the row is written to the output band.

6. Finally, let's test the code. Edit your `if __name__ == '__main__':` block:

```
if __name__ == '__main__':
    base_path = "../../data/landsat/"
    base_name = 'LC80140282015270LGN00_B'

    bands_numbers = [4, 3, 2]
    bands = itertools.imap(
        compose_band_path,
        itertools.repeat(base_path),
        itertools.repeat(base_name),
        bands_numbers)

    dst_image = "../output/color_composition.tif"
    create_color_composition(bands, dst_image)
```

7. Now run it. After it's done, open the image (`color_composition.tif`) in the `output` folder. You should see this beautiful color image:

You can play with the numbers that we passed to the `adjust_values` function. Try changing the lower limit and the upper limit; you will get different variations of brightness.

Processing specific regions

Now, let's change our code to crop the image for us, so we can have a better view of the details of the region around Montreal. It's something like we did before. But instead of cropping the image after processing, we will only process the region of interest, making the code much more efficient.

1. Edit the `create_image_generator` function:

   ```
   def create_image_generator(dataset, crop_region=None):
       if not crop_region:
           cols = dataset.RasterXSize
           rows = dataset.RasterYSize
           xoff = 0
           yoff = 0
       else:
           xoff = crop_region[0]
           yoff = crop_region[1]
           cols = crop_region[2]
           rows = crop_region[3]
       for row_index in xrange(yoff, yoff + rows):
           yield dataset.ReadAsArray(xoff=xoff, yoff=row_index,
                                     xsize=cols, ysize=1)
   ```

   Now, the function receives an optional `crop_region` argument and only yields rows of the region of interest if it's passed. If not, it yields rows for the whole image.

2. Change the `create_color_composition` class to work with the cropped data:

   ```
   def create_color_composition(bands, dst_image, crop_region=None):
       try:
           os.remove(dst_image)
       except OSError:
           pass
       datasets = map(gdal.Open, bands)
       img_iterators = list(itertools.imap(
           create_image_generator, datasets,
           itertools.repeat(crop_region)))

       if not crop_region:
           cols = datasets[0].RasterXSize
           rows = datasets[0].RasterYSize
       else:
   ```

```
        cols = crop_region[2]
        rows = crop_region[3]

    driver = gdal.GetDriverByName('GTiff')
    new_dataset = driver.Create(dst_image, cols, rows,
                                eType=gdal.GDT_Byte,
                                bands=3,
                                options=["PHOTOMETRIC=RGB"])
    gdal_array.CopyDatasetInfo(datasets[0], new_dataset)
    rgb_bands = map(new_dataset.GetRasterBand, [1, 2, 3])
    for index, bands_rows in enumerate(
            itertools.izip(*img_iterators)):
        for band, row in zip(rgb_bands, bands_rows):
            row = adjust_values(row, [1000, 30000])
            band.WriteArray(xoff=0, yoff=index, array=row)
```

Note that when `img_iterators` was created, we replaced the `map` function by `itertools.imap` in order to be able to use the `itertools.repeat` function. Since we need `img_iterators` to be a list of iterators, we used the `list` function.

3. Finally, edit the `if __name__ == '__main__':` block to pass our region of interest:

```
if __name__ == '__main__':
    base_path = "../../data/landsat/"
    base_name = 'LC80140282015270LGN00_B'

    bands_numbers = [4, 3, 2]
    bands = itertools.imap(
        compose_band_path,
        itertools.repeat(base_path),
        itertools.repeat(base_name),
        bands_numbers)

    dst_image = "../output/color_composition.tif"
    create_color_composition(bands, dst_image,
                             (1385, 5145, 1985, 1195))
```

4. Run the code. You should now have this nice image of Montreal:

False color compositions

Color compositions are a great tool for information visualization, and we can use it even to see things that would be otherwise invisible to the human eye.

Landsat 8 and other satellites provide data in ranges of the spectrum that are reflected or absorbed more or less by specific objects. For example, vigorous vegetation reflects a lot of near-infrared radiation, so if we are looking for information on vegetation coverage or plant growth, we should consider this band.

Besides the computational analysis of different bands, we are able to visualize them by replacing the red, blue, and green components by other bands. Let's try it as follows:

1. Just edit the `if __name__ == '__main__':` block, so we use the near infrared (band 5) as the green component of the RGB image:

   ```
   if __name__ == '__main__':
       base_path = "../../data/landsat/"
       base_name = 'LC80140282015270LGN00_B'

       bands_numbers = [4, 5, 2]
       bands = itertools.imap(
   ```

```
            compose_band_path,
            itertools.repeat(base_path),
            itertools.repeat(base_name),
            bands_numbers)

    dst_image = "../output/color_composition.tif"
    create_color_composition(bands, dst_image,
                             (1385, 5145, 1985, 1195))
```

2. Run the code and look at the output image:

Processing Big Images

3. You can have many other combinations. Just change the `band_numbers` variables to achieve different results. Try changing it to [6, 5, 2]. Run the code and look at how the farm fields stand out from the other features.

> You can check out more interesting band combinations by clicking on the following links:
> `http://landsat.gsfc.nasa.gov/?page_id=5377`
> `http://blogs.esri.com/esri/arcgis/2013/07/24/band-combinations-for-landsat-8/`

Summary

As we did with the points of interest, we managed the problem of excessive computational resource consumption by splitting the load into pieces. Specifically, instead of reading and processing whole images, we created Python iterators that allowed us to iterate through these images one row at a time without hitting the memory limit of the computer.

With this technique, we were able to process three Landsat 8 bands at a time to produce fancy colored images valuable for data visualization.

At this point, we are able to split our processing tasks into pieces that can be processed independently. We can do this with vectors, with database access, and now, with images as well.

With this, we completely paved the road for the next chapter, where we will be sending each of these pieces to be calculated at the same time by a different processor core performing the so-called parallel processing.

10
Parallel Processing

In this chapter, we will take another step in code optimization; we will experiment with the possibility of using multiple processor cores to perform calculations.

Using the satellite images from the previous chapter, we will use Python's multiprocessing library to distribute tasks and make them run in parallel. As an example, we will experiment with different techniques to produce true color compositions from Landsat 8 data, with better resolution and a greater level of detail.

To achieve our objects, we will go through these topics:

- How multiprocessing works
- How to iterate through two-dimensional image blocks
- Image resizing and resampling
- Parallel processing in image operations
- Image pan sharpening

Multiprocessing basics

The implementation of Python that we are using, CPython, has a mechanism called **global interpreter lock** (**GIL**). GIL's purpose is to make CPython thread-safe; it works by preventing the code from being executed by more than one thread at once.

With that limitation, multiprocessing in Python works by forking the running program (for example, making a copy of the state of the program) and sending it to another computer core. As a consequence, the new process comes with an overhead.

Parallel Processing

Let's try a simple code:

1. First, make a copy of the previous chapter folder in your `geopy` project and rename it to `Chapter10`.
2. Clean the `Chapter10/output` folder (delete all files in it).
3. Expand the `Chapter10/experiments` folder, right-click on it, and create a new Python file. Name it `parallel.py`.
4. Add this code to this new file:

   ```
   # coding=utf-8

   from datetime import datetime
   import multiprocessing as mp

   def an_expensive_function(text):
       for i in range(500):
           out = "{} {} {}"
           out.format(text, text, text)
       return "dummy output"
   ```

   This is a simple function that receives text and performs string formatting multiple times. The only purpose of this function is to consume CPU time, so we can test whether we can speed up our code by running parallel processes.

5. Now, create an `if __name__ == '__main__':` block at the end of the file so we can test the code and measure its execution time.

   ```
   if __name__ == '__main__':
       texts = []
       for t in range(100000):
           texts.append('test text')

       t1 = datetime.now()

       result = map(an_expensive_function, texts)

       print("Execution time: {}".format(datetime.now() - t1))
   ```

   This code makes a list of `100000` strings, then this list is mapped to the function; this means that `an_expensive_function` is called `100000`. Note that here we are using a simpler technique for measuring the execution time for this piece of code; `t1` holds the start time and in the end it's subtracted from the current time. This avoids the overhead of using a profiler and is also more suitable for what we are going to do than the `timeit` module.

6. Run the code and check the result in the console:

   ```
   Execution time: 0:00:35.667500

   Process finished with exit code 0
   ```

My computer took approximately 35 seconds to run the function 100,000 times; probably your results will be different. If your computer is much faster, change this number to get an execution time of at least 10 seconds. Take note of your result.

1. Now edit the `if __name__ == '__main__':` block so we can execute this code in parallel:

   ```
   if __name__ == '__main__':
       texts = []
       for t in range(100000):
           texts.append('test text')

       multi = True

       t1 = datetime.now()

       if multi:
           my_pool = mp.Pool(processes=8)
           result = my_pool.map(an_expensive_function, texts)
       else:
           result = map(an_expensive_function, texts)

       print("Execution time: {}".format(datetime.now() - t1))
   ```

   The `Pool` class represents a pool of worker processes; they stand by, waiting until we submit some jobs to be done.

   In order to use all of your processor cores, you need to create the same number as, or more than, the number of cores of your processor. Or, if you don't want to fully load your computer processor, use fewer processes than the number of cores. This is done by changing the `processes` argument.

   We put the code in an `if` block so we can easily switch between parallel and single processes.

2. Run your code and see the difference:

   ```
   Execution time: 0:00:08.373000

   Process finished with exit code 0
   ```

   The code ran approximately four times faster for me.

Parallel Processing

3. Now, open your Task Manager, or your system monitor and open the CPU load graphs.
4. Run the code again, using `multi=True`, and take a look at the CPU load graph:

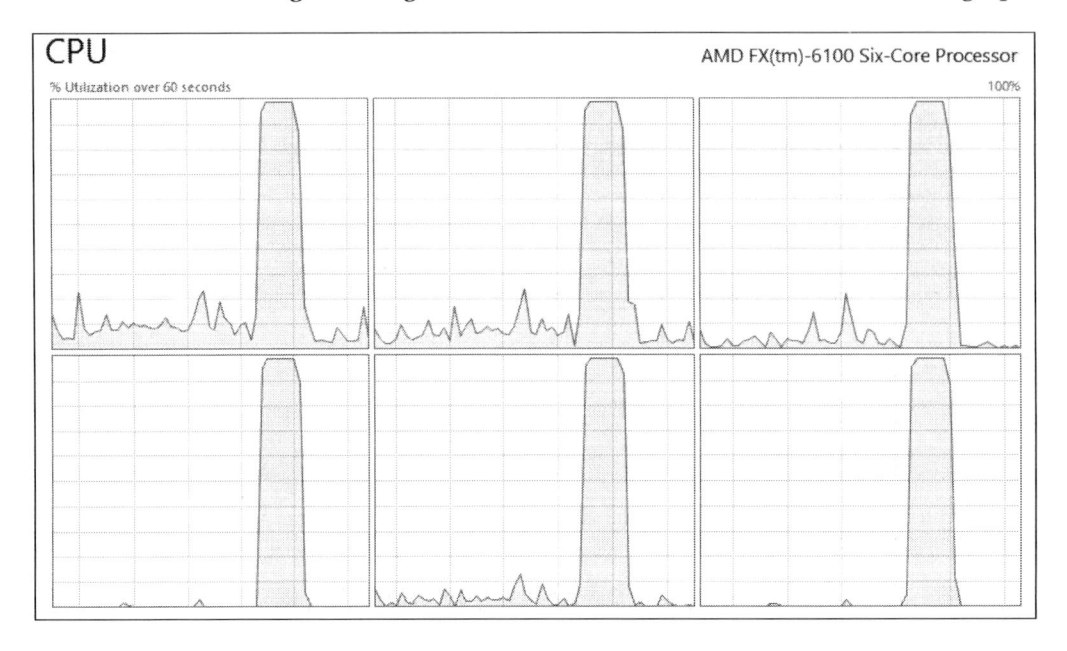

5. Change to `multi=False` and run it again. Inspect the graph now:

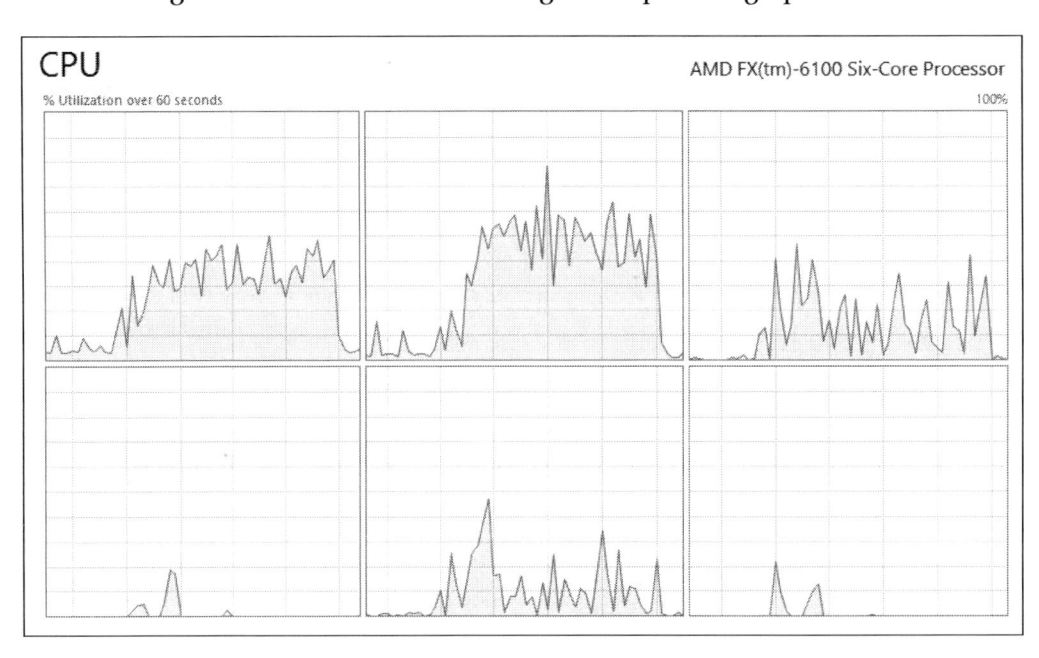

Note that when using multiprocessing, all cores were fully occupied for a short period of time. However, when using a single process, some of the cores are partially occupied for a long time. This pattern may vary according to the computer architecture.

Block iteration

The TIFF format is a versatile image format that can be customized for very diverse needs. The file is composed of a **Header**, at least one **Image File Directory,** and any amount of **Image Data**. Explaining it in a simple way, the header tells where the first directory is on the file. The directory contains information about the image, tells how to read the data related to it, and tells where the next directory is. Each combination of a directory and image data is an image, so a single TIFF file may have multiple images inside it.

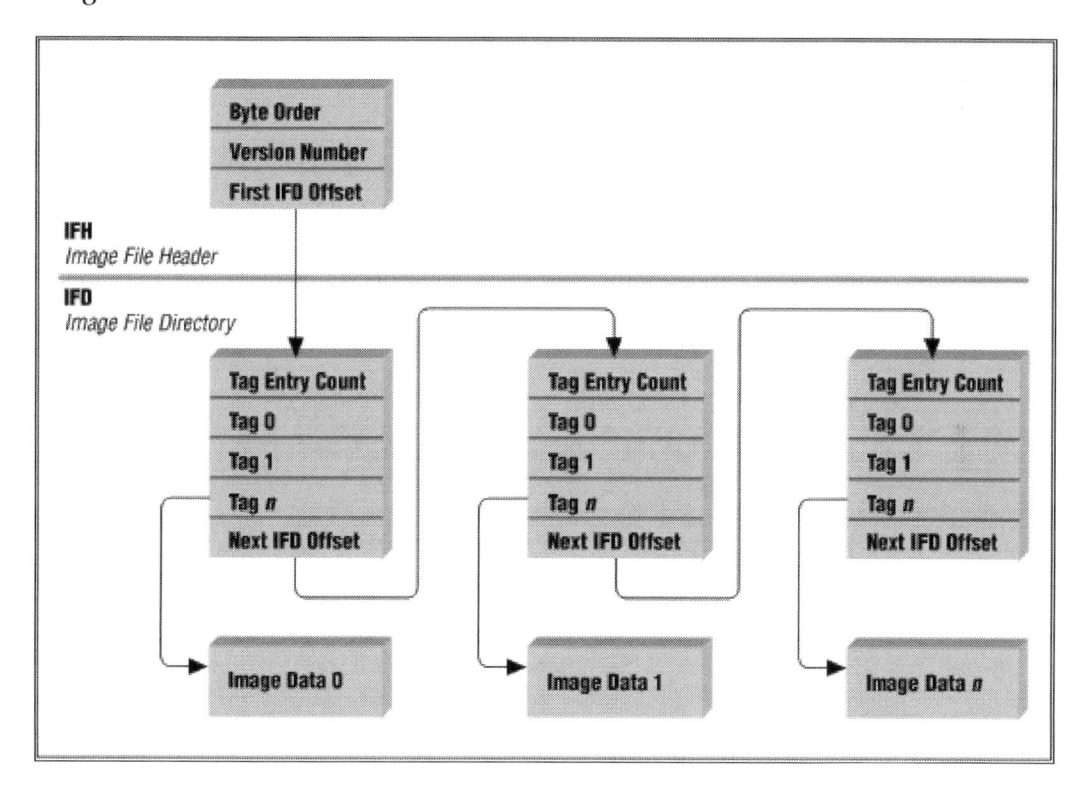

Each image data (a whole image) contains blocks of data (that is, parts of the image) that can be read separately, each one representing a specific region of the image. This allows the user to read the image by chunks, just like we did.

Parallel Processing

The blocks of data are indivisible; in order to return data from an image, the program that is reading it needs to read at least one whole block. If the desired region is smaller than a block, the whole block will be read anyway, decoded, and cropped; the data will then be returned to the user.

The blocks of data can be in strips or in tiles. Strips contain data for an entire image row and may be one row or more in length. Tiles have width and length (which must be a multiple of 16) and are interesting because they allow us to retrieve specific regions with no need to read entire rows.

In our previous examples, we programmed a function that was able to read images one row at a time; now we will improve that function in order to read blocks of any size. This will allow us to make fancier stuff with the images in the upcoming topics.

This time, we will take a different approach to how we iterate the image.

1. Inside your Chapter10/experiments folder, create a new file named block_generator.py.
2. Edit this file and insert the following code:

```
# coding=utf-8
import os
from pprint import pprint
from osgeo import gdal, gdal_array


def create_blocks_list(crop_region, block_shape):
    """Creates a list of block reading coordinates.

    :param crop_region: Offsets and shape of the region of
    interest.
        (xoff, yoff, xsize, ysize)
    :param block_shape: Width and height of each block.
    """
    img_columns = crop_region[2]
    img_rows = crop_region[3]
    blk_width = block_shape[0]
    blk_height = block_shape[1]
    # Get the number of blocks.
    x_blocks = int((img_columns + blk_width - 1) / blk_width)
    y_blocks = int((img_rows + blk_height - 1) / blk_height)
    print("Creating blocks list with {} blocks ({} x {}).".format(
        x_blocks * y_blocks, x_blocks, y_blocks))

    blocks = []
```

```
            for block_column in range(0, x_blocks):
                # Recalculate the shape of the rightmost block.
                if block_column == x_blocks - 1:
                    valid_x = img_columns - block_column * blk_width
                else:
                    valid_x = blk_width
                xoff = block_column * blk_width + crop_region[0]
                # loop through Y lines
                for block_row in range(0, y_blocks):
                    # Recalculate the shape of the final block.
                    if block_row == y_blocks - 1:
                        valid_y = img_rows - block_row * blk_height
                    else:
                        valid_y = blk_height
                    yoff = block_row * blk_height + crop_region[1]
                    blocks.append((xoff, yoff, valid_x, valid_y))
        return blocks
```

3. Before some explanation, let's see this function working. Add the `if __name__ == '__main__':` block at the end of the file with this code:

```
if __name__ == '__main__':
    blocks_list = create_blocks_list((0, 0, 1024, 1024), (32, 32))
    pprint(blocks_list)
```

4. Run the code. Since we are running a different file from before, remember to press *Alt* + *Shift* + *F10* to select the file to run. Check the output:

```
Creating blocks list with 1024 blocks (32 x 32).
[(0, 0, 32, 32),
 (0, 32, 32, 32),
 (0, 64, 32, 32),
 (0, 96, 32, 32),
 (0, 128, 32, 32),
 (0, 160, 32, 32),
 (0, 192, 32, 32),

...

 (992, 928, 32, 32),
 (992, 960, 32, 32),
 (992, 992, 32, 32)]

Process finished with exit code 0
```

Parallel Processing

The sole purpose of this function is to create a list of block coordinates and dimensions; each item on the list contains the offset and the size of a block. We need the size because the blocks on the edges may be smaller than the desired size.

The intention of this design choice, instead of iterating through an image directly, was to hide this low-level functionality. This function is extensive and unintuitive; we don't want it mixed with higher-level code, making our programs much cleaner. As a bonus, we may gain a little speed when iterating multiple images because the list only needs to be produced once.

1. Now, let's adapt the function to copy the image. To use the iteration by blocks, add this code to the file:

   ```
   def copy_image(src_image, dst_image, block_shape):
       try:
           os.remove(dst_image)
       except OSError:
           pass

       src_dataset = gdal.Open(src_image)
       cols = src_dataset.RasterXSize
       rows = src_dataset.RasterYSize

       driver = gdal.GetDriverByName('GTiff')
       new_dataset = driver.Create(dst_image, cols, rows,
                                   eType=gdal.GDT_UInt16)
       gdal_array.CopyDatasetInfo(src_dataset, new_dataset)
       band = new_dataset.GetRasterBand(1)

       blocks_list = create_blocks_list((0, 0, cols, rows), block_shape)
       n_blocks = len(blocks_list)

       for index, block in enumerate(blocks_list, 1):
           if index % 10 == 0:
               print("Copying block {} of {}.".format(index, n_blocks))
           block_data = src_dataset.ReadAsArray(*block)
           band.WriteArray(block_data, block[0], block[1])
   ```

2. Edit the `if __name__ == '__main__':` block to test the code (we are also going to measure its execution time):

   ```
   if __name__ == '__main__':
       base_path = "../../data/landsat/"
       img_name = "LC80140282015270LGN00_B8.TIF"

       img_path = os.path.join(base_path, img_name)
   ```

[292]

Chapter 10

```
        img_copy = "../output/B8_copy.tif"

        t1 = datetime.now()
        copy_image(img_path, img_copy, (1024, 1024))
        print("Execution time: {}".format(datetime.now() - t1))
```

3. Now, run it and check the output:

    ```
    Creating blocks list with 256 blocks (16 x 16).
    Copying block 10 of 256.
    Copying block 20 of 256.
    ...
    Copying block 240 of 256.
    Copying block 250 of 256.
    Execution time: 0:00:26.656000

    Process finished with exit code 0
    ```

    We used blocks of 1024 by 1024 pixels to copy the image. The first thing to notice is that the process is extremely slow. This happened because we are reading blocks smaller than the size of the blocks in the image, resulting in a lot of reading and writing overhead.

    So, let's adapt our function in order to detect the block size and optimize the reading.

4. Edit the `copy_image` function:

    ```
    def copy_image(src_image, dst_image, block_width=None,
                   block_height=None):
        try:
            os.remove(dst_image)
        except OSError:
            pass

        src_dataset = gdal.Open(src_image)
        cols = src_dataset.RasterXSize
        rows = src_dataset.RasterYSize

        src_band = src_dataset.GetRasterBand(1)
        src_block_size = src_band.GetBlockSize()
        print("Image shape {}x{}px. Block shape {}x{}px.".format(
            cols, rows, *src_block_size)
        block_shape = (block_width or src_block_size[0],
                       block_height or src_block_size[1])

        driver = gdal.GetDriverByName('GTiff')
    ```

[293]

Parallel Processing

```
        new_dataset = driver.Create(dst_image, cols, rows,
                                    eType=gdal.GDT_UInt16)
        gdal_array.CopyDatasetInfo(src_dataset, new_dataset)
        band = new_dataset.GetRasterBand(1)

        blocks_list = create_blocks_list((0, 0, cols, rows), block_shape)
        n_blocks = len(blocks_list)

        for index, block in enumerate(blocks_list, 1):
            if index % 10 == 0:
                print("Copying block {} of {}.".format(index, n_blocks))
            block_data = src_dataset.ReadAsArray(*block)
            band.WriteArray(block_data, block[0], block[1])
```

We separated the block shape arguments into width and height, and made them optional. Then we got the size (shape) of the block that is defined in the image. If the block width or height are not passed as arguments, the image values are used instead.

We have a hint that this image is divided in stripes. Remember that when we copied the image one row at a time, it was fast. So, we are going to test reading multiple rows at a time.

5. Edit the `if __name__ == '__main__':` block:

```
if __name__ == '__main__':
    base_path = "../../data/landsat/"
    img_name = "LC80140282015270LGN00_B8.TIF"

    img_path = os.path.join(base_path, img_name)
    img_copy = "../output/B8_copy.tif"

    t1 = datetime.now()
    copy_image(img_path, img_copy, block_height=100)
    print("Execution time: {}".format(datetime.now() - t1))
```

6. Run the code and see the difference:

```
Image shape 15401x15661px. Block shape 15401x1px.
Creating blocks list with 157 blocks (1 x 157).
Copying block 10 of 157.
Copying block 20 of 157.
Copying block 30 of 157.
...
Copying block 130 of 157.
```

```
Copying block 140 of 157.
Copying block 150 of 157.
Execution time: 0:00:02.083000

Process finished with exit code 0
```

It's confirmed that, for Landsat 8 images, each block is one row of the image. And by reading whole lines, we achieved the same level of speed as before.

You can play with the block height parameter; instead of reading 100 lines, try reading 1 or 1,000 lines and see if it has any influence on the execution time.

Improving the image resolution

In order to obtain a better image for visual analysis, we can combine different techniques to increase the image resolution. The first one changes the size of the image and recalculates the missing data by interpolation. The second one uses a band of higher resolution (band 8, in our case) — combined with bands in a lower resolution — to produce an improved true color map.

Image resampling

Image resizing or resampling is a technique to change the size of the image. By doing this we change the number of pixels in it (that is, the number of samples) or vice-versa.

As the size of an image is increased, we need to give a value to pixels that didn't exist before. This is done by interpolation; the new pixel value is given based on the value of its surrounding pixels. That's why we needed two-dimensional chunks.

In our first trial, we will resample one 30m-resolution band into a 15m-resolution image. Since we will perform a lot of tests, let's start by creating a practical way of viewing and comparing our results. To do that we will crop the image and save it to disk so we can easily visualize the same region.

1. Edit the imports at the beginning of the file:

   ```
   # coding=utf-8

   from datetime import datetime
   import os
   import itertools
   import numpy as np
   from pprint import pprint
   import functools
   ```

Parallel Processing

```
import multiprocessing as mp
from osgeo import gdal, gdal_array
from images import adjust_values, compose_band_path
from images import create_color_composition
import cv2 as cv
```

2. Add this new function to your file:

```
def crop_and_save(image_path, prefix=""):
    dataset = gdal.Open(image_path)
    array = dataset.ReadAsArray(4209, 11677, 348, 209)
    array = adjust_values(array, (10000, 30000))
    array = array.astype(np.ubyte)
    preview_path, preview_file = os.path.split(image_path)
    preview_file = "preview_" + prefix + preview_file
    cv.imwrite(os.path.join("../output/", preview_file), array)
```

This time we will zoom the image to downtown Montreal, including the Mount Royal and the Old Port. As a reference, the next image is a high-resolution image extracted from Bing maps of our region of interest:

3. Now, add the resampling function to your file:

```
def resample_image(src_image, dst_image,
                   block_width=None, block_height=None, factor=2,
```

```
                interpolation=cv.INTER_LINEAR):
    """Change image resolution by a factor.

    :param src_image: Input image.
    :param dst_image: Output image.
    :param block_width: Width in pixels of the processing blocks.
    :param block_height: Height in pixels of the processing
blocks.
    :param factor: Image size multiplier.
    :param interpolation: Interpolation method.
    """
    t1 = datetime.now()
    print("Start processing -> {}".format(dst_image))
    try:
        os.remove(dst_image)
    except OSError:
        pass
    src_dataset = gdal.Open(src_image, gdal.GA_ReadOnly)
    cols = src_dataset.RasterXSize
    rows = src_dataset.RasterYSize

    src_band = src_dataset.GetRasterBand(1)
    src_block_size = src_band.GetBlockSize()

    # print("Image shape {}x{}px. Block shape {}x{}px.").format(
    #     cols, rows, *src_block_size)
    block_shape = (block_width or src_block_size[0],
                   block_height or src_block_size[1])

    driver = gdal.GetDriverByName('GTiff')
    new_dataset = driver.Create(dst_image, cols * factor,
                                rows * factor,
                                eType=gdal.GDT_UInt16)

    gdal_array.CopyDatasetInfo(src_dataset, new_dataset)
    band = new_dataset.GetRasterBand(1)
    blocks_list = create_blocks_list((0, 0, cols, rows), block_shape)
    new_block_shape = (block_shape[0] * factor,
                       block_shape[1] * factor)
    new_blocks_list = create_blocks_list((0, 0,
                                          cols * factor,
                                          rows * factor),
                                         new_block_shape)
```

Parallel Processing

```
        n_blocks = len(blocks_list)
        for index, (block, new_block) in enumerate(
                zip(blocks_list, new_blocks_list), 1):
            #if index % 10 == 0:
            #    print("Copying block {} of {}.".format(index, n_blocks))
            block_data = src_dataset.ReadAsArray(*block)
            block_data = cv.resize(block_data, dsize=(0, 0),
                                   fx=factor, fy=factor,
                                   interpolation=interpolation)
            band.WriteArray(block_data, new_block[0], new_block[1])
        return dst_image, t1
```

This function creates an output dataset that is scaled by the defined factor. It reads each block from the source image, changes its size by this same factor, and writes it to the output. Note that the size of the output block is also recalculated and scaled by the multiplying factor. The method of interpolation is optional and by default uses linear interpolation.

Instead of just testing this function, let's generate previews of every possible interpolation method, so we can visually compare it and see which one returns the best result. Since we will do this using multiprocessing, we also need a callback function so we can time the execution of each job.

4. Add this function to your file:

```
def processing_callback(args):
    t2 = datetime.now() - args[1]
    print("Done processing {}. {}".format(args[0], t2))
```

5. Finally, edit the `if __name__ == '__main__':` block:

```
if __name__ == '__main__':
    base_path = "../../data/landsat/"
    img_name = "LC80140282015270LGN00_B4.TIF"
    img_path = os.path.join(base_path, img_name)

    interpolation_methods = {
        "nearest": cv.INTER_NEAREST,
        "linear": cv.INTER_LINEAR,
        "area": cv.INTER_AREA,
        "bicubic": cv.INTER_CUBIC,
        "lanczos": cv.INTER_LANCZOS4}

    output_images = []
    multi = True
    my_pool = mp.Pool(processes=8)
```

```
            total_t1 = datetime.now()
            for name, inter_method in interpolation_methods.iteritems():
                out_image = "../output/" + name + '_B4.tif'
                output_images.append(out_image)
                if multi:
                    my_pool.apply_async(
                        resample_image, (img_path, out_image),
                                        {'block_height': 100,
                                         'interpolation': inter_method},
                                        processing_callback)
                else:
                    result = resample_image(img_path, out_image,
                                            block_height=100,
                                            interpolation=inter_method)
                    processing_callback(result)
            if multi:
                # Close the pool, no more jobs.
                my_pool.close()
                # Wait for all results to be ready.
                my_pool.join()

            print("Total time: {}".format(datetime.now() - total_t1))
            map(crop_and_save, output_images)
```

Here we used another technique for adding jobs to a queue. With `apply_assinc`, we added each job one at a time, telling that we wanted the calculations to happen asynchronously. In the end, `my_pool.join()` make the program wait until all the jobs in the pool are complete.

6. With `multi = True` (multiprocessing enabled), run the code and look at the output:

```
Start processing -> ../output/bicubic_B4.tif
Start processing -> ../output/nearest_B4.tif
Start processing -> ../output/lanczos_B4.tif
Start processing -> ../output/linear_B4.tif
Start processing -> ../output/area_B4.tif
Done processing ../output/nearest_B4.tif. 0:00:33.924000
Done processing ../output/area_B4.tif. 0:00:37.263000
Done processing ../output/linear_B4.tif. 0:00:37.700000
Done processing ../output/bicubic_B4.tif. 0:00:39.546000
Done processing ../output/lanczos_B4.tif. 0:00:41.361000
Total time: 0:00:42.264000

Process finished with exit code 0
```

Parallel Processing

7. Now, disable multiprocessing by setting `multi = False` and run the code again:

```
Start processing -> ../output/bicubic_B4.tif
Done processing ../output/bicubic_B4.tif. 0:00:02.827000
Start processing -> ../output/nearest_B4.tif
Done processing ../output/nearest_B4.tif. 0:00:07.841000
Start processing -> ../output/lanczos_B4.tif
Done processing ../output/lanczos_B4.tif. 0:00:09.729000
Start processing -> ../output/linear_B4.tif
Done processing ../output/linear_B4.tif. 0:00:09.160000
Start processing -> ../output/area_B4.tif
Done processing ../output/area_B4.tif. 0:00:09.939000
Total time: 0:00:39.498000

Process finished with exit code 0
```

Comparing the output of both of the trials, we see a different pattern of execution. When using multiprocessing, all the processes are started, they take a long time to execute, and finish almost together. When not using multiprocessing, each process starts and finishes before the next one.

On my computer, it took longer to execute the code when using multiprocessing. This happened because our jobs used intense reading and writing and my hard drive was the **hardware bottleneck** and not the CPU. So, when using multiprocessing we added a lot of extra labor and also enforced concurrent reading and writing of files, reducing the HD efficiency.

There is no way to overcome hardware bottlenecks when the hardware is used at full capacity. As happened in this example, we needed to write 2.30 GB of resampled image data, so the program will take at least the time needed to write 2.30 GB to disk.

The following screenshot of my task manager was taken during the program execution and illustrates the described situation:

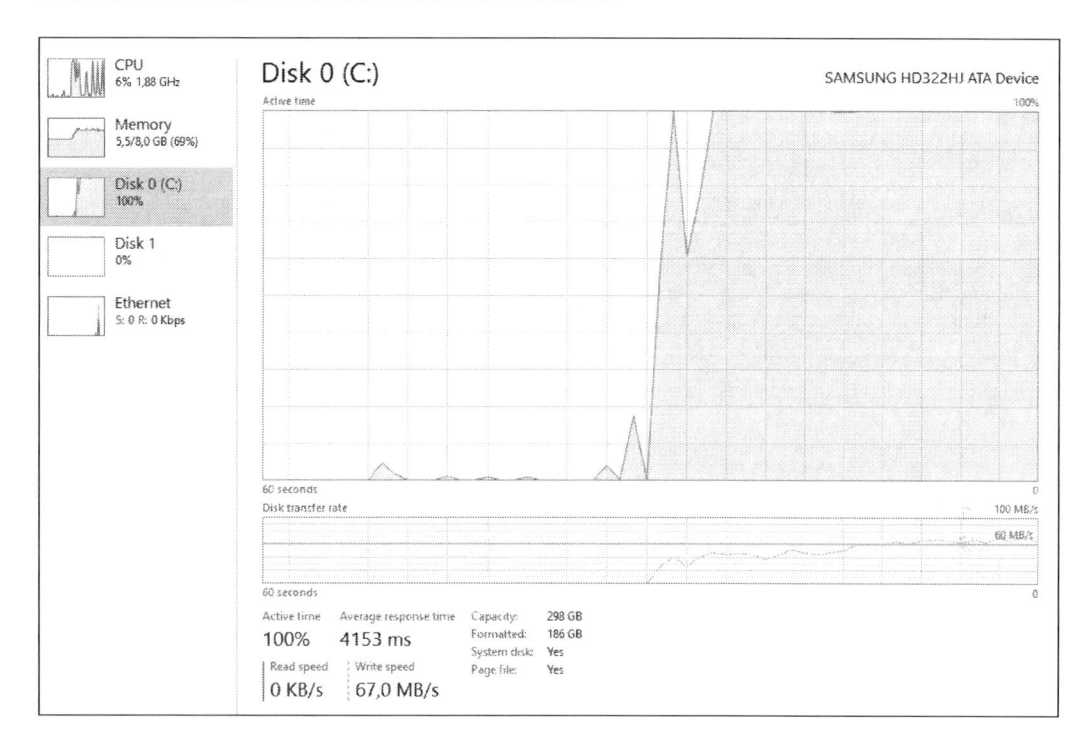

These results may vary from computer to computer, especially if you are using a configuration with more than one storage media, where the IO could also happen in parallel.

Open your `output` folder and see what we have:

- Area interpolation:

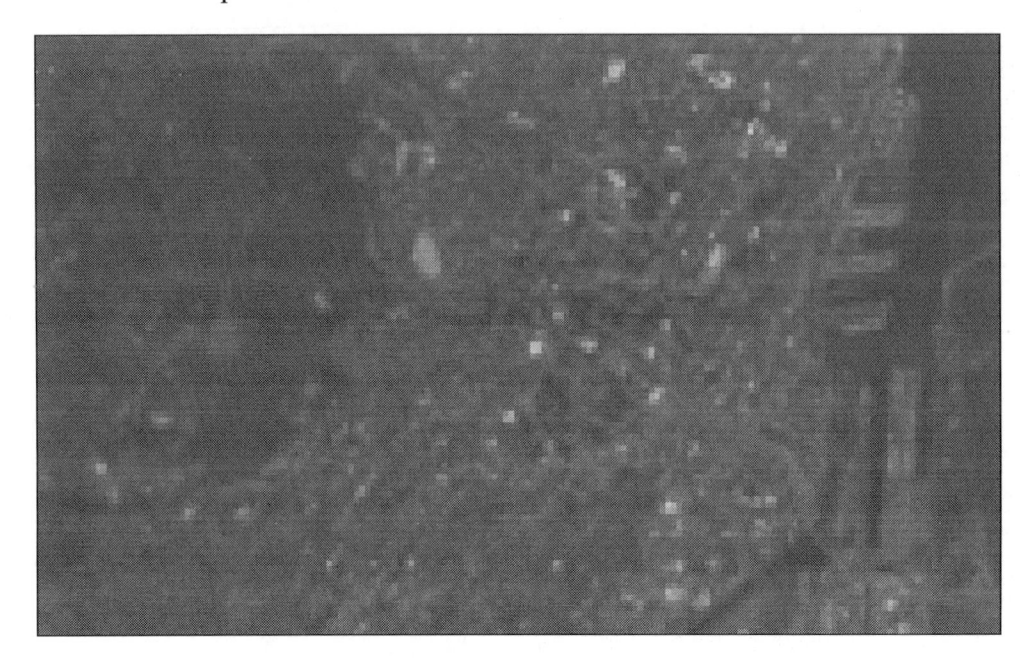

- Bicubic interpolation:

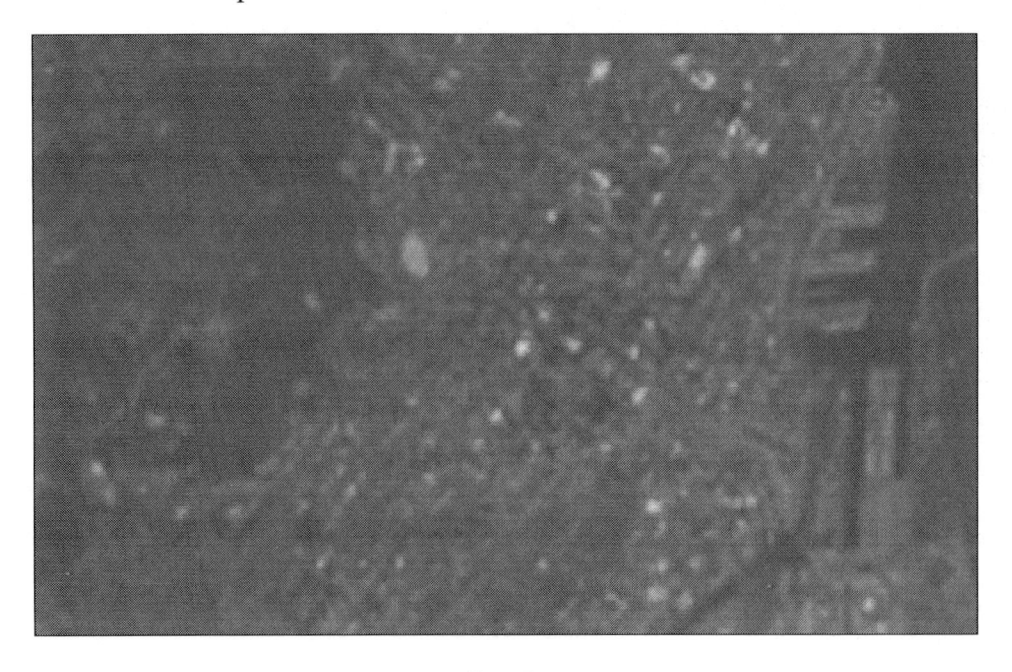

- Lanczos interpolation:

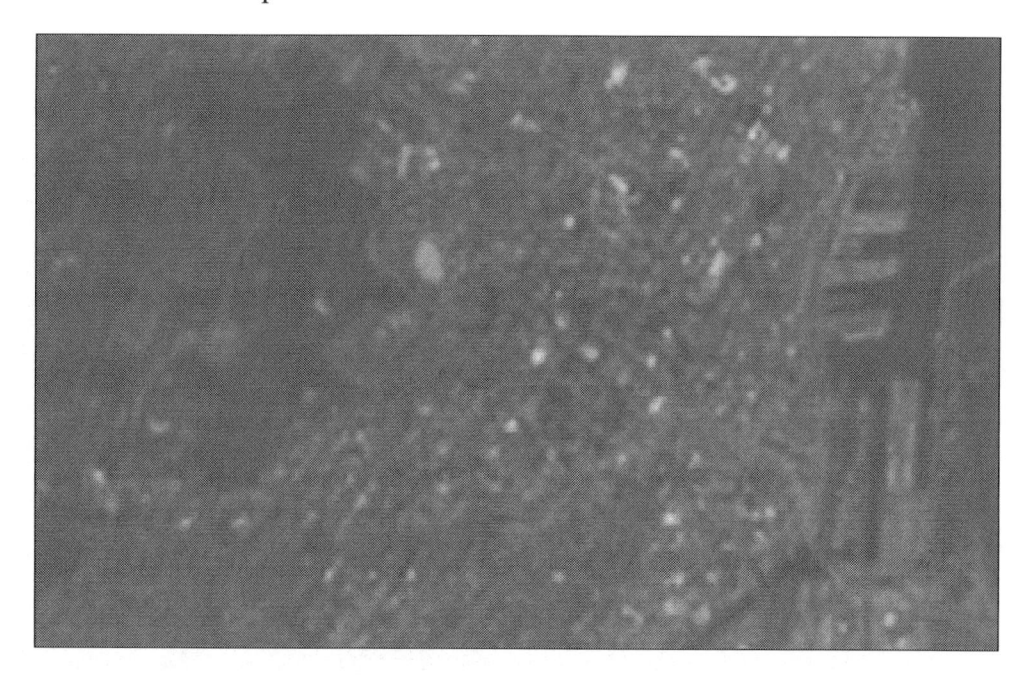

- Linear interpolation:

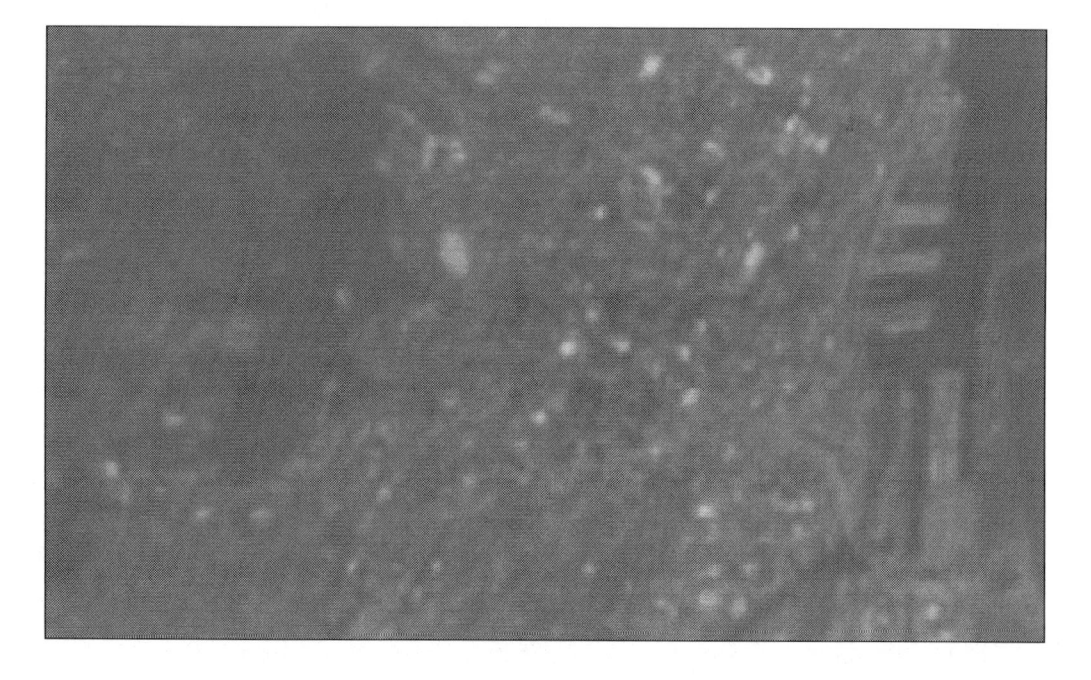

- Nearest interpolation:

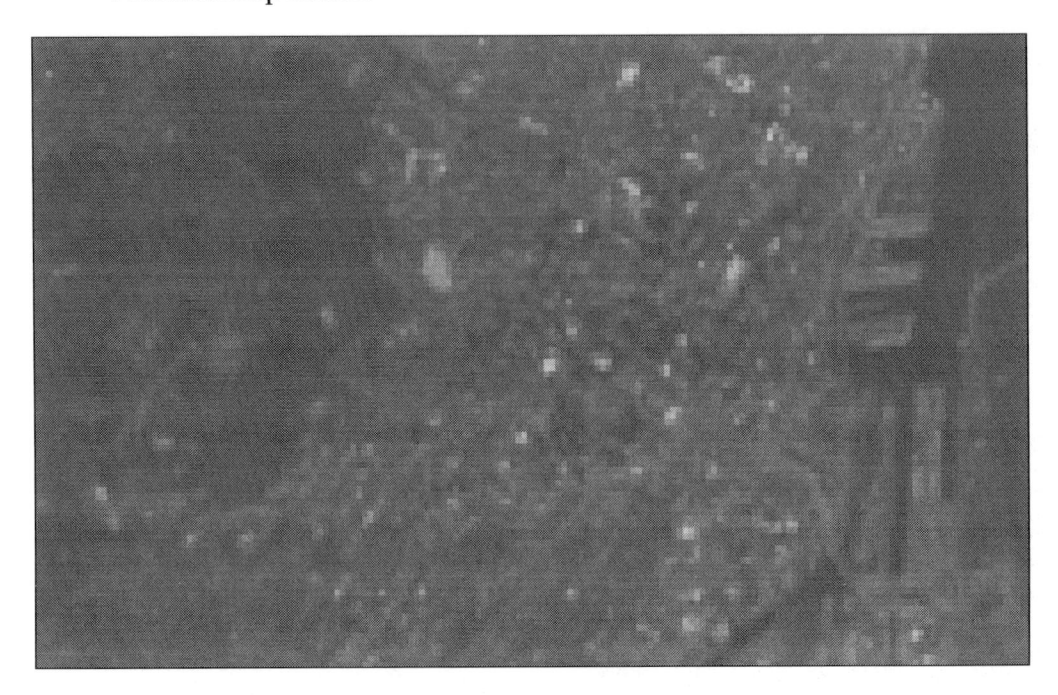

- And finally, look at band 8, the panchromatic band, with 15m resolution, as a reference:

Pan sharpening

With the resampling, we were able to produce images with pixels of 15 meters, but we've achieved little improvement in the details of the objects in the image.

To overcome this limitation, a technique called **pan sharpening** can be used to produce color images with a better resolution. The principle is to use the panchromatic band (Landsat band 8) to improve the resolution of the composition.

Here we will use a method that consists of changing the color representation of an image from RGB to HSV—Hue, Saturation, Value.

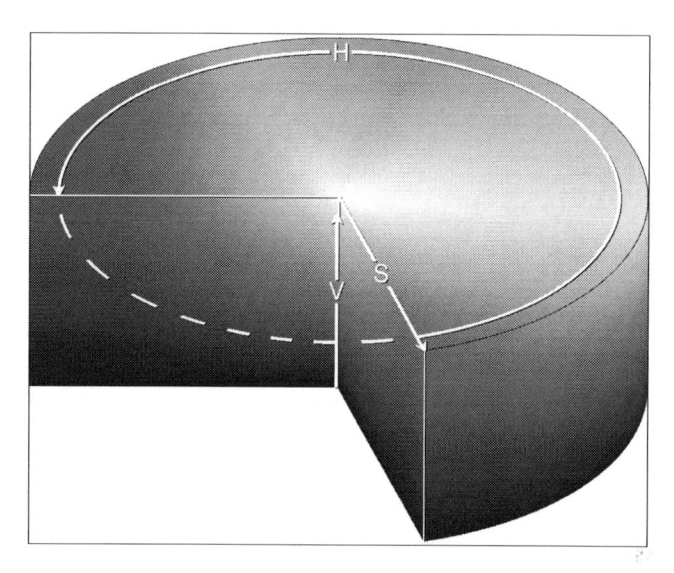

As can be seen from the image, the value component could be interpreted as the brightness or intensity of the color. So, after the color representation is transformed, the value component can to be replaced with the higher-resolution panchromatic band, resulting in an image with better definition.

To do that, we need to produce a true color composition with the RGB bands, like we did before, but this time with the resampled images. Then we change the color representation, replace the value component, transform the color representation back to RGB, and save the image to disk.

1. Since we have most of the function ready, start by editing the `if __name__ == '__main__':` block. Remove the older tests and add this code:

   ```
   if __name__ == '__main__':
       base_path = "../../data/landsat/"
       base_name = 'LC80140282015270LGN00_B'
   ```

Parallel Processing

```
bands_numbers = [2, 3, 4]
bands_paths = itertools.imap(
    compose_band_path,
    itertools.repeat(base_path),
    itertools.repeat(base_name),
    bands_numbers)

output_images = list(itertools.imap(
        compose_band_path,
        itertools.repeat("../output/"),
        itertools.repeat("15m_B"),
        bands_numbers))

# 1) Resample RGB bands.
for source, destination in zip(bands_paths, output_images):
    resample_image(source, destination, block_height=200)

# 2) Create a true color composition with the resampled bands.
# This image is only for comparison.
create_color_composition(list(output_images),
        '../output/preview_resampled_composition.tif',
        (4209, 11677, 348, 209))

# 3) Crop all the bands.
output_images.append(
    "../../data/landsat/LC80140282015270LGN00_B8.TIF")
for source in output_images:
    crop_and_save(source)

# 4) Use the cropped images for pan sharpening.
band8 = "../output/preview__LC80140282015270LGN00_B8.TIF"
bgr_bands = itertools.imap(
            compose_band_path,
            itertools.repeat("../output/"),
            itertools.repeat("preview__15m_B"),
            bands_numbers)
pan_sharpen(list(bgr_bands),
        band8, "../output/pan_sharpened.tif")
```

The procedure to generate the iterator with the file names is the same as used before.

In Part 1, the resampling of the RGB bands will be made using the default linear interpolation.

Chapter 10

In Part 2 we will create a true color composition with the resampled RGB bands. We won't use this image to perform the pan sharpening; we are creating it only to compare the results.

We crop all the bands in Part 3. By doing this, we are also adjusting the values of the grayscale from 16 bits to 8 bits. Finally, the pan sharpening is performed in Part 4.

2. Now add the pan_sharpen function to your file:

```
def pan_sharpen(bgr_bands, pan_band, out_img):
    bgr_arrays = []
    # Read the images into Numpy arrays.
    for item in bgr_bands:
        array = cv.imread(item, flags=cv.CV_LOAD_IMAGE_GRAYSCALE)
        bgr_arrays.append(array)
    pan_array = cv.imread(pan_band, flags=cv.CV_LOAD_IMAGE_GRAYSCALE)

    # Create the RGB (BGR) composition and convert it to HSV.
    bgr_composition = np.dstack(bgr_arrays)
    hsv_composition = cv.cvtColor(bgr_composition, cv.COLOR_BGR2HSV)

    # Split the bands and remove the original value component,
    # we wont use it.
    h, s, v = np.dsplit(hsv_composition, 3)
    h, s = np.squeeze(h), np.squeeze(s)
    del v

    # Use the panchromatic band as the V component.
    pan_composition = np.dstack((h, s, pan_array))

    # Convert the image back to BGR and write it to the disk.
    bgr_composition = cv.cvtColor(pan_composition, cv.COLOR_HSV2BGR)
    cv.imwrite(out_img, bgr_composition)
```

The process is simple. The joining and splitting of the bands is done with NumPy's `dstack` and `dsplit` functions. The color conversion is done by the `cvtcolor` function. Note that OpenCV uses a sequence of BGR bands instead of RGB.

3. Run the code and open the color compositions in the output folder to see the results.

- The resampled composition:

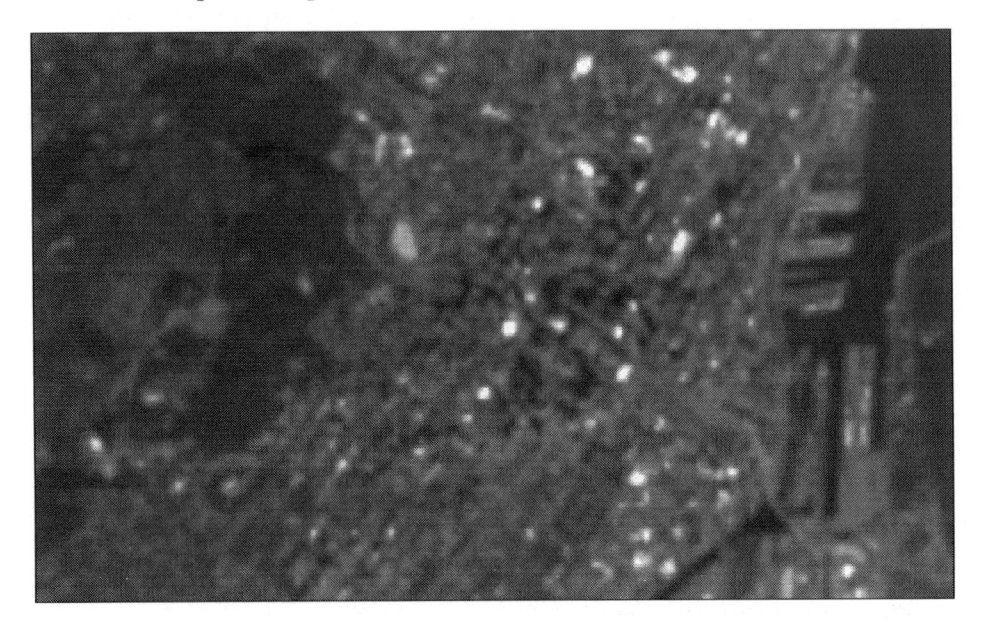

- The image with pan sharpening:

I would say that we achieved impressive results. The pan sharpened image is very clear and we can easily identify the city's features on it.

Summary

In this chapter, we saw how to distribute jobs into multiple processor cores, allowing the program to use all the available computing power.

Although parallel processing is a great resource, we found in our examples that it's not applicable for all situations. Specifically, when the bottleneck is not the CPU, multiprocessing may downgrade the program speed.

In the course of our examples, we took low-resolution satellite images and were able to increase their resolution and level of detail through resampling and pan sharpening, obtaining images of much greater value for visual analysis.

Index

A

abstraction 60, 61
Advanced Spaceborne Thermal Emission and Reflection Radiometer (ASTER) 168
alpha blending 210
app
 integrating with 117-120
app search capabilities
 improving 83
area of all countries
 calculating 19-23
attributes and relations
 filtering by 109-113
attribute values
 obtaining 97-99

B

basic statistics, raster data
 about 191, 192
 data, preparing 193
 histograms, calculating 198, 199
 making, lazy property 199, 200
 other statistics, calculating 199
 output information, formatting 196-198
 quartiles, calculating 198, 199
 simple information, printing 194-196
block iteration 289-294
book project
 creating 12-14

C

closest point
 searching 49-54

code comments 30
code profiling 222, 223
color classified images
 creating 201, 202
 right colors, selecting for map 203-210
context manager 38
coordinate system
 transforming 18-23
countries
 sorting, by area size 24, 25
current location
 setting 46-49

D

data
 filtering 235
 filtering, boundaries used 253, 254
 importing 232-234
 making homogeneous 60
 searching for 251, 252
database
 information, storing on 223, 224
 populating, with real data 247-250
database inserts
 optimizing 237-239
data miner app
 creating 217, 218
data parsing
 optimizing 239-241
digital elevation models (DEM)
 about 168
 reference 168
docstrings 30

[311]

E

ElementTree 249
ESRI shapefile 57
execution time
  measuring 218-222

F

file
  content, preparing for analysis 43
  contents, obtaining 41, 42
  opening 41, 42
filters
  chaining 115, 116
first example
  programming 15-18
  running 15-18
function
  combining, into application 43-45

G

GDAL
  about 5
  installing, on Ubuntu Linux 8
  installing, on Windows 8
geocache point
  abstracting 61-63
geocaching app
  application entry point, creating 31-34
  application tree structure, creating 28
  basic application structure, building 28
  code, documenting 30
  functions 29
  methods 29
geocaching data
  abstracting 63
  converting, into Geocache objects 75-77
  direct download 34
  downloading 34
  downloading, from URL 37, 38
  downloading manually 39-41
  download link 39
  geocaching data sources 35
  GPX attributes, reading 67-72
  homogeneous data, returning 72-74
  importing 64-67

  information, fetching from REST API 36, 37
  multiple sources, merging 77, 78
  REST API 35
GeoDjango 226
geographic data
  representing 56, 57
geometries
  representing 57-60
geometry relationships
  about 106
  contains 108
  crosses 107
  disjoint 109
  equals or almost equals 108
  intersects 109
  touches 107
  within 108
geo objects
  exporting 145-148
Geospatial Data Abstraction Library. *See* GDAL
global interpreter lock (GIL)
  pan sharpening 285
GPX format 57

H

hardware bottleneck 300
hill shading 179
histogram
  for colorizing maps 213-215

I

IDE
  about 11
  installing 11
  installing, on Linux 11
  installing, on Windows 11
image compositions
  creating 273
  false color compositions 280, 281
  specific regions, processing 278, 279
  true color compositions 274-277
image processing pipeline
  building 181, 182
image resolution
  image resampling 295-304

improving 295
pan sharpening 305-308
images
  blending 210-212
  iterating, through whole image 270-273
  memory usage 263-266
  numerical types 166, 167
  opening, GDAL used 266-269
  opening, with OpenCV 164, 165
  processing, by chunks 266
  representing 162-164
Integrated Development Environment (IDE) 1
iterables 270
iterator 270

J

Java Topology Suite (JTS) 87
JSON (JavaScript Object Notation) 57

L

Landsat 8 images
  about 259
  obtaining 259-263
lazy evaluation 199
lines
  importing 99-101
Linux
  IDE, installing 11

M

Map Maker app
  creating 149-151
  PythonDatasource, using 151-156
  using, with filtering 158, 159
Mapnik
  about 8, 122
  experiments, performing with 122
  installing 8
  installing, on Ubuntu Linux 9
  installing, on Windows 8
  map, making with pure Python 122-124
  map, making with style sheet 124-126
maps
  layers, adding 136-138

style options 131
styling 131
massive data
  importing 236
mosaicking 169
multiple attributes
  filtering by 113, 114
multiprocessing
  about 285
  basics 285-289

N

new functionality
  integrating, into application 79, 80
Noun Project
  reference 140
Numpy
  about 5
  installing 5
  installing, on Ubuntu Linux 5
  installing, on Windows 5
Numpy documentation
  reference 171

O

Object Relational Mapping (ORM)
  creating 225
  environment, preparing 226
  manager, customizing 228-232
  models, changing 227, 228
OGR drivers 6, 7
Open Computer Vision (OpenCV) package 130
Open Geospatial Consortium (OGC) 85
OpenStreetMap 60
OpenStreetMap points of interest
  importing 242-246
OpenStreetMap wiki
  URL 252
Operational Land Imager (OLI) 258
other packages
  installing, from pip 10
  installing, on Ubuntu Linux 10
  installing, on Windows 10
Overpass API 243

P

painter model 134
pan sharpening 305
PEP-8
  about 20
  URL 20
pixel 163
Poços de Caldas 168
points of interest (POI) 242
polygons
  importing 89-97
  working with 84
PostgreSQL
  URL 224
processing pipeline 181
profiling 222
Python
  installing 2
  installing, on Ubuntu Linux 2
  installing, on Windows 2
Python glossary
  reference 143
Python objects
  using, as source of data 141-145
Python package
  about 3
  installation, for Ubuntu Linux 5
  installation, for Windows 4
  installing 4
  package manager 3
  repository, for Windows 3
  required software 4

R

raster data
  basic statistics 191, 192
  information, extracting from 191
RasterData class
  creating 182-189
relief shading 179
remote sensing images
  cropping 176-178
  mosaicking 169-173
  processing 168
  shaded relief image, creating 179, 180
  values, adjusting 174, 175

REST (Representational State Transfer) 35
reStructuredText
  reference 30

S

satellite images
  about 257
  working with 257, 258
Scalable Vector Graphics (SVG) file 140
Shapely
  about 9, 87
  for handling geometries 87, 88
  installing, on Ubuntu Linux 10
  installing, on Windows 9
spaghetti data 59
Spatialite extension 224
spatial reference system
  units, converting 101-105
SQLite database 224
statistics
  displaying, with colors 212
style options, maps
  line styles 134, 135
  map style 131, 132
  point styles 139, 140
  polygon style 132-134
  text styles 135
SVG transformations
  reference 140

T

tables
  generating 232-234
test data
  removing 246
Thermal Infrared Sensor (TIRS) 258
TIFF format 289

U

Ubuntu
  URL 224
Ubuntu Linux
  GDAL, installing 8
  Mapnik, installing 9
  Numpy, installing 5

    other packages, installing 10
    Python, installing 2
    Python package, installing 5
    Shapely, installing 10
U.S Geological Survey (USGS)
    EarthExplorer 259
utility functions
    creating, for generating maps 126, 127
    data source, changing at runtime 127-130
    map, previewing automatically 130, 131

W

well-known binary (WKB) 85
well-known text (WKT) 85-87
Windows
    GDAL, installing 8
    IDE, installing 11
    Mapnik, installing 8
    Numpy, installing 5
    other packages, installing 10
    Python, installing 2
    Python package, installing 4
    Shapely, installing 9

[PACKT] open source
PUBLISHING — community experience distilled

Thank you for buying
Geospatial Development By Example with Python

About Packt Publishing

Packt, pronounced 'packed', published its first book, *Mastering phpMyAdmin for Effective MySQL Management*, in April 2004, and subsequently continued to specialize in publishing highly focused books on specific technologies and solutions.

Our books and publications share the experiences of your fellow IT professionals in adapting and customizing today's systems, applications, and frameworks. Our solution-based books give you the knowledge and power to customize the software and technologies you're using to get the job done. Packt books are more specific and less general than the IT books you have seen in the past. Our unique business model allows us to bring you more focused information, giving you more of what you need to know, and less of what you don't.

Packt is a modern yet unique publishing company that focuses on producing quality, cutting-edge books for communities of developers, administrators, and newbies alike. For more information, please visit our website at www.packtpub.com.

About Packt Open Source

In 2010, Packt launched two new brands, Packt Open Source and Packt Enterprise, in order to continue its focus on specialization. This book is part of the Packt Open Source brand, home to books published on software built around open source licenses, and offering information to anybody from advanced developers to budding web designers. The Open Source brand also runs Packt's Open Source Royalty Scheme, by which Packt gives a royalty to each open source project about whose software a book is sold.

Writing for Packt

We welcome all inquiries from people who are interested in authoring. Book proposals should be sent to author@packtpub.com. If your book idea is still at an early stage and you would like to discuss it first before writing a formal book proposal, then please contact us; one of our commissioning editors will get in touch with you.

We're not just looking for published authors; if you have strong technical skills but no writing experience, our experienced editors can help you develop a writing career, or simply get some additional reward for your expertise.

Learning Geospatial Analysis with Python

ISBN: 978-1-78328-113-8　　　　Paperback: 364 pages

Master GIS and Remote Sensing analysis using Python with these easy to follow tutorials

1. Construct applications for GIS development by exploiting Python.

2. Focuses on built-in Python modules and libraries compatible with the Python Packaging Index distribution system – no compiling of C libraries necessary.

3. This is a practical, hands-on tutorial that teaches you all about Geospatial analysis in Python.

Python Geospatial Development
Second Edition

ISBN: 978-1-78216-152-3　　　　Paperback: 508 pages

Learn to build sophisticated mapping applications from scratch using Python tools for geospatial development

1. Build your own complete and sophisticated mapping applications in Python.

2. Walks you through the process of building your own online system for viewing and editing geospatial data.

3. Practical, hands-on tutorial that teaches you all about geospatial development in Python.

Please check **www.PacktPub.com** for information on our titles

Python Geospatial Development Essentials

ISBN: 978-1-78217-540-7 Paperback: 192 pages

Utilize Python with open source libraries to build a lightweight, portable, and customizable GIS desktop application

1. Develop a GIS application that you can easily modify and customize.
2. Optimize your GIS application for user productivity and efficiency.
3. Discover Python's many geospatial libraries and learn how they can work together.

ArcPy and ArcGIS – Geospatial Analysis with Python

ISBN: 978-1-78398-866-2 Paperback: 224 pages

Use the ArcPy module to automate the analysis and mapping of geospatial data in ArcGIS

1. Perform GIS analysis faster by automating tasks, such as selecting data or buffering data, by accessing GIS tools using scripting.
2. Access the spatial data contained within shapefiles and geodatabases, for updates, analysis and even transformation between spatial reference systems.
3. Produce map books and automate the mapping of geospatial analyses, reducing the time needed to produce and display the results.

Please check **www.PacktPub.com** for information on our titles

Made in the USA
San Bernardino, CA
06 December 2017